# BUDDHISM IN A DARK AGE

# BUDDHISM IN A DARK AGE

## Cambodian Monks under Pol Pot

### Ian Harris

University of Hawai'i Press
Honolulu

**Library of Congress Cataloging-in-Publication Data**
Harris, Ian Charles.
Buddhism in a dark age : Cambodian monks under
Pol Pot / Ian Harris.
pages cm
Includes bibliographical references and index.
ISBN 978-0-8248-3561-3 (pbk. : alk. paper)
1.  Buddhism—Cambodia—History—20th century.
2.  Buddhist monks—Cambodia—History—20th century.
3.  Communism and Buddhism—Cambodia—History—
20th century.  I. Title.
BQ466.H365 2013
294.309596'09047—dc23

Designed by Janette Thompson (Jansom)

Printed by Integrated Book Technology, Inc.

*Na paro paraṃ nikubbetha*
*Nātimaññetha katthacinaṃ kañci*
*Vyārosanā paṭighasaññā*
*Nāññamaññassa dukkham iccheyya*

Let none deceive or decry
His fellow anywhere;
Let none wish others harm
In resentment or in hate

*Karaṇīyametta Sutta* v. 6

# CONTENTS

# ACKNOWLEDGMENTS

This work came to life in 2003 as a research project at the Documentation Center of Cambodia (DC-Cam), Phnom Penh. In due course I was able to organize my findings into a semicoherent scheme, and this further transmogrified into a monograph (Harris 2007) published by DC-Cam some four years later. That monograph forms the basis of the present significantly revised work, and I would like to register my appreciation to Youk Chhang, director of DC-Cam, both for giving his permission for this to occur and for his support and encouragement over the years.

In terms of archival sources, I have relied heavily on the DC-Cam's own holdings, but I have also used materials held at the National Archives of Cambodia and the Library of the Buddhist Institute, Phnom Penh, as well as various repositories in the West, most notably the Echols Collection on Southeast Asia at the Kroch Library, Cornell University; the Bibliothèque Nationale, Paris; and the libraries of the Institute of Southeast Asian Studies in Singapore, the School of Oriental and African Studies, Institut National des Langues et Civilisations Orientales, and the École Française d'Extrême-Orient. I would like to thank the staff at all of these institutions for their assistance.

The photographs reproduced in this book come from a variety of sources. The majority are from the DC-Cam archives. These have been collected from around Cambodia over the last few decades, usually in small batches donated by unidentified individuals who were not the copyright holders. Despite my best efforts it has been impossible to trace their legal owners, many of whom we must suppose lost their lives during the period covered in this study. Unless otherwise credited, the images belong to the author.

Prum Phalla assisted me in most of the fieldwork conducted in connection with the project, and I know that we share vivid memories, both positive and negative, of our peregrinations around rural Cambodia. I would like to offer him special gratitude for his consistent application to the task at hand, his equanimity, and his impressive driving skills. My thanks also extend to Osman Ysa and the rest of the staff of DC-Cam for their hospitality and friendship.

As I write, the trial of senior surviving Khmer Rouge leaders in the Extraordinary Chambers in the Courts of Cambodia for the Prosecution of Crimes Committed during the Period of Democratic Kampuchea is in progress in Phnom Penh. This has sharpened my awareness of the responsibilities that go with historical work of this sort, and I have done all I can to ensure that I have approached my sources in an open and objective manner. At various times I have received helpful advice and criticism from David Chandler, Chin Channa, Youk Chhang, Penny Edwards, Steve Heder, Ven. Ky Sovanratana, Henri Locard, and Ashley Thompson. I have incorporated the vast majority of their suggestions into the body of this work, but I am, nevertheless, aware that they may not agree with all of my interpretations.

The inception of this work overlapped with my time as Senior Scholar at the Becket Institute, St. Hugh's College, Oxford, and I would like to record my appreciation of Jonathan Rowland and the Becket Fund for Religious Liberty, Washington, D.C., for providing me with the time and the funding to get started. Support to cover the time spent in Cambodia came from the British Academy Committee for South East Asian Studies, the Spalding Trust, and grants to DC-Cam from the Swedish government and the United States Agency for International Development, to all of which I am greatly indebted. The initial writing stage was made possible by the award of a sabbatical term from the University of Cumbria, and the revisions were accomplished during a very happy and fruitful period spent as Senior Visiting Research Fellow at the Asia Research Institute, National University of Singapore.

Finally I would like to thank Pam Kelly and Ann Ludeman at the University of Hawai'i Press for their editorial support, Rosemary Wetherold for her conscientious copyediting, and my wife, Gwen, for putting up with years of absence and Buddhist-related obsession.

Toronto<br>
Seventh day of the waxing moon, month<br>
of assoc, year of the rabbit, BE 2555<br>
4 October 2011

# NOTE ON TRANSLITERATION

There is no universally recognized means for rendering Khmer terms in Roman characters, but there are two systems currently favored by scholars. The first, the Franco-Khmer method, is a modernization of practices employed during the French colonial period, and although not perfect in representing Khmer orthography, it provides a good indication of pronunciation. The second, originally proposed by Saveros Lewitz (1969) and modeled on the transliteration of Pāli and Sanskrit, gives an accurate representation of orthography but is an unreliable guide to pronunciation.

I have chosen to use the latter in this book, with some limited exceptions. These relate firstly to a handful of terms that would simply look strange to readers already familiar with more conventional renderings, such as *achar* (*ācāry*), Angkar (*aṅgkār*), and *wat* (*vatt*). For various reasons, attempts to impose Lewitz's system on the transcription of personal names and placenames have also proved problematic, but I have made every effort to offer them in a form that reflects conventional usage.

The issue of monastic names and rankings is somewhat complicated. In most cases I have avoided ecclesiastical titles, except where they are relevant to the context. In any case, they are often quite difficult to translate into intelligible English. To indicate an individual's monastic status, I have simply given a personal name preceded by the anglicized abbreviation "Ven." (for "Venerable").

The transliteration of Pāli and Sanskrit terms accords with accepted academic conventions.

Unless otherwise noted, translations are mine.

# INTRODUCTION

In the course of writing this book, I began to realize that it was, in part, a semiconscious homage to Holmes Welch's very fine *Buddhism under Mao*. While I cannot claim that author's experience or breadth of knowledge, I intend that this offering will, however imperfect, stand as a memorial to the many Cambodian Buddhist monks and laypeople, both named and unknown, who lost their lives or had their futures traumatically altered by the tragedy that overwhelmed their country in the 1970s. The choice to present periodic lists of personal names and places in the form of a litany reflects this. Although this may appear repetitious, it has been done for a specific purpose and, I hope, will require no apology.

The period covered in this study extends to either side of Democratic Kampuchea, the catastrophic regime that exercised power in Cambodia from April 1975 until January 1979. Early in my research Ven. Tep Vong, the country's most senior monk, sought to convince me that any inquiry into the crimes committed on such a massive scale by the communists should not neglect the significance of the overthrow of Sihanouk in March 1970.[1] This perspective derives, in part, from Tep Vong's own role as a significant participant in the People's Republic of Kampuchea (PRK), Democratic Kampuchea's successor regime. But it would be remiss of me to ignore another essential ingredient in his thinking. This is linked to a traditional Buddhist perception that the security of the state requires the protective presence of a monarch carrying out his responsibilities in accord with the Buddha's teachings. Whatever members of the international community and the Cambodian intelligentsia of the late 1960s may have thought, the vast bulk of the Cambodian population, especially those living in the country-side, regarded Sihanouk as precisely such a righteous ruler. His ousting as head of the state, then, was envisioned in cosmological terms, and Buddhist traditionalists interpreted his downfall in an apocalyptic manner. Through this one act the entire structure of Cambodian political life, together with the natural environment in which it was situated, would be fatally disrupted.

As a scholar of Buddhism, I am not unsympathetic to this reading of Cambodia's recent history, but I think that there are other equally important reasons for beginning a study of Buddhism under Pol Pot at a much earlier stage than the start of the Democratic Kampuchea period. The most significant of these is that almost immediately after Sihanouk's fall the new government of the Khmer Republic began to lose large swaths of the country to the communist insurgents who would come to be known as the Khmer Rouge. As the Lon Nol–led regime continued its fitful existence, so the proportion of the country under Phnom Penh's control shrank rapidly to little more than some of the major towns and the road corridors connecting them with the capital.

Meanwhile, in the "liberated areas" controlled by the Khmer Rouge the extreme policies that were to come to the outside world's attention in the late 1970s were already being tried out. Manipulation and repression of the Buddhist monastic order, allied to a cruelly antipathetic attitude to the faith and practice of the laity, commenced in some regions of the country almost five years before the beginning of Democratic Kampuchea. If we are to understand the regime's mature policy on the question of religion, we must begin our study at its very inception.

The Democratic Kampuchea period was relatively short-lived. It came to an end, at least as far as the control of Phnom Penh and the apparatus of national government was concerned, in early January 1979, when the National Front for the Salvation of Kampuchea, supported by the military and political resources of the Democratic Republic of Vietnam, invaded the country. The PRK was established soon after and lasted until the end of the following decade, when, largely as a result of the collapse of the Soviet Union, Vietnam was obliged to withdraw its economic support.

Given the horrors of the previous period, it might be supposed that the PRK would have garnered an overwhelming degree of popular support. But this was not so, for the new government was backed by a neighboring state that had come to be regarded by many as Cambodia's traditional enemy. For this reason the PRK had to work hard to establish its legitimacy, and one of the means by which this was accomplished was a relatively rapid reestablishment of the Buddhist monastic order (*saṅgha*). But since this had to be accomplished within a communist framework, the various pre-1970 freedoms could not be easily condoned and the reborn *saṅgha* was placed under some of the same severe restrictions previously imposed upon it by the Khmer Rouge. The ending of the Democratic Kampuchea period, then, does not represent a decisive rupture with the past, at least as far as the treatment of Buddhism is concerned, and this is the principal reason that this study takes us through to the end of the 1980s.

It is important to recognize that Buddhism in Southeast Asia has never been a disembodied conceptual system devoid of purchase on historical and political reality. Neither can it be regarded as a purely passive entity, a mere uncomplaining recipient of actions initiated by powerful individuals or corporations located beyond the religious domain. Both positions are caricatures that relate to Western conceptions of the nature of Asian religiosity rather than to social reality. They are also connected with a reluctance to accept Buddhism as a localizable "total fact." What I mean here is that when we look at Buddhism, we tend to focus on its philosophical and scholastic superstructure while ignoring the ways in which it has operated on a far wider level to sustain and inform the cultures with which it formed a whole. It has achieved its sociocultural character by the provision of educational and welfare facilities, certainly. But it has also acted through more direct involvement in the apparatus of state.

Buddhism has never been an entirely otherworldly religion of "Being-within-itself," nor are Buddhists a "people outside history." This Hegelian and Weberian *imaginaire* is premised on a modern and essentially European conception of a separation between church and state, yet it has been influential in the discounting of Buddhism's political dimension. This is surprising, given that, as individuals possessed of mobility, moral authority, and traditional learning, Theravāda monks have been significant figures in the exercise of political power. Throughout the last two centuries such figures were active in campaigns to both accelerate and hinder the transplantation of modernity in Southeast Asia. They also acted as effective creators of new social organizations and political institutions.

It has become a commonplace to claim that the passivity inherent in Theravāda Buddhism, especially its monastic segment, has made it ripe for cynical and consistent exploitation by successful power holders. I do not wish to entirely deny this assertion, but it is only a part of the picture, and this book would give only one side of the story if it stood merely as a catalogue of atrocities directed against the monastic order by the Khmer Rouge. Certainly, I intend to supply this information in significantly greater and more accurate detail than attempted by any previous writers. But I wish to balance my account with a demonstration, admittedly controversial for some, of the ways in which Buddhist categories were also imported into the ideology and practice of the Cambodian revolutionary movement. It is a modest aspiration that, in so doing, this work will prompt future scholars to pay more serious attention to the indigenous factors that constituted the worldview of one of the most destructive political regimes of the modern period.

By emulating and seeking to surpass the disciplined morality of the *sangha,* the Khmer Rouge created a moral and social order based on an inversion of Buddhist virtues. This new dispensation rapidly undermined the traditional authority of the Buddhist monk and evoked fear and trembling in the hearts of those who continued to value Buddhist ideals. Many did not survive the terrible events of the late 1970s, and Buddhism as an institution was completely destroyed by the time that Pol Pot fell from power. But it remains a moot point whether all aspects of religion were annihilated during Democratic Kampuchea.

As Albert Camus eloquently noted many decades ago, for totalitarian regimes mass murder transmogrifies into the only sign of the sacred possible in a completely desacralized cosmos. More prosaically, a small body of monks did survive the period with their vocations intact, Buddhist symbols maintained their protean character, and apotropaic elements deeply embedded in Cambodia's religious continued to provoke meaningful responses even in the most extreme circumstances. All of these factors would ultimately ensure Buddhism's relatively rapid reestablishment.

The persecution of Buddhism is not a modern phenomenon. According to legendary sources contained in the *Aśokāvadāna,* the tradition was suppressed by Puṣyamitra Śuṅga (r. 185–151 BCE) quite soon after its first ascent to prominence in ancient India. This ruler's motivations are unknown, but he is said to have attacked monasteries, destroyed stupas, put bounties on the heads of monks, and ordered their execution (Strong 1983). During this unstable period in its early history, the fear of persecution appears to have combined with core doctrinal notions stressing the omnipresence of impermanence in such a way that Buddhism developed into a religion that accepted the necessity of periodic phases of decline (Chappell 1980), and prophecies, attributed to the Buddha, that predicted various calamities adversely affecting the practice of religion are found in almost all Buddhist cultures.[2]

A number of factors have fostered negativity toward Buddhism from its inception until the present day. One of the more enduring of these is straightforward doctrinal antipathy, a significant element in the history of South and East Asia, where Buddhist monks have been obliged to compete in a multireligious marketplace in which Brahmanism, Daoism, Confucianism, Islam, and Christianity have variously occupied prominent and occasionally hostile positions. Social and political critiques have also been widespread. Complaints that monks contribute nothing to society, that they undermine its social institutions, that they are too influential, that they seek to overthrow the established order, or that they are unpatriotic are nothing new. Xenophobia and nationalism may also play important roles in fostering hostility toward a religion that has its origins in India.

State persecution on economic grounds has also been a significant factor in most of the regions in which Buddhism has flourished. A common pattern is that a period of general prosperity leads to expansion in the religious sphere and to a subsequent concentration of wealth within the *sangha* through a growth in lay donations, typically taking the form of increased landholding and commercial activity. But the *sangha* has often stood outside the system of taxation, so this process has tended to decrease the revenues available to rulers. This change in the power relationship between *sangha* and state may easily be deemed unpalatable by the latter.

A simple solution for improving the overall rate of economic performance is to confiscate monastic lands and return monks to the lay life. But in Asia such activity is often given a Buddhist justification: the ruler is engaging in a "purification" of the *sangha* in an attempt to root out unsuitable or heterodox elements. Four separate emperors persecuted Buddhism in China between the fifth and tenth centuries for such reasons. The best-known of these events is the Great Suppression of 845 CE, conducted during the reign of the Tang emperor Wuzong, who, having just concluded an expensive military campaign, had powerful reasons for replenishing his treasury (Ch'en 1956). Coincidentally, at almost exactly the same time, the Tibetan king Langdarma (r. ca. 838–841) launched a campaign against Buddhism—defrocking monks and closing monasteries—possibly because he belonged to a different religious persuasion (Karmay 2003).[3] But Langdarma's victory was short-lived. He was assassinated by a Buddhist monk.

All of the elements of traditional anti-Buddhism successfully migrated into the modern period, although now they were supplemented by a scientific and rationalist spirit imported from the European Enlightenment. As James Ketelaar (1993, 14) notes, with specific reference to the Japanese context, "it would be much easier to compose a list of those who were *not* ardently opposed to Buddhism in the nineteenth century." During the Meiji restoration, moreover, a campaign to "abolish Buddhism and destroy Śākyamuni" (*haibutsu kishaku*) in the joint names of Shintō and modernism nearly succeeded in bringing about the tradition's total eradication in Japan. The level of bloodshed during the campaign fortunately was not high. The same cannot be said of Stalin's almost complete liquidation of the Mongolian monastic order during the 1930s (Bawden 1989; Moses 1977), which when taken together with the events of the Chinese Cultural Revolution are probably the closest historical parallels to those with which this book is concerned.

Before the Chinese Cultural Revolution, the Communist Party's policy was "to protect Buddhism, while at the same time keeping it under control and utilizing it in foreign policy" (Welch 1972, 1).[4] A Chinese Buddhist Association ensured that the country's Buddhists would "participate, under the leadership of the People's Government, in movements for the welfare of the motherland and the defence of world peace; . . . help the People's Government fully to carry out its policy of freedom of religious belief; . . . link up Buddhists from different parts of the country; and . . . exemplify the best traditions of Buddhism" (quoted in ibid., 20). This all sounded quite laudable, but we must bear in mind that "defending world peace" actually involved providing concrete support for the Korean War, while contributing to the "policy of freedom of religious belief" meant that Buddhist monks were expected to stop preaching in public places.

Subsequently monks were transformed into fully contributing members of the economic realm as the Party passed a number of agrarian reform laws, the last of which, in 1950, decreed that monastic lands should be confiscated.[5] As a consequence, around 90 percent of China's approximately half a million monks disrobed in the 1950–1958 period. From the early 1950s, Buddhist monasteries were beginning to be used for non-monastic purposes, while monks were encouraged to cleanse their beliefs of "pessimism and escapism" by learning the basic elements of Marxism-Leninism. As a result the *saṅgha* was obliged to reduce or entirely abandon traditional religious practice, and the intensity of lay Buddhist activity also massively contracted.

In Tibet the policy on religion was pursued in its purest form, an international report of 1960 observing that the Chinese intended to "allow only that degree of freedom of religious belief which was compatible with complete acceptance of communism, *in short, none at all*" (my italics; International Commission of Jurists 1960, 14). The same work opined that the communists intended to weaken Buddhism in Tibet as a prelude to its total eradication.

But there is some evidence that monks "of the poorest class" may have been treated less severely than those from well-to-do families, and the report's authors made the point that a case can be made, as the communists themselves did, that most of the measures need not be regarded as "necessarily directed against religious belief" as such (ibid., 36).

In 1940 Mao had written that communists "may form an anti-imperialist and anti-feudal united front for political action with certain idealists and even with religious followers, but we can never approve of their idealism or religious doctrines."[6] A significantly restricted form of Buddhism, then, might be employed to convince the people of the Party's bona fides. But in the long run no form of Buddhist-Marxist syncretism would be tolerated, in part because belief in the inerrancy of the Party line, and in the quasi omniscience of Mao, would soon begin to take on an almost religious quality (MacInnes 1972, 286–287). The door was now open for the Cultural Revolution, the initial phases of which were taken up with violent though sporadic attacks on religious institutions. This practice was followed by a more coherent policy of persecuting "counterrevolutionary" groups, such as the Buddhist *saṅgha,* so that by September 1966 virtually all monasteries in China had closed, the first time that this had happened since 845 CE.

I shall attempt to argue that the path taken by the Khmer Rouge in its approach to the religious question had a logic largely determined by the indigenous cultural context. But the reader will have little difficulty in detecting parallel patterns and processes across the two communist states. The degree to which the mode of suppression during Democratic Kampuchea was determined by the events of the Cultural Revolution is, however, in need of further investigation. One observation we can make with absolute confidence is that neither regime was successful in transforming into an enduring reality its desire for the construction of a new society freed from the shackles of religion. The Chinese leadership began to dissociate itself from the worst consequences of such an extreme policy as the Cultural Revolution, which was running out of steam. From the early 1970s "the frenzy of destruction" diminished, even though "the political terror could not be resolved until the death of the senile Chairman in 1976" (Reinders 2004, 194). We begin to detect some limited, officially controlled reordinations of previously disrobed Chinese monks soon after. Although the mechanisms driving the process were rather different in Cambodia, movement in the same general direction occurred there, and the Buddhist monastic order gradually reemerged, admittedly still with many restrictions, following hard on the invasion of the country by a neighboring communist state.

## A Note on Sources

Ideally the writing of this book and the research on which it is based should have been conducted at a point somewhat nearer to the events it seeks to describe. Although by the late 1970s I was beginning to develop an interest in the state of contemporary Buddhism in Asia, Cambodia was at that time still part of a French field of academic influence, and significant knowledge of its distinctive form of Theravāda was largely hidden from English-language scholarship. Indeed, I accepted the very infrequent and rather sketchy media accounts of what was happening to organized Buddhism under the Khmer Rouge at face value, and it was only much later that I started to realize that the situation was more complex. In particular I came to suspect that statistics concerning the number of monks liquidated and pagodas destroyed that started to emerge in the aftermath of Democratic Kampuchea might have been plucked out of thin air, often in an attempt to reinforce some specific ideological line.

This book represents a belated effort to look into the matter in more detail, but I would fall at the first hurdle if I did not make clear the problematic nature of much of the primary source material that I present. When researching an earlier book, *Cambodian Buddhism: History and Practice* (2005), I had made some initial attempts to interview surviving members of the *saṅgha* regarding their experiences under the Khmer Rouge. These early probings made me realize that a far more rigorous effort would be necessary to build up an accurate and properly nuanced picture of the history of Buddhism between 1970 and the end of the communist period, not the least because a discernible process of mythification about the recent past was already well under way in Cambodian society. Although I was relatively unfamiliar with fieldwork when I started out, I quickly discovered what anyone experienced in conducting personal interviews with witnesses to traumatic events already knows—an interviewee's impressions can be astonishing sharp and vivid in some respects but vague in the extreme as far as supporting details are concerned.[7] This makes such tasks as trying to establish a chronology of events, for example, very problematic. And the setting of specific incidents against an objective calendar may be even more confusing. That many of my informants were monks or Buddhist laymen and laywomen of advanced age and, in some cases, declining mental faculties further complicates the matter.

No interview, however lucid, coherent, and convincing, can stand as evidence in isolation. It must be weighed against the utterances of other informants and used only when a certain configuration of veracity emerges. It seems to me that there is as much art as there is science to this activity, and I would be foolish not to admit that I have occasionally been convinced of the honesty of an informant's account by strongly subjective factors. But I have been fortunate in being able to correlate, and in many cases verify, the results of my interviews with materials collected by Ben Kiernan, Chantou Boua, Sharon Brown, and others in 1986 during a US Social Science Research Council's Indochina Studies Program project coordinated by David Hawk, a former executive director of Amnesty International USA and a founder of the Cambodian Genocide Commission.[8]

I have been able to significantly complement the insights gained from interview sources by drawing on the enormous collection of unpublished materials now held at the Documentation Center of Cambodia (DC-Cam).[9] The size of this archive makes it more than likely that I will have missed much relevant material, and on this ground alone the picture that I present must be regarded as provisional. But there are other methodological complexities that make it necessary to take a cautious line. One of the obvious problems when drawing inferences from documentary sources of the kind held at DC-Cam is that we often require a far better insight into the circumstances and context in which they were composed before we can be certain of their significance. But this is not always possible.

The most prominent of these difficulties relates to the "confession" transcripts and attached interrogator reports extracted from prisoners of the state security organization of the Communist Party of Kampuchea (CPK) at the notorious Tuol Sleng prison in Phnom Penh, also known as Office S-21. These statements were invariably collected as part of the process that led to the torture and execution of individuals as enemies of the revolution and of Angkar, its controlling revolutionary organization. It can be confidently asserted that these documents were composed under the most extreme duress of a kind and horror that can only be dimly imagined. Indeed, one often feels an intense sense of voyeuristic unworthiness when simply reading and commenting upon them. An initial and entirely natural response to the information contained within these documents would be to bracket it out of any equation related to historical and legal reliability.[10] But this appears to me to be an overreaction, for there is much material here that, with careful contextualizing and cross-referencing to other sources, may enrich our understanding.

Other DC-Cam documents with specific relevance to this study were composed in less disturbing conditions, but they also raise significant questions concerning objectivity. In this category we must include diverse sources such as Lon Nol government intelligence reports[11] and items of Khmer Rouge correspondence, such as reports from low-ranking cadres to officials, directives from superiors to their subordinates, and requests for information or assistance—this last category is sometimes called the Khmer Rouge telegrams. Also available are large quantities of biographical writings that record personal details of Party members or of prisoners;[12] reports and minutes of various CPK political and military committees; the personal notebooks of some 520 CPK cadres, soldiers, and other officials; copies of three Democratic Kampuchea–period Party magazines;[13] and around 95 films and instructional videos produced by the regime or, in some cases, by visiting film crews from friendly communist states.

Foreign source materials, especially those detailing official connections between Democratic Kampuchea and China and Vietnam, provide additional insights into the period, as do post–Democratic Kampuchea, Khmer-language materials such as the vast quantity of survivor petitions—also called the Renakse (*raṇasirsa,* or "front") documents—that were addressed to PRK officials after the fall of Pol Pot.[14] We should add to these the increasing body of survivor memoirs, both published and in draft form, many of which tell the harrowing stories of individuals who were mere children during Democratic Kampuchea, and the growing collection of DC-Cam interview transcripts and mapping reports. It is clear that all such materials can be relevant in gaining a better understanding of the fate of Buddhism during the period, but it is equally the case that they must be used with considerable care.

Finally, the records of the 1979 trial of Pol Pot and his associates cannot be ignored. On 15 July 1979, only seven months after the overthrow of Democratic Kampuchea, the country's new People's Revolutionary Tribunal passed its first law (Decree Law No. 1), designed to pave the way for the trial of what was termed "the Pol Pot and Ieng Sary clique" on a charge of genocide. The definition of genocide was drawn quite widely and did not correspond with the terms of the 9 December 1948 Convention on the Prevention and Punishment of the Crime of Genocide, although it did include reference to the "smashing" of religion (Heder and Tittemore 2004, 11n17). As far as Buddhism was concerned, five charges were specified by the tribunal:

1. That at the same time that they were emptying Phnom Penh, the revolutionaries moved swiftly to destroy the central bureaucracy of Buddhism. It was asserted, for example, that the Mahanikay *saṅgharāja* (chief monk), Ven. Huot Tat, and other monks in his entourage were taken to Oudong by car on 18 April 1975 and promptly eliminated.
2. That between 17 and 19 April 1975 all centers of Buddhist culture and learning throughout the country were closed down, resulting in the destruction of the country's cultural patrimony.
3. That the followers of Pol Pot "insulted, tortured and persecuted, individually and collectively, more than 100,000 monks[15] among which were the order's influential backbone of between four and five thousand senior monks and lay religious specialists (*achar*s)."
4. That everyone who refused to abandon his or her religion was exterminated.[16]
5. That the revolutionaries totally abolished the functions of Cambodia's *wat*s and destroyed precious objects and relics. (Groupe de Juristes Cambodgiens 1990, 218–219)

The tribunal was a brief affair, lasting a mere five days, between 15 and 19 August 1979.[17] The principal defendants were believed to be in hiding in Thailand and did not participate in the proceedings. No evidence was put forward on their behalf, and key figures in the legal process had declared Pol Pot and Ieng Sary guilty before the trail began. They were, indeed, found guilty of a wide range of crimes that went well beyond the normal definition of genocide, and were sentenced to death in absentia. An order was also given for the confiscation of their property. The trial clearly suffered from many shortcomings. Furthermore, many of the documents and testimonies submitted to the tribunal appear to be compromised by factual errors. Nevertheless, some of this documentation is relevant to the theme of this study and may also be consulted with care.

# CHAPTER ONE

# Unraveling of the Buddhist State

## Sihanouk and Buddhist Socialism

Following King Sisowath Monivong's death in April 1941, an adolescent prince, Norodom Sihanouk, came to the Cambodian throne under close French tutelage. This unenviable position ensured that he was discredited in the eyes of Cambodians who were opposed to foreign control. Among this group were powerful sections of the newly radicalized Buddhist *saṅgha,* some of whom were to become influential in the emergence of organized anticolonialism.[1]

In the late 1930s the French had attempted to romanize and rationalize written Khmer. Among certain segments of the *saṅgha* the idea provoked open hostility. Many monks regarded the reform as an attack on both traditional learning and the status of traditional monastic educators, even though it seems that the romanization decree was never intended to apply to religious writings. Against this background Ven. Hem Chieu, a prominent Pāli teacher based at Wat Unnalom, Phnom Penh, was arrested on 17 July 1942 and charged with eight offenses, including the planning of an anti-French uprising, involvement in secret meetings with the Japanese, and "using witchcraft to make Cambodian troops invincible." Found guilty on all charges, he was imprisoned on the notorious prison-island of Poulo Condore, where he died in 1943 at the age of forty-six. Angered that Hem Chieu had been defrocked without the necessary Buddhist rituals, around one thousand people, half of whom were umbrella-carrying monks, gathered for a demonstration on 20 July 1942. Sihanouk later derided the demonstration as the "Umbrella War."

Sihanouk certainly seems to have shared some of the presuppositions of the French. He viewed Buddhism as "a sweet religion whose doctrines of resignation are marvelously suited to a tired people" (Armstrong 1964, 30), but he also appreciated that it might be employed as a means of constructing a new sense of nationhood. As he grew more confident in his new role, Sihanouk became anxious to shrug off French influence, but his ability to exercise power was frustrated by a hostile National Assembly and by the depredations of various rebel groupings. His solution was to rebrand himself as the "father of Cambodian independence" and steal the fire from competing nationalist organizations.

The strategy was a success, in part because events in Vietnam meant that the colonial grip on Indochina was fast unraveling. The French relinquished authority over Cambodia in October 1953, and Sihanouk ruled as king of an independent state until 1955, when he abdicated in favor of his father, Suramarit. Now free to enter the political arena as a private citizen, Sihanouk quickly formed a political movement—the People's Socialist Community (*saṅgam rāstra niyam*), or Sangkum—and, against a background of violence,

Prince Norodom Sihanouk inaugurating a *wat*, late 1960s. (Documentation Center of Cambodia)

intimidation, and fraud, won all of the seats in the 1955 elections to the National Assembly. The Sangkum's ideology called for the creation of a Buddhist-oriented community (*saṅgam niyam braḥ buddhasāsanā*) and stressed mutual help and the promotion of the welfare of the poor, premised on the notion that the nation's flourishing depended on a Buddhist approach to good governance.[2]

A great increase in Buddhist patronage, especially in the field of education, occurred as a result of this policy of "Buddhist socialism." In 1955 the Preah Suramarit Buddhist High School evolved out of the old colonial-period École Supérieure de Pāli. The latter institution had been lauded as a "school for the nation" in the March 1941 edition of *Nagara Vatta,* a newspaper closely associated with Son Ngoc Thanh and other members of the new anticolonialist intelligentsia.[3] The Université Bouddhique Preah Sihanoukreach was established four years later. Meanwhile the monastic population grew by 72 percent, from 37,531 in 1955 to 61,014 in 1967,[4] and the prince officiated at the establishment of many new or refurbished Buddhist *wats*.[5]

In his upbeat inaugural address to the Sixth Conference of the World Fellowship of Buddhists, held in Phnom Penh in November 1961, Sihanouk claimed that the Buddha's teachings were compatible with the fundamental principles of rationality and scientific thought and that they had sustained and comforted the Cambodian people when "brute force and violence [had] set out to annihilate them" (Norodom Sihanouk 1962, 27). But as his reign progressed, Sihanouk began to lose the support of younger *saṅgha* members, many of whom had entered the order expecting to take up secular careers at the end of their studies. As economic stagnation worsened, these aspirations were frustrated, and, with ample leisure to discuss their grievances, their disaffection increased at a time when the prestige associated with the traditional monastic life was fast eroding.

The Sangkum's Buddhist veneer soon looked decidedly thin. Many policies appeared at odds with fundamental Buddhist ethics, especially after the establishment of a government casino resulted in a number of high-profile suicides due to bankruptcy. But more worrying was the alacrity with which the authorities turned to extrajudicial violence in dealing with political opponents. Sihanouk's own brutal treatment of Preap In, an ex–Democratic Party member and associate of Son Ngoc Thanh, was a case in point. Preap In's arrest, public display in a cage, and execution by firing squad in January 1964 caused particular dismay among Buddhists.[6]

Antigovernment manifestations in the capital in August 1964 prompted Sihanouk to comment that they were "the work of our pro-communist

Khmers, who have not hesitated to press even our monks to parade in the streets, thereby infringing the fundamental discipline of their apostolate."[7] It is certainly the case that copies of Mao's Little Red Book were circulating in Phnom Penh monasteries (Chandler 1999, 79), but Sihanouk was also badly shaken by a number of inauspicious events, including the death of twenty-four passengers in a train crash and the collapse of a funerary structure (*men*) containing the body of Chuon Nath, the country's recently deceased chief monk (*saṅgharāja*) (Meyer 1971, 92, 95).

When the prince left Phnom Penh for France on 5 January 1970, he assured the public that he would be back in Cambodia by April, in time to plow "the first furrow of the agricultural year." This was not to be. Yet before his fall from power, he had already admitted that Buddhist socialism

Sihanouk with Ven. Chuon Nath (*right*), chief monk of the Mahanikay (1946–1969).
(Documentation Center of Cambodia)

was a failure. Characteristically he placed the blame for this on the religion's emphasis on nonviolence, neutrality, and compassion—all of which had been insufficiently robust to deal with the corruption and international intrigues that Cambodia was obliged to face—rather than on his own mercurial character and unpredictable political maneuvering.

## Exit the King: Lon Nol and Religious War

When Lon Nol declared Cambodia a republic on 9 October 1970, he sent a message to the patriarchs of the two monastic orders, assuring them that "the present radical change of political rule is not meant to be prejudicial to Buddhism, which remains the state religion as it has up till now" (Agence Khmère Presse 1970b). To emphasize the point, he had a monument erected to the glory of the Khmer Republic outside the Royal Palace in Phnom Penh, with the following inscription: "Buddhism teaches us to be honest, to reject selfishness and to promote mutual assistance. Above all, it is a symbol of liberty, equality, fraternity, progress and well being" (quoted in Yang Sam 1987, 50). At around the same time, Bunchhan Mul, the new regime's minister of religious affairs and a veteran of the 1942 Umbrella War, attended a conference of Buddhist leaders in Seoul, where he opined, "[Sihanouk's] socialism was Buddhist in name only; it was diverted from its original

Bunchhan Mul, prison mug shot, 1942. (Documentation Center of Cambodia)

correct path—in other words, the teachings of the Buddha were not adhered to. The ex-dictator merely sought to use Buddhism as an instrument for his personal Machiavellian, autocratic, and despotic policy" (Agence Khmère Presse 1970a, 10).

Lon Nol believed in a reborn Cambodian nation that would lead the entire region of mainland Southeast Asia into an era of peace and prosperity rivaled only by the civilization of Angkor. Like most Khmer, he held a strong belief in the efficacy of magic, and soon after the coup, he called on those trained in the occult arts to use their powers to help defeat the communist enemy (Chandler 1991, 205). Indeed, the battle with Vietnam and the increasing number of homegrown rebels was conceived in millenarian terms, with Lon Nol himself cast as a sort of a Buddhist messiah.[8] These ideas were also connected with the historical mission of a so-called Khmer-Mon race[9] and a perception that its "atheistic" enemies were demons (*damil*)[10] for whom the normal requirements of Buddhist ethics need not apply. As such, they might be killed without compunction. Indeed, in a pamphlet entitled *Campāṃṅ sāsanā* (The religious war; 1970), a work that appears to have been influenced by earlier Khmer Buddhist prophecies,[11] Lon Nol openly declared that "the current war in Cambodia is a religious war."

Lon Nol termed his heady potion of politics and religion "Neo-Khmèrisme," and he seems to have thought that it would "contribute to prolong[ing] the Buddhist era for five thousand years." Through its application, furthermore, socialism would be achieved without "savage class struggle and sending monks to work in the ricefields,"[12] a clear reference to the situation in areas of the country already "liberated" by the communists.

Although the religious war rhetoric was primarily intended to apply to the communists, it had other consequences. A call to "chop down the Vietnamese" (*kāp' yuon*) resulted in many atrocities,[13] while *Campāṃṅ sāsanā* cynically stated, "For the present our Vietnamese brothers will have to return to South Vietnam. . . . Houses abandoned by [them] . . . will be taken care of by their neighbors. . . . We must not do anything that contradicts Buddhism" (Lon Nol 1970). By the time the pogroms had subsided, only some seven thousand of an original population of sixty-five thousand predominantly Vietnamese Catholics remained in Cambodia. A significant proportion had been killed; many of the rest had fled to Vietnam. Ironically, Catholics living in the zones already liberated by the communists were unharmed (Ponchaud 1990, 135–141).

## Politicizing the *Saṅgha*

In late March 1970 the Chinese and Vietnamese communist parties had proposed the formation of a National United Front of Kampuchea (FUNK) to bind Sihanouk to a fledgling Communist Party of Kampuchea committed to the fight to oust Lon Nol. Three prominent Cambodian leftists— Khieu Samphan, Hou Yuon, and Hu Nim—issued a statement in support of Sihanouk on 26 March 1970. Addressed "to the Samdech Chiefs of the two Buddhist sects, to venerable monks at all levels, to all our dear countrymen," it noted that "monks at all levels . . . are compelled to serve the policy of the reactionaries" (quoted in Caldwell and Tan 1973, 398). FUNK's political program[14] accused the Khmer Republic of vilifying and distorting the views of "honest intellectuals [and] monks." Furthermore, it asserted that the future of the country was tied to the protection and continued prospering of Buddhism, which was to remain the state religion after FUNK had regained control. Other religions—Islam, Catholicism, Protestantism, Caodaism, and tribal religions—were also to be guaranteed their freedom (ibid., 374, 378).

A follow-up *Declaration of Patriotic Intellectuals,* written by a group that included Khieu Samphan, Son Sen, and Pol Pot, was issued from the liberated zone on 30 September 1971. It noted that monks had previously "enjoyed freedom to exercise their religious rites in peace, freedom to do their studies and *to lead the population toward the road of independence, neutrality and peace* [my italics]," while deploring that monasteries in the Lon Nol–controlled zone had been deployed as barracks, arms depots, and military posts. The document somewhat hypocritically concluded, "What a pity to see monks being forced to leave their places of worship. . . . These traitors [i.e., government troops loyal to Lon Nol] have even tried to force monks to participate in anti-religious and anti-national elections. . . . They force monks to accompany them in their propaganda activities" (quoted in ibid., 418–419).

Such developments intensified the polarization of the *saṅgha,* as some monks supported the coup leaders, some remained dyed-in-the-wool monarchists, and others had already joined the communist cause. The government sought to use pliant monks to counteract communist propaganda in the countryside, and this tactic was fairly effective, especially in Pursat, Svay Rieng, and Takeo provinces (Corfield 1994, 93).

The governor of Battambang province, Sek Sam Iet, was a strong Lon Nol supporter, and it seems that Battambang's chief monk (*megaṇ*), Ven. Pon

Sompheach, an important figure in the nation's ecclesiastical hierarchy and a past director of the Pāli High School in Phnom Penh, followed his lead. In any case many members of the local populace wanted the country to modernize, and they thought that Lon Nol would be able to achieve this.[15] However, the success of the communists' propaganda, combined with the government's rapid decrease in popularity, soon meant that special measures were required to control the monkhood. A number of my informants reported the presence of individuals who were acting as putative government spies in their pagodas by late 1972,[16] and this is corroborated by surviving intelligence reports, three of which appear to be permissions given to named monks to work undercover in regions controlled by the communists. Interestingly, one of the three, Ven. Chan Dy, from Samraong Knong commune, Sangke district, seems to have been a student of Ven. Pon Sompheach.[17] Chan Dy had the monastic status of *anugaṇ* (deputy chief monk), but his cover was eventually blown and he was executed in either 1973 or 1974. Apparently, some of his ex-students invited him to their base in a flooded forest, where they became angry and killed him.[18]

On the other side of the equation, a deep-rooted connection between segments of the *saṅgha* and the highest levels of the state, traditionally embodied in the person of the king, ensured that many monks were very suspicious about the new turn of events. For reasons associated with its origins in the Bangkok court, members of the aristocratic and monarchist Thommayut order[19] were deeply affected by the fall of Sihanouk. We certainly know that a significant group of such monks had planned a protest march in Phnom Penh immediately after the coup, and this was prevented only by the swift intervention of Ven. Huot Tat, the country's supreme patriarch (Yang Sam 1987, 42).

Lon Nol's relations with senior members of the monastic hierarchy were problematic from the start. Thus it was only with great difficulty and after consistent pressure that he was able to get a statement from the two patriarchs, Huot Tat[20] and Tep Loeung,[21] condemning the actions of the Vietcong and North Vietnam in invading Cambodia, mistreating monks, and destroying *wats*.[22] Later they were pressured into declaring that the abolition of the monarchy would have no adverse effect on the position of Buddhism (*Cambodge Nouveau* 1970c). But these two dignitaries refused to support a change of name for the Université Bouddhique Preah Sihanoukreach, the Buddhist institution established by the previous head of state (Meyer 1971, 81) or to "excommunicate" Sihanouk for collaboration with the communists.[23] Indeed they both attended a press conference given by Professor Keo An at the Phnom Penh Law Faculty on 25 February 1972, during which he denounced both Lon Nol and Prince Sirikmatak (Corfield 1994, 126).[24]

Suspicion and resistance were not confined to the capital. In June 1971 a monk called Nget Tuon had been arrested by government forces and accused of propagandizing the people at Wat Kam Pheng and neighboring monasteries in Kirivong district in support of Sihanouk.[25] Under interrogation, he claimed that the Khmer Rouge had accused one of his fellow monks of hating the royal family, who were by that time in alliance with the communists. He also admitted that he supported communist ideology and opposed the Khmer Republic because it colluded with America and South Vietnam in bombing Cambodian villages and pagodas. Moreover, he told his interrogators that on 10 May 1971 he had been present—whether willingly or otherwise we do not know—at a meeting of 447 monks and *achar*s from Kampot, Takeo, and Kampong Speu, at Wat Ang Andet in Kampot province. The event had been organized by Ta Mok, Phok Chhay, and other senior communists to encourage monks to teach the people the principles of the revolution.[26]

In the context of the civil war, the Khmer Rouge's arguments had an explanatory power. Many ordinary monks, both before and after liberation, were convinced that the CPK would "defend the country and religion" against foreign aggression. As Nuon Chea (1987, 12) later asserted, they

Ven. Huot Tat, chief monk of the Mahanikay, 1969–1975.

Ven. Tep Loeung, chief monk of the Thommayut (1966–1975), with Sihanouk (*right*). (From *Kambuja* 1969, 74)

"held aloft our banner even if they did not like communism." That sections of the *saṅgha* went over to the side of the communists was further enhanced by Sihanouk's support for the movement as part of a united front against Lon Nol. Presumably, this is the reason a very frightened Sihanouk shared a

Sihanouk and audience, including monks, in the liberated northwest, March 1973.
(From *Samdech Sihanouk's Inspection Tour of the Cambodian Liberated Zone* 1973, 26)

platform with a group of monks when he visited Pol Pot in his northern zone headquarters in March 1973.[27]

A typical cadre of the time was described as someone who had been a monk for five years and then a low-level official in local government before becoming a Khmer-language inspector at a pagoda school (Thion 1993, 13–15). We also know that, in the liberated zone, monks tended to make the first speeches at political gatherings, and only after these preliminaries did local Party workers step up to the podium (Mak Phœun 2003, 52–53). Indeed, monks and ex-monks were particularly successful in recruiting peasants, who seem to have been more convinced by their sermons than by speeches given by communist officials. Without these monastic recruitment officers the path to victory would have been much harder to achieve.

But Lon Nol also had his monastic supporters, such as Ven. Khieu Chum (1907–1975), an especially effective cheerleader during the early Khmer Republic period.[28] From his early twenties Khieu Chum had lived at Wat Langka, Phnom Penh, where his preceptor was the pagoda's abbot (*cau adhikār*) and influential modernist monk, Ven. Lvī Em. Chum soon became become part of Hem Chieu's inner circle and later participated in the Umbrella War. Fearing that the French wanted to arrest him, he fled to the Dangrek Mountains, where he stayed with Son Ngoc Thanh, already a significant figure in the anticolonial movement and a sworn enemy of the Cambodian monarchy.

Around the time Cambodia gained its independence, Khieu Chum returned to Phnom Penh, where his activities caused some consternation in the Royal Palace. Indeed, the monk had known Lon Nol and some of his

Ven. Khieu Chum.            Ven. Lvī Em.            Ven. Hem Chieu.

associates well before the 1970 coup and may actually have been one of the plotters. So it was natural for him to broadcast his support for those involved in ousting Sihanouk soon after the coup had occurred. He specifically argued that Buddhism showed a marked preference for republican forms of governance and that, in any case, the Buddhist religion (*sāsana*) should not be required to depend on the monarchical structures that had been so decisively rejected by the Buddha when he renounced his life as a prince to follow the calling of a recluse. Cambodia, furthermore, had suffered from "thousands of years of absolutism, arbitrariness and tyranny,"[29] and this was another reason why the people should embrace the Khmer Republic.

As soon as Lon Nol had consolidated his power, he suggested that Khieu Chum take up the post of a two-star army general! The monk refused but offered to advise the new government on anything within his broad area of expertise. Indeed, it seems that he ended up writing many of Lon Nol's speeches, and in early March 1971 he chaired a committee to write the manifesto of the Khmer Republic. He was also tasked with bringing about a rapprochement between Lon Nol and Son Ngoc Thanh (Corfield 1994, 108). The latter was appointed prime minister in March of the following year.[30]

This period represents the zenith of Khieu Chum's political influence. He wrote extensively on political issues and was a frequent speaker on national radio.[31] However, his activities were not always helpful to the government, and he seems to have become disillusioned as time went on. In 1973 he and Ven. Pang Khat, a fellow veteran of the 1942 monks' demonstration,[32] encouraged Phnom Penh students to protest against certain aspects of the regime, possibly unaware that the Khmer Rouge had infiltrated some of the student groups involved. Ven. Huot Tat was forced to issue him a reprimand (Corfield 1991, 5).

## Monks and Monasteries in the Conflict Zone

In early September 1970 a letter circulated by Leang Hap An, president of l'Association des Écrivains Khmers, condemned the destruction of sacred literature, other religious artifacts, and more than one hundred monasteries by the Vietcong and North Vietnam (*Cambodge Nouveau* 1970a). He also listed a number of chief monks who had been tortured, brutalized, or murdered. A companion document, entitled *Appeal Made by the Buddhist Association of Cambodia Concerning the Aggression Committed by Vietcong–North Vietnamese Forces against Peaceful and Neutral Cambodia* (1970) and written by but not attributed to Bunchhan Mul, was issued by the Buddhist Association of Cambodia. It made a powerful case. As might be expected from an author who occupied the post of minister of religions and cults, the *Appeal* defended the overthrow of Sihanouk on the grounds that he had been unwilling to prevent a Vietcong and North Vietnamese (VC/NV) military presence in Cambodia. It claimed that on 28 March forty thousand well-armed communist troops had launched brutal attacks against administrative buildings, schools, hospitals, and pagodas[33] and backed this up with photographs of the damage caused at a pagoda in Skoun, Kampong Cham, and to the modern temple of Phnom Chisor, in Takeo province. The document also asserted that many monks and lay Buddhists had been killed in the conflict, while the aggressors had used pagodas as military bases. Government forces, on the other hand, were pious Buddhists who would not attack these locations even though the enemy had "been seen to push the monks and lay-Buddhists to the forefront of their troops towards the battlefield" (Buddhist Association of Cambodia 1970, 3–4).

The *Appeal* also made reference to putative anti–Lon Nol manifestations, but it maintained that "elements of the North Vietnamese–Vietcong armed forces, on 23 March 1970, [had] violently forced the pious Cambodian population in the provinces of Kampong Cham, Prey Veng and Takeo to revolt and march in demonstration against the present Government of Cambodia" (ibid.). In actual fact we know that some of the participants in the Kampong Cham event were monks (Ponchaud 1989, 170) and that additional demonstrations involving *saṅgha* members took place throughout September and October 1971.[34] It is difficult to be certain about the political affiliations of the participants, assuming that they had any, but there is little doubt that by early 1972 a large swath of monastic opinion was turning against the blatant corruption of the Khmer Republic.

From the beginning of the conflict, government officials had been compiling statistics related to the treatment of the structural and human causalities inflicted on Buddhism by the enemy. A press conference of 23 June 1971, chaired by Bunchhan Mul with the assistance of Lon Non, accused the communists of prohibiting religious practice and of taking up military positions in some sixty pagodas in the vicinity of Tram Khnar village, Takeo province. Monks had been warned that if they did not work, they would not be able to eat. For this reason, the grounds of one pagoda, Wat Slap Leng, had been turned into a market garden (Ministère de l'Information 1971, 42–43). However, the first substantial digest of statistics was published by the Ministry of Information and signed by Bunchhan Mul in October 1971. It listed numbers of monks killed (thirty), wounded (thirty), or abducted (thirteen) by the enemy from 18 March 1970 until 31 July 1971, and 204 pagodas damaged or destroyed in the same period. Various atrocities committed against Buddhist personnel were also recorded—namely, twelve men, including five named monks, taken away from Wat Preah Phos, Battambang province, on 20 April 1971; cannon fired at Wat Ang Po in Kampong Speu on 22 May 1971, gravely wounding Ven. Kong Soth; five monks and six novices arrested at Wat Mongkol Monichot, Kampong Thom province, on 1 June 1971; Wat Kampong Popil, in Prey Veng, hit by heavy artillery on 2 June 1971, killing two monks; and the previously mentioned Wat Chisor, Takeo province, hit by shellfire on 12 June 1971, injuring two named monks and destroying the *brah vihāra* (principal sanctuary), the *sālā chān'* (a building with several functions), and four *kuṭi*s (huts) (Ministère de l'Information 1971, 6–11, 25–28, 45).

In December 1972 an extended article by Dik Keam appeared in *Cambodge Nouveau*. It repeated some of the incidents of communist persecution already mentioned in official sources, but it also referred to an undated forced gathering of monks from Takeo, Kampong Speu, and Kampong Chhnang provinces; the eye gouging and execution of Ven. Om Po, the *cau adhikār* of Wat Bali Chas, Takeo province, on 4 November 1970; the undated killing of an unnamed *cau adhikār* at Wat Sen Monorom, Mondulkiri province; and the fatal shooting of Ven. Pom Sam in Kampong Cham on 11 September 1970 and Ven. Ham Phou of Wat Ang Metrey, Takeo province, on 10 December 1970.[35] The article called on the Lon Nol government to protect cultural goods and monasteries, particularly those that were old or of special cultural significance, in line with the Hague Convention of 1954.

On 12 September 1971 the residents of Baray district, Kampong Thom, organized a demonstration against VC/NV aggression that was attended by many monks (Ministère de l'Information 1971, 53). Nine days later Huot Tat led a silent march in front of Phnom Penh's Buddha relic shrine after government soldiers discovered a mass grave containing a thousand bodies.[36] The two Buddhist patriarchs also issued a joint declaration dated 9 October 1972, condemning a VC/NV attack on the Chrui Changvar bridge, which linked the capital with Kampong Cham and points farther north. The attack had taken place two days earlier, during *bhjuṃ piṇḍ,* the annual festival for dead ancestors.[37] It seems as though hostilities were amplified during this somber period of the religious calendar. Indeed, when the National Army regained territory around Siem Reap commune, Kandal province, on 26 September, it discovered that Wat Khleang Moeung had been completely destroyed, with statues of the Buddha scattered in nearby fields and trenches. It seems that, several nights earlier, communist forces torched school buildings donated by the United States, and local people felt so insecure that they took to spending the night at Wat Kork Kak, a pagoda better supported by alms than most others in the area. For this reason Wat Kork Kak continued to function, but most other local *wat*s were not so fortunate and *bhjuṃ piṇḍ* could not be celebrated in their precincts.[38]

A little over a month later Lon Nol made a pilgrimage to Kampong Speu to pay homage to monks killed by the communists, including Ven. Sao Sokhom, *anugaṇ* of Phnom Srouch, who died on the night of 1 November 1972 when a grenade was thrown into the pagoda's main shrine hall. Sao Sokhom's remains were subsequently brought to the capital and ceremonially incinerated before the Buddha relic shrine (Dik Keam 1972, 26).

Another engagement between communist and government troops on National Route 5 in late August–early September 1972 illustrates something of the confusion of warfare and its impact on the Buddhist *saṅgha*. It appears that when Lieutenant Colonel Rak Phan, commander of Special Brigade No. 5, left Prey Phdeak with government forces on 28 August, they were attacked by an enemy force of some three to four thousand soldiers, hiding in nearby Doung Saoy village. Two government T-28 planes were called in, but they hit the wrong target, destroying Wat Pongea Keo instead and resulting in a number of lay and monastic fatalities, including a certain Ven. Soum (*Koḥ Santibhāb* 1972b). Villagers, however, attributed the death of that pagoda's *cau adhikār*, Ven. Ong Pan, to North Vietnamese forces, although it is clear from the confused nature of the account that blame cannot be easily attributed to one side rather than the other.

Both sides in the conflict certainly occupied pagodas for military purposes. Lon Nol soldiers were based at the old royal monastery of Wat Veang Chas, Oudong, until it was eventually captured by the enemy.[39] Government troops also used Wat Norea, Battambang, as a training center, while nearby pagodas like Wat Po Veal were employed as barracks until hostilities started in earnest, around 1973–1974.[40] Wat Samraong Meanchey in Kampong Thom province, on the other hand, was badly destroyed by government forces after the revolutionaries' arrival in 1970. Its monks were obliged to move a number of times before they settled uneasily at Wat Tbong Damrei.[41]

As the civil war began to rage, more and more monks displaced by the fighting began to congregate in the monasteries of the main cities. The monasteries in Phnom Penh were packed with young men, many of whom were seeking to avoid military service. According to official records, 430 monks had sought refuge in the capital's *wat*s by late July 1971 (Ministère de l'Information 1971, 12–24), but the real number is likely to have been much higher. A typical story is that of Ven. Puth Neang, who escaped to Phnom Penh after living as a monk in the liberated zone in Kampong Cham province (*Cambodge Nouveau* 1973a). The overcrowding of city *wat*s made it very difficult to engage in traditional monastic pursuits, but Buddhist education was somehow maintained at all levels. Nevertheless, rapidly deteriorating economic conditions meant that there was great pressure to shift the monastic curriculum toward the acquisition of relevant skills, with many young monks demanding to have more science in the curriculum so that monastic qualifications would be brought into line with secular qualifications. As has already been noted, this meant that many of the better-educated urban monks rapidly lost whatever enthusiasm they might once have had for the Lon Nol regime.[42]

By the end of 1972 an economic crisis was in full swing. Because of the rising prices of goods, the government agreed to increase the salaries of all government officials, but monks who worked as teachers were exempt from the provision. Their salary had been fixed at 300 riels a month, and this was a significant cause for complaint. One newspaper, *Rāstracakr* (1972a), called for monks to have a raise to at least 1,000 riels monthly, prompting Ven. Phai Sampov, principal of the school at Wat Damrei Sa, Battambang, to write a letter to the paper in support of the proposal, noting that the current pay of monk teachers equated only to the cost of two postage stamps.[43] While matters of monastic remuneration were being debated, however, Cambodian communist forces were gaining in strength, especially after the failure of the government's Chenla II campaign (Sak Sutsakhan 1980, 72–73). Now adequately trained and supplied with weaponry, they took over from North Vietnamese forces, and three of the latter's four divisions withdrew into Vietnam, leaving only the fourth to control the border area in Kampong Cham province. From that point on, the Communist Party of Kampuchea, better known as the Khmer Rouge, would control the revolution.

From the beginning of 1974, enemy pressure on the capital intensified (Sak Sutsakhan 1980, 125). On 8 January, Lon Nol received a letter from Ven. Kim Sang, the chief of the Theravāda Buddhist Association of

Kampuchea Krom, a strongly Khmer area within South Vietnam's Mekong Delta region. In it, the monk expressed his sorrow at the communist bombardment of Phnom Penh, and especially the destruction of various monasteries (*Le Republicain* 1974a, 2). On 14 February, Tep Loeung and Huot Tat appealed to the United Nations and other international organizations to use their influence to bring an end to aggressive acts perpetrated by the VC/NV and their lackeys. The monks also solemnly, although perhaps not wholeheartedly, reaffirmed their support for the Lon Nol government. Huot Tat and officials from the Ministry of Cults and Religions also visited the capital's Boeung Salang school on 19 February to distribute food and clothing supplies to those affected by particularly heavy shelling (*Le Republicain* 1974b, 1–2).

## Final Days of the Buddhist State

The auguries for organized Buddhism were not good. Lon Nol had suffered a stroke in early 1971 and never fully recovered. A superstitious populace, discovering that he had lost the use of his right arm—the arm he had used to sign the order to depose Sihanouk—took this as a bad omen. Much of Lon Nol's time was now spent listening to the military advice of Buddhist holy men who promised supernatural solutions to the conflict.[44] Meanwhile prophecies that had circulated in Cambodia for at least a hundred years began to take on a more urgent significance. Describing a "*bodhi* tree with [a] flat stump," one such prophecy noted, "The roots do not grow . . . a poisonous cobra hides quietly at the same place" (quoted in Yang Sam 1987, 51). Rumors that one of the great heroes of the past, such as Po Kambo, Sivotha, or *anak tā* (ancestral spirit) Khleang Moeung, would soon be returning to take a decisive part in the war were also widespread (Kiernan 1996, 374). A millennial tinge may also be discerned in the construction of a wooden palace near Phnom Penh by some Buddhists to serve as the headquarters of the coming Buddha, Maitreya.

On 13 February 1974 General Chantaraingsey, the governor of Kirirom and Kampong Speu, welcomed seventeen monk refugees from Wat Kraing Chek, some fifteen kilometers north of Kampong Speu town in a zone controlled by the revolutionaries. They spoke of the danger posed to Buddhism by atheistical communists, and they reported that some of their fellows had been sent as cannon fodder to the front. Those who had resisted had been summarily executed (*Le Republicain* 1974c, 3, 6).

# CHAPTER 2

# Buddhism and the Origins of Cambodian Communism

## The Formative Period

From its foundation in 1930, the Indochinese Communist Party (ICP) had made sporadic attempts to recruit the first generation of Cambodian anticolonialists. Two young monks appear to have been involved with the first known Khmer communist, Ben Krahom (Kiernan 1981, 161–162), and another shadowy figure, a twenty-eight-year-old Khmer from Kampuchea Krom called Thach Choeun, apparently joined the ICP in 1932. According to French intelligence sources, Thach Choeun had also been a monk in Takeo province.

But while the authorities took an interest in early Chinese and Vietnamese communist cells, they regarded the Khmer as "nonchalant and undisciplined" (Morris 1999, 30), and this made it difficult for them to believe that the Khmer could be significant players. In the words of one intelligence officer, the Cambodians "know how to gather together only on pagoda feast-days and for funeral ceremonies, which are not very suitable for intrigues" (quoted in Kiernan 1981, 161). The first stirrings of an anticolonialist movement in the Umbrella War and its aftermath had, indeed, been largely devoid of leftist elements, but this would change when Son Ngoc Minh created the Unified Issarak Front (*samāgam khmaer īssara,* or UIF) in April 1950.[1]

Son Ngoc Minh (ca. 1910–1972) is also known as Achar Mean, but there has been some confusion about his true identity.[2] The name is clearly a nom de guerre formed by combining "Son Ngoc Thanh" and "Ho Chi Minh." It is plausible that he was born Pham Van Hua (Lamant 1987, 93, 95) somewhere in Kampuchea Krom, an ethnically Khmer region of the Mekong Delta, and that at some stage he was ordained there as a Buddhist monk. Eventually he

moved to Phnom Penh and became a Pāli teacher at Wat Unnalom. The like-
lihood is that after the Umbrella War he fled to Kampong Chhnang province,
where he made contact with an ICP cell in the neighboring Thai-controlled
provinces of the northwest (Kiernan 1985, 44). Others claim that Son Ngoc
Minh was admitted to the ICP around September 1945 and by March of the
following year was commanding a Vietnamese-backed resistance group in
Battambang that was designed to draw French forces away from southern
Vietnam (Engelbert and Goscha 1995, 27n10, 33).

In the late 1940s the ICP had decided to give its Khmer compatriots
greater autonomy by dividing the country into four fields of operation. Son
Ngoc Minh was moved to Kampot province, where, by the early 1950s, he
took charge of the Southwestern Zone.[3] The neighboring Southeastern Zone
was commanded by fellow ex-monk Tou Samouth (ca. 1915–1962) (Short
2004, 39).[4]

Son Ngoc Minh, in black (*right*). (Documentation Center of Cambodia)

One Vietnamese official likened Tou Samouth to "an old monk, sweet and good-natured" ("Recherche sur le Parti Cambodgien" n.d.), and another source described both Son Ngoc Minh and Tou Samouth as "influential" and "authoritative" Buddhist monks (Khmer Peace Committee 1952, 13). Tou Samouth was also known as Achar Sok. Like Son Ngoc Minh, he came originally from Kampuchea Krom and had lived as a monk at Wat Unnalom, where he appears to have been well versed in Buddhist learning, had a reputation for oratory, and taught Pāli. He also became part of the circle of Mlle. Suzanne Karpelès, who was the French director of the Buddhist Institute, an important center of intellectual and political debate (Khing Hoc Dy 2006–2007). It seems that Tou Samouth fled Phnom Penh soon after Wat Unnalom was bombed by a US B-29 warplane on 7 February 1945, an event in which some twenty monks and bystanders were killed (Kiernan 1985, 48).[5]

Phnom Penh office of H. E. Chea Sot, with photographs of Son Ngoc Minh (*top left*) and Tou Samouth (*top right*), November 2004.

On 17 April 1950 the Unified Issarak Front organized a first National Congress of the Khmer Resistance at Wat Kampong Som Loeu. Some two hundred individuals, around half of whom were Buddhist monks, attended.[6] In June of the same year a political school named after hero and martyr Ven. Hem Chieu was also established in the southwest (Steinberg et al. 1959, 107). That the UIF viewed itself as contiguous with the earlier phase of monastic opposition to colonial rule seems clear from its sponsorship of a three-day Khmer Buddhist conference in February 1951. A play detailing the life of Hem Chieu was performed at this event. Somewhat later, in February 1953, a group calling itself the Achar Hem Chieu Unit was held responsible for the assassination of the governor of Prey Veng (Kiernan 1985, 93–94, 130).

By 1951 the ICP had split into three national parties for Vietnam, Laos, and Cambodia, respectively. The resulting Vietnam Workers' Party (VWP) had some difficulty in recognizing the communist credentials of the Khmer People's Party (KPP),[7] on the grounds that the KPP was merely the "vanguard party of the nation gathering together all the patriotic and progressive elements of the Khmer population" rather than the "vanguard party of the working class."[8] This seems to suggest that the Vietnamese were disappointed by the motivation of Cambodian revolutionaries, who, to a great

Issarak monks. (Documentation Center of Cambodia)

extent, remained close to the Buddhist-inspired nationalism of the 1940s. The statement also points to Vietnamese worries about the ideological purity of a party that admitted members of the *sangha*.[9]

But a number of monks—such as the Wat Unnalom–based Ven. Prom Samith, who accompanied Son Ngoc Minh on a November 1951 preaching tour of monasteries in Kampuchea Krom—did join the struggle.[10] They would ensure that Khmer Krom monasteries became fertile recruiting grounds. Early successes included the establishment of an Issarak Buddhist Studies School with an initial intake of thirty students. Some senior monks were also won over to the cause (Kiernan 1985, 93). Just as importantly, a region with a prior history of millennial and anticolonial activity was being co-opted into the struggle for an independent Cambodian state.[11]

Son Ngoc Minh explicitly linked the nationalist cause with the protection of Buddhism, arguing, "The Cambodian race is of noble origin. It is not afraid of death when it is a question of fighting the enemy, of saving its religion, of liberating its fatherland. The entire race follows the Buddhist doctrine which places death above slavery and religious persecution." Furthermore, Son Ngoc Minh asserted, such a struggle conformed to "the aspirations of the Buddhist religion."[12] This insistence on the jeopardy facing Buddhism was a clear extension of monastic suspicions of French reform measures in the early 1940s. But the indirect reference to a holy war was something new.

By the end of 1952 the UIF was "boiling over with revolutionary spirit, with love for . . . country, race and religion." By the early fifties an Issarak Monks' Association was active in twenty-four monasteries and claimed a membership of more than seven hundred monks in Prey Veng province alone.[13] But it was difficult for them to become full members of the Party. As part of the "exploiting class," monks had to serve a nine-month probationary period before earning full Party membership rights (Kiernan 1985, 94).

The case of Kong Sophal (also known as Keu) is a particularly interesting example of someone with strong Buddhist connections who would subsequently go on to a leadership role within the communist movement. Born in 1927 in Battambang province, he was five when his family moved to Oudong district, Kampong Speu province. When he was in his teens, his mother sent him to study at Wat Dambok Mean Leak, but after a while his famous uncle, Ven. Hem Chieu, took him to live at Wat Unnalom. After Hem Chieu's arrest and imprisonment by the French, Kong Sophal continued to live at Wat Unnalom until 1945. He joined the Party in 1958, possibly recruited by Saloth Sar (also known as Pol Pot), and became very popular with monks because of his kinship with the great national martyr.[14] In due course he became a revolutionary youth leader and played a major role in the organization of the 1967 Samlaut uprising,[15] eventually joining the Party's influential Standing Committee in 1978. Kong Sophal was arrested for treachery and transferred to S-21 in November 1978.

The S-21 confession of Yuk Chuong (alias Chon), dated 23 December 1978, gives a further picture of the role that monks played in the early years of the movement.[16] As a child, Chon had studied at a *wat* school in his native district, but he moved to the Lycée Yukunthor in Phnom Penh in 1960. His athletics instructor was Kong Sophal, and through him he was introduced to Son Sen, who would later rise to become Democratic Kampuchea's defense minister. Chon was subsequently inducted into the Party's Youth League by an individual living at Wat Botum Vaddei. His first mission was to work with students at Yukunthor, but after leaving school in 1966, he linked up with other Party members, some of whom were students at the Buddhist University. Chon, it seems, had helped organize an antigovernment demonstration outside the Royal Palace, though it was something of a dud. A few young men did turn up, but only one monk participated. Apparently there had been a Party order not to let monks get mixed up in the action.

The Communist Party of Kampuchea (CPK) was established in September 1960. Tou Samouth became its first secretary and Nuon Chea his deputy.[17] As we have seen, Tou Samouth had received a fairly traditional Buddhist education, and younger members like Saloth Sar (Pol Pot), who had been trained in the French system, may have been attracted to him for this very reason (Chandler 1999, 43).[18] However, Tou Samouth's mysterious death in July 1962 left the Party bereft of any significant figure connected with higher levels of traditional learning, and this may have been one of the factors that would in due course contribute to the extreme anticlericalism of the Democratic Kampuchea period (1975–1979).[19] It is certainly the case that after Tou's disappearance few senior communists could trace an unbroken lineage back through the old ICP to the events of 1942.[20] In some cases, they may not have wished to.[21]

Whatever the nature of post-1962 Cambodian communism, the break with tradition did not come abruptly. While working as acting secretary of the Party's Central Committee, Saloth Sar gave a number of seminars in Phnom Penh in late 1962, shortly before escaping into the maquis. Ven. Sok Chuon, who had been a Buddhist monk for ten years at the time, remembers the future Pol Pot speaking persuasively about the "new society" to an audience of around fifty individuals, thirty of whom were monks from three monasteries in Phnom Penh. He also recalled Pol Pot defending the Buddha on the grounds that he "had never sold anything" (Chandler 1999, 62).

Despite an early affection for Buddhism, by the 1960s the Party was beginning "to shed its Buddhist mantle" (Keyes 1994, 55). A document probably written as the basis for discussions with the Vietnamese in Hanoi during June 1965 represents an important transition point. Referring to the approximately seventy thousand monks in the country, of whom sixty thousand were "young and strong," the document's authors note the potential for revolutionary activity among those with a peasant background. They assert that despite the monkhood's feudal influence over the people "the revolution must understand this problem in depth in order to win over the monks and transform them into an important political force" (quoted in Engelbert and Goscha 1995, 130). In response Le Duan, the general secretary of the Communist Party of Vietnam, advised, "In Kampuchea, if we are going to build up the [national democratic] front in the villages, then we have to join with religious [forces; otherwise] . . . the bourgeoisie class will use religion in order to draw the peasants away from us. . . . [W]e must think carefully in order to have a correct religious policy" (quoted in ibid.). Le Duan's rejoinder may, perhaps, reflect concerns about Sihanouk's own manipulation of Buddhism during the Sangkum period.

## Senior Communists: "From Monks to Murderers"?

The future Pol Pot went to Phnom Penh to live with his cousin, one of King Monivong's many concubines, when he was five years of age. It seems likely that he spent a short period as a novice monk at Wat Botum Vaddei, the chief monastery of the aristocratic and royalist Thommayut order situated a stone's throw from the Royal Palace, for about one year when he was fifteen.[22] Pol Pot himself claimed to have spent six years in a monastery, two of them as a monk, but most commentators have regarded this as an exaggeration (Short 2004, 21). Nevertheless, he was said to have absorbed the ideals of "disciplined personal transformation, rebirth and enlightenment" (Chandler 1999, 6) from this Buddhist background, and his frequent attacks on individualism and—rather more puzzlingly, given subsequent events— his emphasis on kindheartedness probably derived from the same source. We know that when he was a student in Paris, he was extolling the virtues of the Buddha, and he even appears to have spoken positively about certain aspects of Buddhism as late as August 1978.

Seen from an indigenous perspective, the period spent in the forest before the Khmer Rouge gained full control of the country gave Pol Pot and his fellow revolutionaries an almost mystical power of the sort obtained by the ascetic heroes of the *Rāmakīrti* and the early Buddhist tradition (Chandler 1999, 76–77). This early experience of wilderness existence also replicated an ancient model of kingship in which a period of renunciation is the ideal preparation for eventual appearance on the political and ritual stage.[23] Indeed, in 1977 Pol Pot asserted that his work with tribal peoples in the forests of the northeast some fifteen years previously had built up the invincible force that prefigured final victory (Quinn 1982, 31). These experiences undoubtedly fed the perception of some Cambodian communists that they were capable of reshaping the world on a massive scale. There are some parallels here with Ho Chi Minh, as Paul Mus once noted, remarking that in the eyes of his followers Ho Chi Minh was not "the bearer of alien teachings [i.e., Marxism] which would require the renunciation of their existing moral norms. On the contrary, he embodied the same values of reverence for . . . divinized soil which the young fighters had been taught to cherish from childhood. Far from being a modernizer or a destroyer of the nation's ancient moral system, Ho was its true fulfillment, a patriot and champion of righteousness" (quoted in Bayly 2000, 616).

Pol Pot came across as a polite and reasonably cultured man. He was known to recite Verlaine and Rimbaud by heart (Martin 1994, 108), and his demeanor was not dissimilar to that of a monk.[24] In 1978 he claimed to live

Pol Pot. (Documentation Center of Cambodia)

with a "Buddhist calm mind" (Stanic 1978), and he often carried a monastic-style fan.[25] One of Pol Pot's long-term followers, In Sopheap, observed, "He was serene, like a monk. For a monk, there are different levels. At the first level, you feel joy. And it's good. Then there's a second level. You no longer feel anything for yourself, but you feel the joy of others. And finally, there's a third level. You are completely neutral. Nothing moves you. This is the highest level. Pol Pot situated himself in that tradition of serenity" (quoted in Short 2004, 340). It is noteworthy that In Sopheap specifically referred to the practice of Buddhist meditation and in particular the attainment of equanimity, the highest of the four divine abidings (*brahmavihāra*), in this attempt to delineate Pol Pot's character.

After the collapse of Democratic Kampuchea, the leaders withdrew to the wilderness once more. With virtually no external support, the rump of extreme Cambodian communism fell back into a mode of life with a strongly renunciatory character. From the late 1980s Pol Pot lived at a forest headquarters, Office 87, a compound described as resembling a Buddhist monastery or hermitage, where he described pure Party members as the "ordained." In teaching sessions delivered in a "monastic style," with primacy given to oral presentation, he characterized the world as caught in a titanic clash between the forces of good and evil. Many of his listeners reported being strongly impressed by what they had heard (Chandler 1999, 175–177). Such an existence and outlook might be read as a warped epitome of the mythical and ascetical ideals that underscored Cambodian culture for many centuries before the opening of the modern epoch.

Pol Pot was not the only senior Khmer Rouge figure to have had more than a passing acquaintance with Buddhism. Ieng Sary, the Democratic Kampuchea vice-premier for foreign affairs, had been born Kim Trang, the son of a village chief in Kampuchea Krom in 1924. But his family lost their economic status, and by the age of fifteen he had moved to Prey Veng, where an elderly *achar* called Ieng took him under his wing. Soon after, the young Ieng Sary learned about the Umbrella War then unfolding in Phnom Penh. It was clearly a formative event, for much later he claimed that this was the first time he came to any understanding of what might be meant by the term "nation" (Short 2004, 30). Son Sen (1927–1997), Democratic Kampuchea's defense minister, came from the same region of Kampuchea Krom as Ieng Sary and was a Buddhist monk before moving to Paris for further education. When he and Ieng Sary returned to Cambodia in mid-1956, they were both assigned duties recruiting monks and students. Son Sen's connection with

Buddhism is reinforced by his having held an administrative position at the Buddhist Institute. In fact he worked on the Tripiṭaka Commission, a body charged with translating the Theravāda Buddhist canon (*tipiṭaka*) from Pāli into Khmer between 1957 and 1959.[26]

One of the most notorious of all Khmer Rouge commanders, Ta Mok, had also been a monk. Born Ung Choeun in Tram Kak district, Takeo province in 1926, he was the eldest of seven children.[27] His family was conspicuously religious. His father, Ung Preak, had been a senior monk teacher at Wat Mohamontrei, Phnom Penh, and the young Mok became a novice at Wat Trapeang Thom, near his home village.[28] A year later he transferred to Wat Mohamontrei, and ten years after that he completed his intermediate training, hoping to join Phnom Penh's prestigious École Supérieure de Pāli. However, it appears that he failed the entrance examination.

By this time Mok was better known as Achar Choeun. He was esteemed as a proficient preacher,[29] but he left the monkhood to join the Khmer resistance soon after the Umbrella War disturbances[30] and by 1949 he was playing a leading role in the Issarak movement.[31] Ta Mok married after the cessation of hostilities, although this did not prevent him from reordaining at Wat Kat Phluk, Kampong Speu, probably around 1954. There is conflicting

Ieng Sary (*center*) and Khieu Samphan (*far right*) with a delegation of Lao officials. (Documentation Center of Cambodia)

evidence on his contacts with organized Buddhism following this event, but Heder (1997, 125) suggests that from there he went to Phnom Penh, where he taught monks and finally enrolled as a student at the Pāli High School. It was here that he met Pol Pot for the first time, probably in the early 1960s (Kiernan 1996, 87). By now Ta Mok was known for his readiness to engage in heated disputes with fellow monks. In particular he argued that traditional Buddhist merit-making rites were expressed in socially unprofitable ways, such as the construction and prettification of monastery buildings. Donations would be better used for the construction of roads and the provision of other public services, an outlook that may, conceivably, have been shared by the historical Buddha.[32]

The early life of Democratic Kampuchea's first minister of information, Hu Nim, is also instructive. In the forced confession obtained before his execution in July 1977, he recalled that as a small boy he was obliged to live in the local pagoda after his father died.[33] The chief monk brought Hu Nim up as his own son and provided the boy's first access to education. In the early 1950s he moved to Phnom Penh, where he studied at the

Son Sen. (Documentation Center of Cambodia)

Lycée Sisowath and lived with a monk at Wat Unnalom. In contrast with hard-line opponents of Buddhism within the Khmer Rouge, Hu Nim was regarded as "OK." His confession informs us that, while residing at Wat Unnalom, he became involved with "the contemptible Son Ngoc Thanh."[34] There would have been nothing especially problematic about this at the time, for Thanh and Minh's Issarak groups cooperated in the early 1950s. But after the Geneva Agreements on Indochina of 1954, Thanh founded the explicitly rightist Khmer Serei with American support, and by the 1960s the CPK and the Khmer Serei were vying for influence at the main monasteries in Phnom Penh. Nevertheless there remained considerable crossover between the two movements. and it would be much later before past connections with Thanh and his circle were regarded as a form of dangerous treachery.[35]

Hu Nim's confession, although it must be used with great care, is of some interest for what it says about Chan Chakrei (ca. 1930–1976). Also known as Prom Sambot, Chakrei has been described as a "flamboyant ex-monk who became commander of the Khmer Rouge 170th Division," operating in the Eastern Zone. It appears that, perhaps as Hu Nim did, he favored "a less extreme communist system, one more tolerant of human failings" (Short 2004, 258). Nevertheless, Chakrei rapidly rose through the revolutionary hierarchy, becoming deputy chief of the General Staff of the Revolutionary Army of Kampuchea in July 1975.

In 1960 Chan Chakrei was a monk at Wat Ampil, Prey Veng province, but in 1963 he moved to Wat Langka, Phnom Penh, to begin studies at the

Hu Nim greeting Sihanouk, March 1973. (From *Samdech Sihanouk's Inspection Tour of the Cambodian Liberated Zone* 1973, 11)

Son Ngoc Thanh.

Pāli High School. It was here that Chakrei was recruited into the Khmer Serei, probably by Khieu Chum, a senior figure at Wat Langka and a close associate of Son Ngoc Thanh from the early 1940s on. It must have been a little later that Chakrei crossed over to the leftists (Chandler 1991, 286–287; Kane 2007, 70; Chandler et al. 1988, 298). In any case Chakrei began to propagandize *sangha* members, and three or four years later he was sent to Zone 24, under the command of Chhouk, also known as Suas Son, who had once been one of Chakrei's fellow students at the Pāli High School.[36]

In early 1974 there had been a quarrel at high levels of the Party over whether it should continue to respect Khmer customs and religion. It seems that a group had crystallized around Chin Y, Chin Ok, and some others who argued that Buddhism should continue to be appreciated and that the people should be granted "the right to do what they want" in terms of religion.[37] The group came to be called the White Khmer (*Khmaer Sa*) or White Scarf Khmer (*Khmaer Kamsan Sa*), and according to Kao Muon, its committee member with particular responsibility for monks, Chakrei had joined the movement soon after it formed.[38]

On 30 August 1976 a Khmer Rouge telegram reported a revolt of "enemies" at Ang Prauch, on the border between Kandal Stung district and Zone 33.[39] It appears that some people had held a demonstration in which banners bearing slogans such as "Long Live Buddhism," "Long Live the White Khmer Front," and "Liberate Earned Rice" were carried. The telegram identified Chakrei as the chief of the rebels,[40] although it seems very unlikely that he was actually present. However, he was detained on 19 May and subsequently transferred to S-21, the highest-ranking individual at that stage to have ended up in that ill-fated place. The reason for his imprisonment was that, on 2 April, a grenade had exploded outside the Royal Palace, and following the interrogation of a low-ranking soldier, Chakrei was implicated in a "plot" that was possibly targeting Pol Pot's headquarters (Chandler 1991, 286–287).[41]

Although it is difficult to get to the bottom of this convoluted series of events or the actual connection between Chakrei and the White Khmer, it looks probable that the rebellion and subsequent execution of Chakrei and other old members of the mid-1950s Pracheachon (*prajājan*) group, such as Keo Meas and Chou Chet,[42] may not have been solely because they were agents of Vietnam, as Angkar claimed, but because they wished to impose a less austere and terrifying socialist regime in which a modicum of Buddhist belief and practice would be tolerated. There were certainly concerns that

Pol Pot, Ieng Sary, and their respective wives and relatives were taking charge of everything and that the government was becoming a family affair (Heder 1983). Whatever the true position, the official line on Buddhism seriously tightened after this point.

As far as religious policy was concerned, the script followed by the Khmer Rouge became increasingly oppressive. The knowledge and experience of senior leaders meant that an extreme approach modeled on the Chinese Cultural Revolution appeared especially attractive. However, not all were persuaded. Some prominent figures were still able to trace a genealogy back to the earliest stages of communist activity in Cambodia, when the movement was given its distinctive form through contact with traditional sources of intellectual expertise largely deriving from the country's indigenous Buddhist background. But as the civil war drew to a conclusion, most of these individuals were being sidelined, and many would soon be dead. The process of change had started in the early 1960s, but by the time Democratic Kampuchea had been established, hard-line antireligious zealots reigned virtually unopposed. Yet, paradoxically, a bricolage of protestantized and rationalistic Buddhist categories, concepts, and practices retained a place in the movement's ideology and continued to inform its actions.

Keo Meas (with black belt) during an anti-Sihanouk demonstration in the Issarak period, location and date unknown. (Documentation Center of Cambodia)

# CHAPTER THREE

# Buddhism and Khmer Communism
## A Shared Conceptual Terrain

### Identifying Parallels

Duch (b. 1942) was the chief of the Khmer Rouge S-21 security facility at Tuol Sleng, where around sixteen thousand persons perished during Democratic Kampuchea.[1] He had been educated at the Lycée Sisowath and in 1959 came in second in the country's national baccalaureate examinations. Subsequently enrolled as a student at Phnom Penh University, he managed, as many poor young men before him had, to find housing at Wat Unnalom—probably in monks' house (*kuṭī*) number 3 (Huy Vannak 2003, 83). During his first period of residence there, in 1961–1964, Duch's political activities came to the attention of the monastery's most senior resident, *saṅgharāja* Chuon Nath, who tried to dissuade him. Somewhat later Duch was reportedly telling friends that "religion is a blood-sucking leech," and he seems to have had some success in encouraging a number of monks to disrobe and join the revolution (Phat 2000).

In 1971, long before his appointment as director of S-21, Duch had imprisoned and interrogated the French scholar François Bizot. Extraordinarily, Bizot had attempted to persuade his inquisitor that the discipline and practice of the Khmer Rouge bore a remarkable resemblance to Buddhism. Bizot noted that both monks and Cambodian communist revolutionaries renounced worldly goods, family, and children and followed a specific, rule-bounded discipline (*vinaya*). Initiation into both organizations involved a ceremony in which the candidate received a new name and a set number of clothing items[2]—seven pieces in the case of a monk, six for the Party member[3]—and both maintained a fairly rigid distinction between fully initiated members and those undergoing apprenticeship. Bizot might have added that the concept of Party age (*āyu pakkh*), something admittedly encountered in communist China, Vietnam, and the USSR, also paralleled Buddhist procedures of seniority, and similarities may even be found in the way Cambodian communists and Buddhists intoned their respective litanies, all the way down to the use of specific trills at the end of each stanza.

According to Bizot's account of what must have been a remarkable dialogue, Duch remained completely unconvinced by the argument. He accused the French scholar of suffering from intellectual delirium and characterized Buddhism in a typically Marxist manner as the opium of the people. For Duch, moreover, Buddhism had contributed to a brutalization of the peasantry, whereas Angkar, by contrast, wished to glorify them. Nevertheless, his rejection was not total. He seems to have accepted that the Cambodian people must "rediscover the source of their morals" (Bizot 2000, 161ff.), and this tantalizing glimpse into the indigenous thought universe as the possible foundation of a revolutionary ethic serves as the starting point in this chapter's effort to establish filial links between the ideology of Angkar and the more traditional Buddhist categories and attitudes that are well established in Cambodian history and culture.

In a 1943 report critical of Buddhism and of the activities of the Buddhist Institute in Phnom Penh, Résident Supérieur Georges Gautier contrasted the French and Buddhist approaches to life: "[The] Protectorate promotes activity, the spirit of enterprise, ambition, and the love of gain, that is to say, the contrary of what Buddhist law prescribes. Cambodians must come out of their dreams and abandon metaphysics. . . ."[4] With one or two modifications this was also the position of the communists, but we should not assume from this that their antipathy toward religion was a straightforward reflection of an anticlericalism derived from European sources. An equally vigorous concern over "nonproductive" aspects of the monastic life is a recurring theme in the history of Asian cultures. The Zen saying "One day without work; one day without food," for example, expresses a deeply rooted indigenous suspicion of the otherworldly spirit.

Well before the outbreak of civil war that ended the short-lived Khmer Republic (1970–1975), the communists were pointing to the economic burden that so many unproductive monks placed on the country. They were "leeches" upon society, and what's more, they promoted the reactionary doctrine of karma, a notion that underpinned belief in the "natural inequality" of persons (Hinton 1998, 110).[5] Such ideas encouraged the masses to passively accept their lot. The traditional conception of wisdom clearly had to be reengineered. In the past, a wise man was someone who understood and endorsed the social hierarchy. In the future, wisdom would be determined by other values. However, such a radical shift in mentality would not be achieved overnight.

One of Saloth Sar's earliest political writings, an article entitled "Monarchy or Democracy," was published in 1952 when he was still a student in Paris. In it, the author, who styled himself the "original Khmer" (*khmaer ṭoem*), visualizes a reconstituted Cambodia in which a "democratic regime will bring back the Buddhist moralism because our great leader Buddha was the first to have taught [democracy]." The future Pol Pot argues that although the Buddha was the son of a king, he left his family home "to be a friend to all men, and to teach people to love one another." This renunciation of kingship, then, stood in sharp contrast to the contemporary French-backed Cambodian monarchy, which was deemed "inimical to Buddhism" because it placed itself "above religion." In Saloth Sar's view, Sihanouk, particularly, had eroded Buddhism's respected position in the country by a variety of policies, including the introduction of ranks into the *saṅgha*.[6]

Saloth Sar's essay makes reference to the French Revolution, which he approvingly notes had "dissolved the monarchy and executed the king,"[7] but he also recognizes Cambodian parallels. Some enlightened monks of the past "always understood very well the nature of monarchy," and, as a consequence, they championed democratic ideals as the only means by which Buddhism's "profound values" could be protected. Indeed, the argument about Buddhism being inimical to monarchy is surprisingly similar to that advanced in rather more detail by Khieu Chum, the prominent Wat Langka–based monk who may have been involved in the successful plot to oust Sihanouk from power in March 1970 (Harris 2008).

Evidence, then, suggests that at this period Saloth Sar shared the same Buddhism-tinged thought universe as earlier figures in the anticolonial movement, Son Ngoc Minh and Tou Samouth, for example. When set in a wider Southeast Asian context this is hardly surprising.[8] In late-1940s Burma the Association of Marxist Monks, for example, was extolling the advent of socialism in Buddhist terms. For those monks Buddhist socialism represented a return to the age of the righteous "wheel-turning king" (*cakkavatti*), while U Ba Swe, in his Burmese Revolution of 1951, was forging an uneasy synthesis in which "Marxist Abhidhamma," as a means of overcoming economic misery, was joined to the higher "Buddhist Abhidhamma," as the final solution to all other forms of suffering (Sarkisyanz 1965, 197, 199).[9]

Similar accommodations between Buddhism and Marxism were also fermenting in Thailand. A good example is that of Samak Burawat, a teacher of philosophy at Mahamakut Buddhist University in the late 1940s to early 1950s. His attempt to transform Buddhism into a "single system of knowledge" (*pen an nung an diawkun*) through its integration with Marxism and social Darwinism resulted in a number of books (Day and Reynolds 2000, 54),[10] while Pridi Banomyong's Impermanence of Society (1957)[11]—the author has been deemed "often stunning in his naivete and disappointing in his simplistic approach to complex ideas" (Morell and Morell 1972, 399)—represented another attempt at Marxist-Buddhist synthesis unified by the central notion of impermanence (*annicang*).

In the early 1960s the Khmer Workers' Party (KWP) ran a newspaper entitled *Pañcasīlā* (literally, "Five Pillars" or "Five Precepts") (Heder 2004, 80). The appellation is a reference to the five principles jointly developed by Nehru and Zhou Enlai in 1954 as a guide to Sino-Indian relations and subsequently adopted by the Non-Aligned Movement.[12] But the newspaper's title would have had particularly strong resonances in Cambodia, for it could also be understood as a reference to the five fundamental lay Buddhist precepts of not taking life, not taking what is not given, abstention from sexual misconduct, abstention from false speech, and abstention from liquor that causes intoxication and indolence. It is possible that the title was specifically chosen to appeal to a variety of constituencies both religious and secular.

A number of key observers have claimed that Pol Pot and his inner circle carefully studied the Chinese Cultural Revolution and that this was the basis of their decision that Buddhist monks had to be defrocked (Heder 1983). Pol Pot and Ieng Sary certainly admitted their debt to China,[13] and there are obvious parallels in the way that Cambodian and Chinese communists manifested hostility toward individual, as opposed to collective, incentives while indulging in a high level of rural romanticism (Quinn 1982, 180ff.). But the extreme violence and terror used to achieve rapid transition to a "pure" society were not deployed in China to the extent used by the Khmer Rouge. While the idea had been vaguely contemplated, money was not abolished[14] during the Cultural Revolution (it is tempting to interpret the abolition as a radicalization of the tenth Buddhist monastic precept, which forbids the handling of gold and silver), and although in the early 1960s Mao had urged millions of city dwellers to join rural communes to maximize production through the *xiafang* (sent-down [to the countryside]) movement, the policy was soon changed when adverse economic consequences became apparent (Kiernan 2006, 199).

Steve Heder (2004, 3) has argued that Khmer Rouge policy was almost entirely modeled on Vietnamese communism. There are certainly obvious parallels in the Vietnamese and Cambodian communist attitudes toward Buddhism, but in Vietnam these were more fully rooted in premodern rivalries between differing religious systems.[15] During and before the Trần dynasty (1225–1400), Buddhism had risen to a position of considerable prestige in Vietnam. But it had its opponents, notably among Confucian officials, who argued that Buddhism encouraged too relaxed a style of government. Throughout the fourteenth century the struggle intensified to the point that donations to pagodas were condemned as a waste of money and manpower, and Buddhism was equated with superstition. As rural governance deteriorated over the period, undermining both familial bonds and village stability, Buddhists were held partly responsible. Indeed, the increase in vagabondage, political disaffection and anarchy during the period was attributed to the influence of Buddhist monks, some of whom were suspected of entering pagodas merely to escape heavy taxation and other forms of unjust treatment. By the end of the fourteenth century, Emperor Hồ Quý Ly was especially concerned about the marauding bands of Buddhist monks. In 1398 he was also responsible for an act of *saṅgha* "purification" by which all monks below the age of fifty were defrocked and forcibly recruited into the army to fight the Cham.

Campaigns to restrict ordination to monks over the age of fifty also occurred in nineteenth-century Vietnam (Nguyên Thê Anh 1993, 106–107, 110), and the communists evacuated towns in the north of the country in the 1947–1954 period.[16] After 1975 those not engaged in production were encouraged to leave Ho Chi Minh City for New Economic Zones, and we know that some revolutionaries harbored hostility to the "jungle of houses" (Quinn-Judge 2006, 209–210). This, in a very general sense, appears to support Heder's thesis that the evacuation of Phnom Penh after its fall to the Khmer Rouge in April 1975 may have been based on Vietnamese precedents, but I do not feel that it satisfactorily addresses the prior political and ritual significance of Phnom Penh. In many ways the emptying of Phnom Penh was a unique event.[17]

Chantou Boua (1991, 228) has suggested that during the 1970–1975 civil war period, it was not entirely "clear what the Khmer Rouge policy was towards Buddhism." The political program that FUNK, the anti–Lon Nol coalition of Sihanouk and the Khmer Rouge, adopted in May 1970 stated that "Buddhism is and will remain the religion of the state." Khieu Samphan, Hou Yuon, and Hu Nim, who made a joint appeal on behalf of FUNK on 9 September 1970, also called on monks and others to liberate the country from the Khmer Republic government. In 1972, furthermore, Ieng Sary wrote a pamphlet that sought to answer the question "Does coexistence between Buddhist monks and progressive and Marxist militants within . . . [FUNK] give rise to serious problems?" Recognizing the "heroic" role of Buddhist *achar*s in former liberation struggles, he observes that *saṅgha* members were "eyewitnesses to the heinous crimes of the US aggressors and lackeys who destroy pagodas . . . and force them into activities banned by the religion" and concludes by declaring his respect for "the rights and liberties of those monks who are sincere and loyal to the . . . [FUNK] and the people" (Ieng Sary n.d., 13–15; my italics).[18]

During an interview conducted by Serge Thion in 1972, the senior communist Vorn Vet halted the conversation to kneel deferentially before some passing monks (Thion 1993, xv).[19] It has been customary to regard such traditional manifestations of respect as part of a deliberately cynical exercise connected with the need to construct a united front at an early stage in the revolutionary process. However, as was noted in the previous chapter, it would be unwise to read the Khmer Rouge as a fully integrated political entity. Chinese sources suggest that there may have been three antagonist Khmer Rouge factions by the time Phnom Penh fell in April 1975 (Slocomb 2003, 37–39), and splits within the movement were, in part, related to views over the future of Buddhism. We have seen that early policy differentiated between monks who could be expected to support the revolution and those who could not. It is perfectly possible that some key cadres may have believed that a new form of Buddhism, purged of superstitious and imperialist elements, would survive the heat of revolutionary change.

We possess some evidence of concern about the issue. One individual complained that Angkar had claimed that it intended to get rid of only capitalists and soldiers, "but now there is no Buddhism, no monkhood, and no schools, no teachers, no markets."[20] Another recruit to the communist cause transferred his allegiance to the Lon Nol government in February 1974, citing as his reason that the Khmer Rouge were curtailing religious freedoms, prohibiting marriage, and obstructing the observance of Buddhist festivals.[21]

One old monk who survived the Pol Pot period maintained that as far as religion was concerned, Hou Yuon and Hu Nim "were all right" but Khieu Samphan had always been "against monks and Buddhism."[22] That Hu Nim was a hard-liner is revealed by his reported remark that "if we are faithful to the people, it does not matter what we do to the Buddhist monks."[23] This assessment is also supported by a lengthy Khmer Republic document detailing the interrogation of a monk from Kandal province by Hu Nim.[24] It reveals that on 25 February 1974 all the chief monks of Sa-ang district were gathered together for a meeting in which they were obliged to discuss a six-point plan apparently drawn up by Khieu Samphan. The six points consisted of a water policy whereby each pagoda had to make between one and ten waterwheels, and monks were expected to construct dams; a cultivation policy specifying that land within pagodas should be cultivated with cotton, potatoes, rice, and bananas to support the local economy; an evacuation policy designed to weed out "false monks"; a donation policy through which a certain *brah grū* (honored teacher) Thong Pim was appointed to collect funds and assorted goods from all the pagodas in the district; a collectivization policy; and a disrobing policy. It appears that an earlier phase of anti-Buddhist propaganda and forced disrobing in 1972–1973 had proved very unpopular, particularly among the people of Sa-ang and Koh Thom, and, as a result, the communists had created a local Ministry of Cults to persuade monks "to love communism," using previously disrobed monks as propagandists.

From this point on, the campaign against Buddhism proceeded more cautiously. An undated Lon Nol government intelligence report,[25] for example, described the Khmer Rouge's indoctrination of a group of youths who were "taught to hate Buddhism." The youths were also told that Buddhism would be eliminated but that they must not communicate this fact to the people. Although forced disrobing may have lessened because of its unpopularity, monks continued to be denounced as beggars[26]—a curious detail, given that "beggar" is the literal and traditionally uncontentious meaning of the term *bhikkhu*! The unpatriotic character of Buddhism as a religion of Indian origin and with suspicious links to a Thailand that "does not belong to the Khmer people" was also highlighted,[27] as was the notion that US imperialists were supporting Buddhism as a means of "sucking the people's blood."[28] Thus the war against American imperialism was also a struggle against Buddhism understood as a form of "imperialist wisdom."[29]

Soon after the 17 April 1975 liberation, Ieng Sary, now the minister of foreign affairs, announced that there would be freedom for all religious groups in the new state of Democratic Kampuchea. This freedom was subsequently enshrined in Article 20 of the Constitution, promulgated on 5 January 1976, which declared: "Every Cambodian has the right to worship according to any religion and the right not to worship according to any religion. Reactionary religion [*sāsanā pratikiriyā*], which is detrimental to Democratic Kampuchea and the Cambodian people, is absolutely forbidden."[30] Khieu Samphan elaborated on this matter in December 1975: "Article 20 stipulates that our people have the right to practice whatever religion they like and the right not to practice any religion at all. Also, as stated in our constitution, our stand is to not allow any foreign imperialists to use religion to subvert us."[31] Most commentators have accepted the interpretation presented in Vietnamese propaganda at the time, which referred to Article 20 as a "dead letter" (Dossier Kampuchéa, 29). However, a softer reading could be held to allow for certain forms of "patriotic" religion. This may explain why, of all the religions that had flourished in Cambodia prior to the Democratic Kampuchea period, only the animism of hill tribes escaped substantial persecution (Etcheson 1984, 151).[32]

Naturally, none of the oracular or prophetic functions of any religions would be tolerated, and the constitution terminated Buddhism's prior status as the religion of the state. But these developments need not be interpreted as a total attack on Buddhism's foundational teachings. The continued existence of an apotropaic Buddhism divested of all foreign or reactionary components was still a remote possibility.

The "Red Standard of the Revolution" (*Daṅ' kraham paṭivatt(n)*) was one of the more popular revolutionary songs of the Democratic Kampuchea period. Focusing on the blood sacrificed by the masses, its first verse includes this refrain: "Blood of workers, of peasants, and of intellectuals: Blood of young men, of monks, and of girls. The blood swirls away and flows upward, gently into the sky, Turning into a red, revolutionary flag!" (Locard 1998, 325). The refrain indicates that the song's author, who may have been Pol Pot himself, still envisaged some monks fighting on the revolutionary side.[33] And as late as August 1978, Pol Pot responded in the following way to a delegation of Belgian communists who asked him about the condition of Buddhism:

In Kampuchea, Buddhism is attached to the people. Monks come from peasant backgrounds. Peasants have joined the revolution and deeply realized the ideals of the revolution, especially in the national liberation when the revolutionary movement was very strong. Peasants are actively involved in the revolution; they provide one part of the manpower to the battlefield and the other to the rice fields. Many monks disrobed to join the revolution. From 1973 or 1974 monks were at a maximum number. Now only a handful of old monks exist. Therefore in Kampuchea religion works its way to align with the revolution. We had pagodas but the enemy destroyed them. Today we try to preserve good pagodas. ("Dialogue between Pol Pot" 2004)

Intriguingly, then, the speech explicitly acknowledges the strong popular support for Buddhism, points to the valued services of revolutionary monks with peasant backgrounds, and identifies the 1973–1974 period as a high-water mark in monastic commitment to the liberation struggle. Pol Pot accepts that some old monks were still in robes in 1978 and that the authorities knew about this and appeared to tolerate the situation. He concludes by attributing the destruction of many pagodas to enemy action and offering the expectation that pagodas of high cultural value will be preserved for future generations.[34] Much of this was not so far from the truth.

## The Nature of Khmer Rouge Ideology

There has been a great deal of discussion of what contributed to the uniquely virulent form of communism displayed during the Democratic Kampuchea period. Some have argued that it was a degenerate form of Maoism, warped by the brutalization (*déraillement*) induced through long years of bloody conflict. Others have invoked the personal neuroses and sexual impotence of some Khmer Rouge leaders. At the more sophisticated end of the spectrum, Karl Jackson (1989, 250) allows that the intellectual genealogy of Khmer communism was multiple, including "Maoism, European Marxism, Fanonism, perhaps Stalinism, and certainly Khmer nationalism," while at the opposite extreme, Kiernan (2006, 201) has concluded that the search for parallels to Democratic Kampuchea is pointless and it would be better to regard the regime as a sui generis phenomenon.

In the following discussion, I try to take a middle path that focuses on both external and indigenous factors. I would certainly not want to claim that dramatic social and political change may never be precipitated solely by foreign influence, but one would expect a careful examination and dismissal of all relevant indigenous factors before such a conclusion is reached. With the exception of one or two vague hints in the literature, it is not clear to me that such considerations have formed a significant part of the scholarly project to understand Cambodia at this crucial point in its history.[35]

Some form of socialism appears to have been an ingredient in the ideology of all of Cambodia's postindependence political systems, up to and including the People's Republic of Kampuchea (PRK). But another unifying factor binding these apparently disparate polities together is that they have all interpreted socialism in distinctively Khmer ways (Slocomb 2006, 388). This seems be one of the reasons why scholarly attempts to situate the Khmer Rouge within mainstream communism have never been entirely satisfactory. Morris (1999, 71) has described the Cambodian revolutionaries as "hyperMaoist" in the sense that they seemed to be trying to "outdo Mao Zedong." However, Mao tended to place his faith in the power of technology to transform the economic conditions of China, whereas the Khmer Rouge opposed all forms of modernist expertise. The political line of the CPK, in contrast, was characterized by an emphasis on the primacy of the human will, with ideological purity taking precedence over material factors such as technology, and this produced a highly unrealistic, almost magical, worldview. To give one example, the Khmer Rouge leaders believed that they would inflict thirty times as many losses as they would receive during the 1978 border dispute with Vietnam, despite massive imbalances in manpower and equipment very much to the advantage of the Vietnamese (ibid., 104). Democratic Kampuchea's large-scale hydraulic works are another case in point. Some have argued that these were inspired by near-contemporary, large-scale socialist civil engineering ventures, like the Soviet Volga-Don Canal project, completed in February 1952 (Sher 2003, 27). This strikes one as mildly absurd, both culturally and historically, given the far more obvious model of indigenous Southeast Asian water control techniques dating back to at least the beginning of the Angkorian period.

Sacha Sher (2003, 22) is too dismissive when he claims that Khieu Samphan's 1959 French doctoral thesis speaks in a "manner fantastical" about the achievements of Angkor. Angkor actually remained an important symbol for the Khmer Rouge, who never entirely repudiated its enchanting influence. It appeared on the flag of Democratic Kampuchea and was mentioned in the national anthem, and visiting dignitaries from friendly nations such as Senegal and Egypt continued to visit Angkor Wat as tourists throughout the regime. The praise was certainly not unequivocal. For the communists Angkor was not a religious site but both a source of national pride, having been "constructed by the people, not by the kings," and a scene of massive exploitation, built by slaves who had been ordered to construct great artificial lakes (*baray*) so that the feudalists might indulge in "nautical and libidinous pleasures" (ibid., 24–26).

Heder (2004, 3) has pointed to the "profound formulaicism" of the Cambodian communists, often "regardless of the facts." He also characterizes Khmer Rouge political and economic analysis as sometimes representing a "rigid ideological orthodoxy bordering on fetishism" (ibid., 74). Doctrinaire forms of governance are clearly found in other Asian communist settings, but there appears to be something distinctively Cambodian about this Khmer Rouge rule "by incantation." During Democratic Kampuchea, Radio Phnom Penh repeated stereotyped phrases with mantra-like regularity, and Pol Pot specifically instructed his information minister, Hu Nim, that the announcers should deliver their reports "like monks who lead the prayers at a *wat*."[36]

The repetitive nature of most Theravāda Buddhist sermonizing is well known, and the ability of the Khmer Rouge to adapt this technique with relatively little modification ensured that they could propagandize in a culturally appropriate manner. A former cadre, interviewed in 1979, in fact grumbled that "Pol Pot and the others were very good at making theory in terms of the 10-point elements, the 8-this, the 6-that, and all the rest of it, but when it came to the basic question of how to end the war they didn't have an answer" (quoted in Chandler 1999, 179). There are striking parallels to Buddhist scholastic categories here.

It seems that Pol Pot and possibly Nuon Chea may have known Stalin's collected works, and it might be argued that these provide a full script for the Democratic Kampuchea experiment. But few other senior figures were familiar with these writings, and many of Angkar's leaders were little short of constituting an "incompetent and half-literate ruling class" (Kiernan 2006, 200).[37] So the ideas that came from the highest level of Angkar were in need of translation into an indigenous idiom. This happened quite early in the history of the CPK, when Khmer student members of the Cercle Marxiste in Paris in the 1950s "interpreted Marxism through the prism of national culture, in their case an intensely normative form of Buddhism" (Short 2004, 65). This Buddhist idiom also manifested itself in a highly puritanical and ascetic outlook that existed long before the communist movement had properly coalesced. Early leaders had emerged from a background that naturally stressed the importance of self-control and renunciation in achieving a purely religious conception of liberation, while some members of the circle were already experimenting with parallel ideas and practices.[38]

In due course a dual emphasis was placed on "independence mastery" (*ekarāj mcās'kar*) and renunciation (*laḥ paṅ'*).[39] The masses were exhorted to renounce both worldly goods and control over their personal destiny. In 1975, Radio Phnom Penh urged its listeners to devote themselves wholeheartedly to the collective good through a series of specifically Buddhist renunciations:

> Renunciation of feelings of ownership [means] . . . that one must concentrate completely on the task at hand without thinking of oneself, as in Buddhist meditation. Renunciation of material goods [implies] . . . detachment from one's wife, one's children, and one's home, just as Buddha once renounced those things.[40] Renunciation of control over one's own life [means] . . . digging out from oneself the roots of pride, contempt for others, and complicated thoughts, as the monks used to preach before. The renunciation of the self is particularly necessary, as it concerns the emotional ties within the family—between husband and wife, parents and children, and children and parents. . . . You must eliminate from your mind all [such] individualistic notions. (Pin Yathay 1980, 222, 227)[41]

The aim seems to have been to systematically uproot all emotional ties as a means of striking at the heart of the old society. An attitude of "cutting off one's heart" (*ṭāc'citt;* Thai *tat cai*) had traditionally meant detachment from the "desires of the world while still living in the world." But for the revolutionaries it came to imply "feeling no emotion" when dealing with one's enemies (Keyes 2006, 29). The notion of heating (*tapas*) oneself to eliminate impurities, a ubiquitous idea in Buddhist literature, was widespread as well. Hinton (2002, 84) also points to the extensive use of the "tempering iron" (*lat'ṭaek*) metaphor. Those deemed insufficiently malleable would need to be hammered into shape, while resistance would result in the "reheating" of self-criticism so that the individual might eventually be "tamed" to serve the revolutionary organization (Hinton 1997, 20). The Khmer Rouge required not active heroism but the renunciation of self.

Whether conscious or not, obvious parallels exist between reported Khmer Rouge forms of execution and the traditional iconography of Buddhist hell. This subterranean region—presided over by Yomareach, the god of the dead who metes out punishments according to each person's previous actions (karma)—is commonly depicted on the walks of pagodas, and most Khmer are familiar with these representations. Such murals appear to be a potent source through which archetypal forms of violence are enacted. Similarly charged motifs can be found in related cultural contexts. The smashing of young children against trees, reported widely under the Khmer Rouge, is part of a well-known lexicon of atrocities purportedly committed by the Vietnamese during the early nineteenth century, and burying an enemy and his entire family up to the neck as a prelude to decapitation, a practice known as "cutting off the family line" (*phtāc' būj*), is an important element in the popular Khmer story of *Tum Teav* (Harris 2005a, 184). Indeed, a variation on the practice is commonly found in Theravāda legal literature.[42]

Post-Democratic Kampuchea pagoda mural depicting Khmer Rouge hell. Wat Intry Samvirak, Kampong Thom town.

Scène de tortures subies par des enfants khmers dans la province de Baray.
(*Satra lbaæk rôba khsat*, str. : 232-234)

Vietnamese killing Khmer children. Illustration from *Sāstrā lpoek rapā khsatr*, vv. 232–234, by Ven. Bâtum Baramey Pich. (From Khin Sok 2002, 93)

Buddhist categories were also widely pressed into service in an attempt to present Marxism to a puzzled population. In the crucial area of party dogma, the central Buddhist concept of dependent origination (*paṭiccasamuppāda*) was employed to translate "dialectical materialism" into Khmer.[43] The three structural elements of the stupa—the base, the bell, and the tip—were likewise compared to the progressive masses, the core organization, and the Party membership.[44] The call to develop a "proletarian consciousness" also made little sense in the agrarian context of most Khmer lives. As Paul Mus (1977, 82) noted, "The era of French colonization . . . left the rural areas of Indochina . . . with less a model than a caricature of capitalism." The conception of a class status based on economic activity was quite foreign to the indigenous mode of thought in Cambodia. But the idea of consciousness (*viññān*), a key Theravāda notion, was sufficiently mutable to be of use. Although it made little sense from a mainstream Marxist perspective, the factor that now defined economic status became a mental attribute, and the "idea that "proletarian consciousness" could be forged, independent of a person's class origins or economic status, became the central pillar of Khmer communism" (Short 2004, 150).[45] In the analysis of the Khmer Rouge, this will or consciousness was specifically linked to another cardinal Buddhist category, that of mindfulness (*sati*). Through the exercise of *sati,* Buddhist practitioners learn to see things "as they are," but in this reworking, potential revolutionaries would learn to use mindfulness to discern the Party's line. The practice had the added advantage that it would also uproot individuality, so that a person's energies could be dedicated to the collective good (Hinton 2005, 194–197).

Personnel were often expected to attend regular criticism and self-criticism sessions in order to root out individualist tendencies, including those related to eating and drinking. This had been a traditional concern of the *saṅgha,* but the Buddhist disciplinary code (*vinaya*) came under criticism and was trumped by the Khmer Rouge. Cadres began to observe a lengthy list of moral rules or Angkar commandments (*vinay aṅgkār*), clearly based on the monastic precepts and partly designed to prove that the revolutionaries were more worthy of the laity's respect than the *saṅgha* was.[46] Ascetic attitudes were reflected in strong disapproval of men who were in love with women or who enjoyed beer. Those who secretly consumed beer were referred to as "CIA drinkers" (Heder and Tittemore 2004, 43). A similar outlook is found in some of the revolutionary slogans of the time, such as "Physical beauty is an obstacle to the will to struggle" (*saṃbaḥ la'a jā upasagg nai chandaḥ prayuddh*) and "Comrade, don't touch women" (*mitt min trūv p"aḥ bāl'nārī phit ḷoey*)" (Locard 1996, 219). Khieu Samphan's statement to the Third

Khmer Rouge smashing children. (Vann Nath painting held at Tuol Sleng Museum)

National Congress of December 1975 that "there are no thieves, drunkards, hooligans, or prostitutes in our country . . . [and] magazines which used to spread the corrupt, perverted culture exist no more" might easily have been uttered by a Buddhist monk.[47] The Constitution of Democratic Kampuchea also contrasted the "cleanliness" of the new order with the "obscenity" of the imperialist past.

A life of sexual continence was the most appropriate means of gaining self-control. The revolutionaries' "sixth moral precept"—the breaking of which involved many types of inappropriate sexual activity, from looking at any woman other than one's wife all the way up to adultery—was very harshly policed.[48] For instance, an ex-monk called Ta Hin, who had been accused of having sex with a woman, only narrowly escaped execution after he claimed that "a god had tricked him into doing it."[49] Both women and men were encouraged to cut their hair short, and women were not allowed to wear jewelry or perfume (Hinton 2005, 193), practices also forbidden to Buddhist monks and nuns. Where unattached adults were concerned, Angkar used a policy of forced marriage to provide a context in which sexual relations might be pursued without social disruption. Polygamy was naturally forbidden (Carney 1977, 11, 47), and attempts to deconstruct the family are another common feature in the reports of survivors. In July 1978, Nuon Chea (1987) complained that many revolutionaries were reluctant to leave their families and flee to another part of the country when the situation demanded. Angkar would therefore act as both mother and father, for it possessed "loving-kindness, the loving-kindness of someone great without measure."[50] Loving-kindness (*mettā*) is, of course a cardinal Buddhist virtue. But although Buddhism is mildly hostile to "familyism," Angkar was considerably more extreme.

Laurence Picq (1989, 48), by virtue of being married to the CPK cadre Suong Sikhoeun, was one of the few Westerners to survive the Democratic Kampuchea period. She describes how even high-ranking individuals and their spouses were separated and forced to live a "barracks lifestyle" (Kiernan 2006, 191). A consequence of this regimentation was that many people experienced an extinction of sexual desire (Pin Yathay 1980, 227). Although an emphasis on ascetic denial had been present in the Chinese Cultural Revolution, this cryptomonastic arrangement appears to have been a distinctive feature of the Khmer Rouge experiment. It may be going too far to claim that the Cambodian revolutionaries saw themselves as forming another religion based on a synthesis of Buddhism and class analysis, but there can be little doubt that internalization of aspects of an older, religiously inspired thought universe was very pervasive during the period. Mao Zedong alluded to that idea when, at a meeting with Pol Pot in Beijing on 21 June 1975, he described Cambodia as being like "a socialist *wat*" (Short 2004, 299).

A tendency to reconfigure and reemploy Buddhist symbolism and modes of thought, all the while against a background of extreme harassment of Buddhist institutions, was common throughout the revolutionary period in Cambodia. The language of the wheel, an ancient symbol of the Buddha's teaching and of the power of the righteous Buddhist monarch (*cakkavatti*), gained new currency as the "wheel of history" (Hinton 2005, 133). It was said that this wheel "never stops and . . . will crush all who place themselves in its path." Some slogans appear to be reworkings of traditional didactic poems on moral themes (*cpāp '*) and related sayings (Locard 1996, 3–4, 236), the very formulae learned by young monks as part of their "practical canon" of training.[51] Thus the saying "Imperialist heart, the mouth speaks only of Angkar" (*citt jā cakrabatra, māt' jā aṅgkār*) is a variation on the more traditional "Heart of Devadatta, mouth of a deity" (*citt jā devadatt, māt' jā devatā*) (ibid., 169–170), which could be more loosely translated as "Sweet words mask an evil heart."[52] The Cambodian version of the story of Rāma, the *Rāmakīrti,* was another source of slogans. "I am truly born from a furrow traced by the plough" (*puggal khñuṃ koet ceñ bī ganlaṅ nǎṅgal soddh saty*) (ibid., 195), for instance, is an edifyingly agrarian reworking of the birth narrative of Rāma's beloved Sītā.[53]

In daily conversation, use of the word "I" (*khñuṃ*) was discouraged, while "thank you," "please," and "sorry" were considered bourgeois affectations and were deemed redundant because there was no need to express indebtedness.[54] This was likewise a feature of the Chinese Cultural Revolution. But Theravāda Buddhism repudiates the concept of an abiding self, and Theravāda monks refrain from enunciating thanks when given alms food. Both of these facts may be germane here.

After the fall of the Khmer Rouge, a belief spread that the terminology employed in its official documentation was not standard Khmer but some special, almost arcane and priestly language incomprehensible to the average person. Scholarly research into the documents of the interrogation and execution facility at Tuol Sleng, S-21, confirms this to some extent. For Heder (1991, 20), they are written in "a peculiar argot that resulted from the attempts of Khmer speakers of Pali and Vietnamese to render into Khmer the vocabulary and syntax of Vietnamese communist phraseology." Heder notes that "the resulting jumble of Pali and Khmer neologisms and fractured syntax is at times unintelligible to even native speakers of Khmer."

Hinton (2005, 49–50) has argued that the "transformative knowledge" claimed by Angkar conferred "on the bearer an aura of potency" and that this secret knowledge was said to be comparable to the enlightenment of a Buddha.[55] In a sense, Angkar took on the role of a new deity. Like the pineapple-shaped, four-headed towers of the Bayon, Jayavarman VII's great pantheon at Angkor Thom, Angkar had eyes that surveyed the land in all directions. It was clairvoyant (ibid., 128–129).

In this respect Angkar's desire to purify society mirrored the soteriological rule of righteous Buddhist kings of previous epochs (Hinton 2002, 63, 69). In Theravāda political thought the role of the righteous, or "wheel-turning," king (*cakkavatti*), of whom the ancient Indian emperor Asoka is the paradigmatic type, is crucial for the proper ordering of the world, in both societal and cosmological terms. Angkar's view that agricultural, economic, and social failures emerge when the people fail to hold to the Party's line occupies identical conceptual territory.[56]

The notion of "attacking" the agricultural environment is a recurring theme in Angkar's project of world control. Martin's (1981, 16) observation that old Buddhist-oriented agricultural rites were being replaced "by the revolutionary chants that accompanied the actions of those engaged in forced labour" is relevant to this context. As a 1977 Party publication observed: "Our experience has been that some places (i.e., villages) are constantly on the attack, and that the people are therefore without worry and constantly have healthy, beaming faces. Some places, however, are not constantly on the attack but are only on the attack two or three months a year. *They wait for the season to arrive*" (my italics).[57] The idea of attack as a means of subjugating the world, as well as speeding up history, is a potent theme in Buddhist esotericism or Tantrism, generally regarded as an important element in the overall character of Cambodian Buddhism (Bizot 1976). In the tantric imagination the general structure of the world reflects the architectonics of the palace of a deity and the palace of his earthly counterpart, the king. Thus, from within his own imaginatively constructed palace, the tantric practitioner acts as one who both conquers space and acts as its overlord (*rājādhirāja*). This "imperial metaphor" (Davidson 2002, 115) rather precisely defines the relationship between Angkar and the natural world.

In December 1975 Khieu Samphan announced, "Our people are working collectively to dismantle the old field embankments and replace them with new high, tall and straight structures forming a great checkerboard net-work throughout the country."[58] On one level this is merely a depiction of rational and scientific agrarian reform, but it should be kept in mind that the repatterning fits very well with traditional Buddhist cosmological specula-tion. The statement also hints at a Buddhist-inspired re-creation of the coun-try as a pure land.[59]

The best example of "pure land" influence in Cambodia is in the con-secration and demarcation of a *wat*'s ritual boundary (*sīmā*). This is the quintessential Buddhist sacred space, where eight stone *nimitta* (markers) are dropped into specially dug pits indicated by the intersections in a check-erboard arrangement made of bamboo poles laid on the ground. The pits are then activated by human blood, an act that may point to an archaic and sacrificial origin of the practice (Giteau 1969, 44).[60] The connection between blood sacrifice and reconfiguration of the environment is highly relevant to

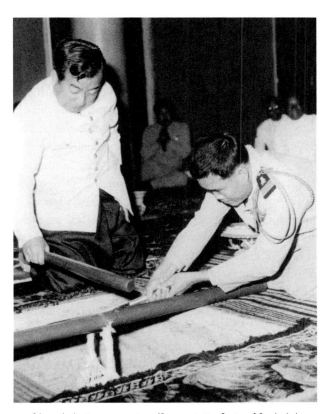

Sihanouk planting a *sīmā* stone. (Documentation Center of Cambodia)

the Democratic Kampuchea context, and it appears that deeply rooted patterns were at work here at a subliminal level.

One of the most widely discussed features of Democratic Kampuchea is that it envisioned the creation of a new world "starting from zero" (*cāp' phtoem bī sūny*). Steve Heder (pers. comm., 15 November 2005) has maintained that "year zero" rhetoric was part of a deliberate effort by Western rightists—he places Francois Ponchaud, the author of *Cambodia Year Zero* (1978), in this category—to discredit the Cambodian revolution as a form of nihilism, when the original concept really referred only to the regime's desire to build the country up from scratch following its destruction by imperialist forces.[61] But the repatterning of the world as a "pure land" coheres well with the Buddhist notion of emptiness (Skt. *śūnyatā*), a Mahayanist concept also known in the Theravāda (Pāli *suññata*). The Pāli abstract noun is derived from the term for "zero" (Skt. *śūnya*), which is more generally employed to denote the primordial state of things before defilement by ignorance.

The desire to return the country to a point before history is certainly somewhat odd, from the perspective of an orthodox Marxist analysis that sees the ideal state as the culmination of linear progress, not as a cyclic return to the most archaic stage of production.[62] The question, therefore, remains open as to the source of this highly romantic ideal. Paul Mus (1952, 303) has argued that for its Asian adherents Marxism was "in effect a catastrophe theory," a system that the Vietnamese in particular had adjusted to fit their preexisting cultural tradition, with its "cyclical instinct" and its conception of the world as a sequence of ruptures and discontinuities (Bayly 2000, 612–613). The same may have also applied in the case of the Khmer Rouge, for it does not seem too great a stretch of the imagination to suppose that indigenous and specifically Buddhist-tinged categories may have colored their conception of history. From this perspective, "starting from zero" would imply the attempt to establish a primordial future state, purified of the defilements associated with foreign powers, and rooted in a cyclical notion of time—a notion quite consistent with the traditional Buddhist understanding of history as an endless cycle of coming into being followed by dissolution.

I am well aware that the arguments presented above will not convince everyone interested in the genealogy of the Khmer Rouge worldview. But I have tried to offer several lines of reasoning that suggest that in a surprising number of ways Buddhist notions appear to have shaped revolutionary categories and practices. Sometimes this influence was explicit, as was the case with the promulgation of the *vinay aṅkār,* while in other contexts the process was reactive in the sense that it led to an inversion of customary Buddhist modes of praxis. Somewhere between these two extremes we find evidence of attitudes and behaviors showing a close family resemblance to Buddhist ways of being. I acknowledge that we are dealing here with quite different tendencies, perhaps pointing in rather different directions, and it is far from my intention to depict the Khmer Rouge as a deviant form of Buddhism. My goal, rather, is to stimulate further informed discussion of the range of influences that may have affected Cambodia's leftist movement.

# CHAPTER FOUR

# Dealing with Monks

## Initial Stages

The communists' first formal contacts with individual pagodas occurred at
differing times, depending on the progress of the conflict. In provinces such
as Stung Treng and certain districts of Svay Rieng, such contact happened
almost immediately after Sihanouk was overthrown. Other provinces fell
under communist influence as the 1970s progressed, while Phnom Penh and
many provincial cities held out until 17 April 1975. However, in some eastern provinces, Buddhist monks had been obliged to deal with the Vietcong
well before the Khmer Rouge arrived on the scene.

Vietcong troops were based in Chan Trea district, Svay Rieng, from at
least 1970 on, and the area was periodically bombed by the United States as
a result.[1] They had also been active in Chhlong district, Kratie, for several
years before the appearance of Cambodian revolutionaries in 1973, and a
local monk remembered helping to transport their weapons after being told
that they were fighting for Sihanouk.[2]

Stung Treng was liberated at the start of the civil war, and at Wat
Srah Keo Monivong in the provincial town the communists responded in
a friendly manner to the pagoda's twenty-odd monks throughout the first
year of occupation.[3] This pattern was repeated in other parts of the country.
In Kampong Speu the communists arrived in 1971, were "very kind," and
were liked by the monks because they claimed to be the "children of *samtec*" (i.e., Sihanouk loyalists).[4] Moreover, even as late as 1975, when the

Khmer Rouge finally arrived in Battambang town, some monks report that they were treated well and were referred to respectfully as "father."[5]

A flavor of these early encounters is provided by the testimony of Ven. Mao Kan, one of the thirty-six monks dwelling at a pagoda in Kampot when the Khmer Rouge arrived in 1970. Nothing much changed at that time, although there was a short battle with Lon Nol soldiers nearby in 1971. Members of the *sangha* were able to go about their business without fear, and some individual Khmer Rouge could be quite supportive. Although the Khmer Rouge never offered alms food in the traditional manner, they often sat down with the monks for conversation, usually on "how to fight the *yuon* [i.e., the Vietnamese]."[6]

Despite the promising start at some pagodas, it was generally only a matter of time before relations cooled. Ven. Ke Kan was appointed the *cau adhikār* of Wat Koh Sampeay, Siem Bok district, around the time the Khmer Rouge arrived in 1970. He later recalled that warm relations persisted until 1973, in part because a cadre's father had been a monk, and that official retained sympathy for the Buddha's teachings. But after 1973 the communists used "hot *dhamma* [teachings]," and although there were no killings, all of the monks were soon defrocked.[7] Meanwhile, around 150 monks had been living at the ancient Wat Nokor Bachey Ba-Ar, Kampong Cham. Things were fine at first, but toward the end of the year the communists began interfering, and the last monk left the *wat* in 1975.[8] Examples of similar deteriorations in relations are legion.[9]

In some localities senior monks were stripped of their ecclesiastical titles, and villagers were urged, very much against their will, to give up using honorific language when addressing them. Elsewhere monks with a nonncompliant attitude toward the authorities were replaced by other monks for whom the peasantry had little or no respect. Numerous reports, some of which are cited below, indicate significant popular resistance to such measures, and some local cadres did take measures to curtail the most vigorous forms of subjugation.

Although popular Buddhist outrage against such restrictions never reached the level found among the Cham Muslim community, it very occasionally surfaced as outright resistance. Throughout 1974, Sun, the district chief of Kang Meas, had been criticizing monks for entering the *sangha* just so they could get fed without working. He prohibited local villagers from offering alms, and it seems that some of them rose up and tried to kill him. They were captured and never seen again. Nevertheless Sun was soon replaced by someone less abrasive.[10]

## Liberation of the Principal Towns

Lon Nol's forces had managed to hold the enemy at bay in all of the districts of Battambang province except Moung Ruessei. This meant that the Khmer Rouge entered Battambang's urban area only a few hours after Phnom Penh was taken on 17 April 1975. A group of monks from the town's Wat Samraong Knong were able to listen to Ven. Huot Tat's broadcast on national radio later the same day. His message that "all Khmer may live in peace now" gladdened their hearts.[11] Meanwhile, government troops flew white flags, and a monk survivor remembers seeing a cadre driving around town on a lorry with a megaphone, calling on all monks to disrobe. The date was 23 April.[12] Things remained fairly quiet, however, and monks were not evacuated immediately. But they could not go on alms rounds and were forced to rely on stored food.[13]

A similar pattern of deceptive calm affected Siem Reap. Ven. Tep Vong, currently Cambodia's chief monk, was the deputy head of Wat Bo, near the center of town, when the Khmer Rouge entered on the evening of 17 April 1975. Over the next three days, he was forced to join a crowd of around five thousand people who were celebrating the great victory at nearby Angkor Wat.[14] The crowd included two groups of monks, one of about thirty from Siem Reap city, and another of about one hundred from the liberated zones. It seems that the two groups did not mix (Locard 2004, 54–55). Victory was announced with great fanfare and to the sound of traditional pagoda music. Monks gathered to chant the traditional Buddhist victory blessing (*jayanto*), and some of their representatives joined lay comrades in giving speeches (ibid., 52–53). However, Ke Pauk, a senior cadre who presided at certain points, introduced a darker element into the proceedings when he said that Buddhism must be crushed.[15] It was after returning from this event that Tep Vong and his fellow monks were moved out of the city. This move may not have happened immediately, for Chantou Boua (1991, 232) has noted that residents of one Siem Reap monastery had their biographies investigated for more than a week before being escorted from the premises.

It is rather more difficult to establish a clear picture of the way events unfolded in Phnom Penh's monasteries after the evacuation order was given, soon after the previous government acknowledged defeat. When Wat Mohamontrei's monks were told to leave, "a few . . . were wounded" in shooting, and one who steadfastly refused to go, Ven. Souh, was later found shot dead in front of the pagoda (Chantou Boua 1991, 230). How many more died under similar circumstances is impossible to tell, but it is worth bearing in mind that, as with the population in general, a significant proportion of monks were old and infirm. The blind monastic who took an overdose, knowing that he would not survive the journey out of Phnom Penh, may not have been unique.[16]

Twenty representatives of the *sangha* were among 311 delegates allegedly present at a Special National Congress held in Phnom Penh on 25–27 April 1975, at which Democratic Kampuchea was founded and Sihanouk was nominated as its head of state. But from this point on, neither radio nor other organs of communication made reference to Buddhism or monks. From the official perspective, they had ceased to exist.

In reality the pressure on institutional Buddhism increased significantly after the fall of Phnom Penh, for Buddhism now was regarded as one of the three mountains—alongside imperialism and reactionary capitalism—that must be leveled to the ground. Its elimination, then, would be part of a wider program to control all aspects of daily existence, in line with Angkar's goal "to push the people to be happy" (Kiernan 1996, 328). But there was no consensus on how this should be achieved. Indeed, some continued to argue for the retention of "money, schools and religion," while reports from the Eastern Zone suggested that Buddhism was still enjoying a fitful existence.[17]

## *Sangha* Organization and Monks with Guns

Given the manner in which the communist movement developed in Cambodia, it is unsurprising that some individual monks were early supporters of the struggle against the Khmer Republic. San Kor commune in Kampong Svay district was liberated soon after the Khmer Republic was established, and until their religious activities were curtailed, many monks backed the revolutionaries (Kobayashi 2005, 506). The Khmer Republic intelligence services were clearly aware that the republic had enemies within the *sangha,* and their reports reflect this concern. In late September 1970, monks from Kien Svay district were observed crossing to the west bank of the Bassac River, where they began to speak in favor of the communists. They also called for no bombing of pagodas and no stationing of troops in pagodas or village houses, abuses that had supposedly been committed by government forces.[18] In October the *anugan* of Koh Sotin district was arranging for the registration of all monks under his jurisdiction by taking their thumbprints. While this was happening, those present were strongly encouraged to accept Sihanouk's Sangkum and to reject the Khmer Republic.[19] By the following year the revolutionaries' propaganda effort was gaining pace. A meeting of 447 monks and *achar*s from Kampot, Takeo, and Kampong Speu provinces in May 1971 took place at Wat Ang Andet in Chhouk district, Kampot province. Allegedly organized by Ta Mok, Phok Chhay, and other senior cadres, its purpose was to encourage monks to teach the people the principles of the revolution.[20]

Such activities are mirrored across much of the liberated zone. On 11 November 1971 about thirty communists entered Wat Sak Sampov, Daun Keo district, Takeo, and propagandized the monks,[21] and in November 1972 troops from Unit 105, commanded by Nem, joined residents of Or and Svay villages in Pursat province to celebrate *kathin*—a ceremony in which laypeople offer new robes to monks as a means of making merit—at Wat Damrei Sa. They also sought to convince those present of the ills of the Khmer Republic.[22]

When Serge Thion visited communist strongholds in early 1972, he reported similar scenes. Only sixteen kilometers from Phnom Penh, the Khmer Rouge were holding evening study sessions at which monks chanted Buddhist verses before the microphone was passed to officials, whose speeches ended with slogans such as "Long live the National Front of Kampuchea presided over by Samdech Norodom Sihanouk" and "Long live the Buddhist religion" (Thion and Kiernan 1981, 69). Thion (1993, 13–14) also mentions a 1972 Front congress for pagoda leaders in which around 350 individuals participated. At one such event an abbot asserted that attacks by Lon Nol's planes made it impossible for monks to fulfill their religious duties and that the Front soldiers' respect for Buddhism contrasted favorably against the profanity and contempt of Lon Nol's forces.[23]

When the Khmer Rouge wrested rural areas from government control, many monks certainly fled, but by no means all. A communist radio broadcast of 1973 claimed that "in the vast and beautiful liberated zone . . . culture, arts and national traditions are developing splendidly among the large popular masses" (quoted in Edwards 1999, 390). This sounds like a typically cynical piece of propaganda, but it probably did reflect the actual feelings of more liberal elements within the liberation struggle. The most prominent of the "national traditions" was Buddhism, and where the *sangha* could be organized so that it promoted the aims of the revolution, it might continue to exist. There was little evidence at this stage of an "ideological commitment to the abolition of Buddhism" (Chantou Boua 1991, 233). But beginning in early 1973, a shift from the relatively spontaneous support of "patriotic monks" to a more structured, centrally directed, and coercive manipulation of the Buddhist order can be clearly detected.

In June 1973 a Patriotic Monks' Association (*brah saṅgh snehā jāti*) started to operate in some locations. Its members effectively constituted a new ecclesiastical hierarchy standing in opposition to the senior clergy based in Phnom Penh. A special cadre (*gaṇah saṅgh*) was often appointed to maintain revolutionary discipline in the *saṅgha* at the level of the *wat* (Ponchaud 1978, 148), and regional conferences took place from time to time. A monk from Kampong Svay district, Kampong Thom, for example, said he had attended a large meeting of such figures in the hilly area of Phnom Kulen in 1974 (Kobayashi 2005, 506n47).

In Kamchay Meas district the Patriotic Monks' Association claimed a membership of around seven hundred, based at thirty-four monasteries (Kiernan 1985, 345–346). Local chapters encouraged mutual surveillance. They also established committees to handle the social, economic, and cultural affairs of the *saṅgha*. Such novel modes of administration curtailed the time that most monks had for more traditional pursuits, such as study, meditation, and the performance of ritual.[24] Instead they were encouraged to become economically active, especially through growing food, the surpluses of which could be supplied to the army. Some, however, were given special assignments. Ven. Ngem Thuok had been forced to disrobe, but in June 1974 he was ordered to put on robes again so that he could more easily gather information in downtown Kampong Cham.[25]

Whether their support for communist policy was genuine or they were acting under duress, the fate of such individuals could be uncertain. According to one informant, four compliant Takeo-based monks were used as "bait or hooks" by the Khmer Rouge. Despite their apparent readiness to propagandize, they were killed when their job had been accomplished.[26] The former chief monk of Wat Sdey Botum in Kampong Cham was more fortunate. The communists had ordered him to supervise all the monks in Zone 30, No. 304 (Prek Koy commune, Kang Meas district), and to prevent them from engaging in traditional learning. However, he disrobed and rallied to the government in mid-1974 after hearing a radio broadcast that assured all monks in a similar position that they would not be punished.[27]

Part of the propaganda process was about encouraging young monks to disrobe and join the revolutionary army. But not all traffic moved in the same ideological direction. In a Tuol Sleng confession dated 22 December 1978, Ong Ol, the ex-head of Hospital P-17, described his participation in a three-day government-backed conference for monks evacuated from the liberated areas. The conference was held at a pagoda in Kampong Tralach district sometime in late 1972 or early 1973. The object of the meeting was to frustrate the communists, and Ong Ol stated that two monks—Naem, who later fled to Phnom Penh, and Tit, who was later the chief of Klong village in Tuol Pich subdistrict—were encouraged to betray the revolution. Monk attendees were also told not to disrobe and join the Khmer Rouge army, on the straightforward grounds that they would likely be killed in action.[28]

In a lengthy but revealing interrogation of Vong Sarin, the former *cau adhikār* of Wat Traeuy Sla, Sa-ang district, the government learned of an early 1974 meeting at Wat Chong Koh, Kandal province. Among those present were Sao Sophal[29] (the director of the local Patriotic Monks' Association committee), Kong (the chief of Sa-ang district), Ven. Thong Pim (Sa-ang's chief monk), and the *cau adhikār*s of all the district's *wat*s. It seems that they discussed a three-point plan, the second item of which concerned the construction of a youth stupa to commemorate those who had died in battle.[30] The most comprehensive account of the situation, however, comes from a monk informant who had been based at Wat Chambak Thom, Me Sa Thngak subdistrict in Svay Rieng. In the early 1970s the Khmer Rouge had generally treated monks well, although they did try to indoctrinate senior members of the order. In the first months of 1973 some cadres had even made donations of alms food. But then things started to take on a darker complexion. Groups of between forty and seventy monks were obliged to attend frequent meetings chaired by revolutionary monks, individuals so powerful that many *cau adhikār*s were "afraid to look in their faces."[31] Exacerbating their fear was that they still owed their loyalty to the provincial chief monk (*megaṇ*) who had been appointed by the Lon Nol government and was now completely cut off at his residence in government-controlled Svay Rieng town.

From 1973 on, the *grū sūtr* (assistant to the *cau adhikār*) at Wat Chambak Thom was a revolutionary monk called Rot. Like most of his comrades, Rot wore an old set of robes and had shoes and a basket made of palm leaves. In this way he could be identified as a "proletarian monk." He was uneducated, and the pagoda's *cau adhikār* lived in fear of him. Rot did many things that were against the Buddha's discipline (*vinaya*). Every month or two, for example, he organized compulsory evening performances of revolutionary song and dance in the *sālā chān'*. Monks were especially incensed when the actors turned their backs on the Buddha while performing. One play concerned a lazy man who just ate and slept while others worked.[32]

When the Khmer Rouge arrived at Wat Samraong Knong, Battambang, the pagoda had a capable *cau adhikār* in Ven. Tep Thang, but another monk was soon appointed in his stead. This appointee received verbal orders about his new work responsibilities from Try and Moeun, two important Front monks representing the district (*brah saṅgh raṇasirsa srok*).[33] We know a little more about Try than about the others. He appears to have come from the liberated zone, possibly from Moung Ruessei district, and some informants believe that he was not a real monk and that he wore robes without authorization. He had two bodyguards, San and Kong, and he kept a pistol in his bag, although he is said to have never used it. Nevertheless, he did order executions.[34] Ven. Uk Mut, at that time a *grū sūtr* at nearby Wat Kdol, seems also to have been a key assistant to Try. However, it is asserted that he was coerced into this role and that he was basically good-hearted. Monks listened to his advice, but they tended to be very suspicious of Try.[35]

Reports of *gaṇah saṅgh* armed with weapons are very common. Clearly a "monk" who felt happy about carrying a gun would not feel constrained to follow traditional monastic discipline, and there are a number of accounts of such individuals riding their own bicycles, driving motorcycles, and so on.[36] In 1973 several monks with pistols were living at Wat Sokunthearam Pong Ro. One of these, named Kim Sokha, had previously been a novice in the pagoda.[37] At neighboring Wat Damnak Pring a gun-toting monk was nominated district chief,[38] and between 1974 and 1975, members of the provincial monks' committee of the liberated zone in Krouch Chhmar district carried guns but also preached the *dhamma*.[39] There is also an intriguing report from Kampong Cham of a monk called Yeum who came from Kang Meas district and had a gun in his bag. But he continued to preach, especially on the theme that if anyone were to capture members of the Lon Nol regime, he would be reborn in paradise.[40]

While some *gaṇah saṅgh* operating at the pagoda or commune level can be identified, identification of those working further up the organization is more difficult. However, it is possible to be more precise in a handful of cases. In Kampong Thom province during 1973–1974 an individual named Pol worked as chief of policy for cults and propaganda in Santuk district,[41] and at the next level down, Keo was responsible for Thnou commune.[42]

In Pursat two individuals, Dem Khon and Kena, are known to have held leadership roles.[43]

It is clear that a certain level of informal monastic support for the revolution in the early civil war period was gradually harnessed and directed by the communists as part of their united-front policy. As new areas were liberated, monks were "invited" to propaganda sessions, and the sympathetic could be recruited into more formal structures of surveillance and control. In time many such "revolutionary monks" formed an alternative *sangha* administration that further undermined links with the national ecclesiastical hierarchy in Phnom Penh. Although some of these individuals may genuinely have believed that their collaboration with the Khmer Rouge offered the best hope for the continued presence of the Buddha's teachings in Cambodia, there can be little doubt that others were severely brutalized by the process and became prime persecutors of their fellow religionists.

## Forced Labor

The requirement that Buddhist monks be expected to work for their living should not, on the face of it, be regarded as a major imposition. Indeed, the practice is far from uncommon in cultures like that of China, where the Mahāyāna form of Buddhism dominated, and even in Cambodia an expectation that monks should willingly engage in the construction of public buildings, roads, and railways was one of the features of Sihanouk's experiment with Buddhist socialism (Lester 1973, 127). But in the Theravāda, fully ordained monks are prevented from engaging in many types of activity by virtue of their rules of discipline (*vinaya*). The digging of the ground, for example, is a monastic offense because it causes the death and injury of small creatures, and *sangha* members therefore are not permitted to perform a host of activities associated with agriculture.

Traditionally, the Theravāda's restrictions on labor have not led to excessive charges that monks are lazy. From an economic perspective the removal of significant numbers of potentially active young men from an overpopulated labor market could be seen in a positive light. But from the religious standpoint the custom has more to recommend it. The path to enlightenment is a difficult route that can be trodden only by a minority. Admittedly, only a very few monks can be said to have achieved this goal, but all members of the *sangha*, almost regardless of their spiritual capabilities, remain symbols of the possibility. Laypeople, by contrast, do not possess the "spiritual capital" of the monks, but in a set of relations deeply embedded in Theravāda culture, the provision of goods and services between these two segments of society ensures their complementarity.

The typical layperson toils on the land to produce food, a portion of which is offered to the *saṅgha*. In this way, he or she supports a religious order that valorizes such actions as highly meritorious. The monk, on the other hand, by temporarily or permanently eschewing worldly activity, broadcasts the salvific message of the Buddha and, as a recipient of alms, provides the best opportunity for lay merit-making. By forcing monks to work, the Khmer Rouge dissolved these well-winnowed relations and, in so doing, greatly shocked a significant portion of Cambodia's population.

It seems to have been particularly easy for the communists to form monks into mobile work units (*calăt*) because the monks were already accustomed to living in a reasonably disciplined manner. In addition they were not married and thus had fewer responsibilities.[44] The *calăt,* then, were formed almost exclusively of celibate groups,—whether monks, young people, widowers, or widows—that retained the same separation of the sexes (male, *calăt yuvajan;* and female, *calăt yuvanārī*) as that found in a monastic setting (Martin 1981, 12).[45] Almost all monks harbored serious regrets over the order to work on the land, but few refused point-blank. However, to resolve the conflict of loyalties between the Buddha and Angkar, many simply disrobed.

The monks of Wat Kdol, on the outskirts of Battambang, were still wearing their robes when they were ordered to plow the fields. As a result the local people said that "the field was yellow."[46] Meanwhile monks at nearby Wat Norea were moved to a neighboring pagoda, where they grew potatoes and other root vegetables.[47] Ven. Oum Sum, a monk at Wat Saravan in Phnom Penh, was forced to leave the city following liberation and wound up in Kampong Cham province, where he worked mixing cow and buffalo manure as fertilizer. He was successful in exceeding norms for vegetable and fruit production, since he had been brought up in a farming community, but he was still mocked by some local cadres for being "cheated by the Buddha for 38 years." When asked, perhaps ironically, whether he was "now awake," he answered that he was.[48]

The raising of animals was a particularly problematic matter. There could be no real objection to monks tending livestock, but slaughtering them infringed a range of Buddhist precepts. At Wat Romduol, Battambang province, Ven. Sor Phak was ordered to look after chickens, but he still believed in the Buddha and didn't want to kill them. He later said that he resorted to a variety of subterfuges in order to avoid slaughtering them.[49] At Wat Kor, Battambang, an old monk pleaded that he was completely prepared to work hard but wanted to be excused from killing animals. His request was refused.[50] There are no recorded cases of monks being executed for expressing these concerns, but it may well have happened. But, as with agricultural work, it was an easier option to disrobe. Ven. Chhuon Vang, for example, was working hard, was not getting enough food, and was especially worried about killing animals. He defrocked, even though a fellow monk became quite angry with him.[51]

Another common task was laboring on civil engineering projects. Siv Sovann had become a novice in 1973. In May 1974 his commune chief, Khim, ordered all the monks at his pagoda to dig a canal. Siv Sovann took the opportunity to disrobe and escape to a government-controlled area.[52] Similarly, a Khmer Republic telegram, dated March 1974, asserted that Angkar was directing monks to work without rest to dig the land, build roads and construct dams,[53] but there was no indication that they were being forced to work harder than everyone else, as was charged, for example, at the August 1979 trial of Pol Pot and Ieng Sary. Several months' later reports also circulated that the communists were using monks and teenagers to build a new road in Kandal province[54] and that monks mobilized from all the pagodas in Cheung Prey district to repair a bombed bridge on National Road 6 worked day and night.[55] Such activities could have an enduring impact on a locality; for example, a drainage canal built by monastic labor near Wat Moha Leap, Kampong Cham province, is to this day called the "monk channel."[56]

One of the more curious reports to emerge in July 1974 was that around four thousand people had been press-ganged into building a stupa for those fallen in battle in Stung Trang district, Kampong Cham. The workers included some four hundred monks from sixty-five pagodas.[57] In late 1975 around sixty robed monks based at Wat Norea, Battambang province, were forced to work on a dam project, and an undetermined number of them died as a consequence. When the project was completed, the survivors were told that if they didn't disrobe, they would have to work even harder in the forest.[58]

It seems probable that not all monks were treated equally and that minor allowances were sometimes made for an individual's capabilities. It was common, though by no means universal, that old and infirm monks were treated less harshly. There is some evidence that the special treatment of old monks may have been formalized, for one survivor, Ven. So Chhem, claimed that he was placed in a work group designated as the "third force" (*kamlāṃṅ dī pī*), the members of which were given light agricultural work because of their age.[59] At Wat Pothi Voan Hanchey Leu, old monks, like all other elderly people, were assigned light tasks such as basket making, while younger ones were obliged to work in the fields.[60] Elsewhere another aging monk, Ven. Non Seng, was detailed to scare away birds from the rice fields. While performing this task, he recited the *dhamma* secretly, being especially careful that the Khmer Rouge did not find out and "give advice."[61]

## Monk Evacuations

Most monks remained, at least for a short time, in their pagodas after the arrival of the Khmer Rouge. But on some occasions—it is difficult to quantify how often—they were moved elsewhere. It seems that in certain regions there may have been a policy to concentrate them into larger groups well before they were forced to disrobe. The most obvious reason for this was that larger assemblies were easier to manage than smaller groups scattered here and there. Maximizing their potential for productive activity was also a more straightforward process under this arrangement. An example is the concentration of personnel from various pagodas in the Battambang area at Wat Samraong Knong. But monks were moved for other reasons as well. Wat Norea was employed as a Khmer Rouge arsenal, and its monks were told they must go elsewhere for their own safety.[62] In another instance, a large group of senior monks were forced to reside together at Wat Ream Keo.[63] The reason for this is unclear, but it would certainly have deprived rank-and-file monastics of effective leadership.

Monk evacuation and concentration started at a fairly early phase of the civil war. In January 1971, for example, forces identified by the Khmer Republic army as Vietcong are alleged to have removed monks forcibly around the pagodas of Angk Snuol district,[64] while in the Oudong area those who had been abandoning Phnom Penh's *wats* for destinations north were detained in a holding center at Daeum Kveth village, on the grounds that they might be government spies (Short 2004, 254). But it should be noted that some concentrations of monks were formed merely by large movements of people attempting to escape from the communists. In 1973 Ven. Hun Khor managed to flee from his home pagoda to Wat Prey Samnang, where many monks from various locations had already congregated.[65] But his was not an isolated case. The flight of monks from their home pagodas had been occurring for several years across large swaths of the country. The most popular destinations for monks uprooted by the fighting were the prominent pagodas of provincial towns, and the populations of these pagodas swelled massively throughout the Khmer Republic.

Because of heavy fighting between the Khmer Rouge and government forces close to his village *wat,* Ven. Soeuy moved from Moung Ruessei district to Wat Damrei Sa in Battambang city soon after being ordained in late 1974. When he arrived, there were already about seventy others eking out an existence in a pagoda designed for far fewer monks.[66] But this increase pales in significance beside the vast growth in the *wat*s of Phnom Penh. The capital city was a major magnet, drawing monks from across the country. By the time the city fell to the communists, Wat Mohamontrei had around 660 monks in residence,[67] Wat Unnalom had swelled from its normal 300 monks to over 1,000, there were 500 at Wat Saravan (Chantou Boua 1991, 230–232), and between 150 and 175 were living at the less capacious Wat Sampov Meas and 100 at Wat Sansam Kosala.[68]

## Fleeing the Country

Cambodia possesses a relatively short coastline, with only one port of any significance. For this reason few people were able to flee by sea. But most of the country's land borders could be crossed with relative ease. Both Laos and Thailand share cultural similarities with Cambodia by virtue of their Theravāda practice, and Bangkok has long been a destination of choice for Cambodian monks keen to improve their level of Buddhist knowledge. It could thus be expected that rather large numbers of monks would cross over once the nature of the communist threat had been recognized. The attractions of Vietnam were rather fewer, in part because of a historically deep-rooted Khmer antipathy to Vietnamese culture. But the Mekong Delta is home to the most substantial of all Khmer minority groups outside Cambodia,[69] and this might have been expected to be an attraction to those living near the border. However, it seems that few monks made the journey.

The Khmer Rouge definitely played upon anti-Vietnamese feelings as a means of dissuasion. One informant suggested that the reason monks did not flee in large numbers was that local officials had circulated a rumor that the Vietnamese would cut open their stomachs and fill them with grass when they arrived.[70] Reeducation centers such as that at Sre Chea near Kampong

Trach, which held around two hundred monks (Quinn 1976, 14–15), were also set up to dissuade potential escapees.[71] But many tried to abscond, nonetheless. At Wat Po Thmei, Chan Trea district, four or five monks ran across the border after attempts were made to disrobe them,[72] and in 1974 at nearby Wat Prey Koki Touch two others managed to get over to Kampuchea Krom, where they remained in robes until their return to their own country in 1980.[73] As we shall see, such individuals, even though they were regarded as a threat by the PRK authorities, were crucial for the reestablishment of Cambodian Buddhism after the Pol Pot period.

An especially vivid account comes from Ven. Nhem Kim Teng.[74] In early 1974 he was a novice at Wat Chambak Thom, Me Sa Thngak subdistrict. The surrounding area had been ravaged by war, and as he later recalled, there were tanks around and some bombing from the air. Many monks were frightened, and some wanted to flee to Kampuchea Krom, but they were very concerned that their *grū sūtr,* a revolutionary monk planted in the pagoda by the Khmer Rouge, would find out. Nevertheless, some did manage to get to Svay Rieng town, where large numbers of monks were congregating. From there they continued their journey to either Phnom Penh or Vietnam. The latter destination was possible because troops loyal to Son Ngoc Thanh were in the vicinity, and they helped the refugees negotiate the border. In all, around five hundred monks and thousands of civilians successfully crossed over.

The situation continued to deteriorate. Bombing and fighting destroyed local pagodas, and many monks were killed. Nhem Kim Teng and his fellow monastics managed to build a temporary retreat in a remote area, but it was soon hit and more deaths ensued. They returned to Wat Chambak Thom, but fear of the *grū sūtr* was no longer sufficient to hold them after the pagoda was also blasted. Traveling to Bavet subdistrict, Nhem Kim Teng crossed the border that same night, staying near the crossing point with five other monks from May 1974 until January 1975. Then he transferred to Saigon, where he stayed at the Cambodian Embassy with his brother and mother.

The family's hope was to get a plane from Saigon to Phnom Penh, but the Cambodian capital fell on 17 April 1975 and the flight was canceled. So Nhem Kim Teng went to stay at Wat Champa Moni, some thirty kilometers from Saigon. It seems that Thach Kong, the pagoda's chief monk, and Thach San, the abbot of nearby Wat Phouloem (another refuge for monks who had recently arrived from Cambodia), were well-known anticommunists who wrote in newspapers and broadcast on the radio. When Saigon was liberated on 30 April, they were both arrested,[75] but Thach Kong had previously advised Nhem Kim Teng to move on to another monastery in Trà Vinh province, where he joined four or five other monk refugees. He stayed there until May 1979 and then returned to Svay Rieng with ten others. They appear to have received a good Buddhist education in Vietnam even though it was under communist control.

As a result of the early influx from Cambodia, the average number of monks per Kampuchea Krom *wat* grew to around thirty-five, with some *wats* housing in excess of one hundred. But once Vietnam had been unified, the thought of getting out of a Cambodia dominated by one extreme socialist regime only to wind up in the hands of another meant that flight to Vietnam lost its attraction. The flow of monks came abruptly to an end, even though it turns out that Theravāda Buddhist practice in Vietnam was not severely restricted during the first few years of communist rule. However, the situation deteriorated after a series of border clashes in 1977–1978, and Khmer monks came under the suspicion of the Vietnamese authorities.

The number of monks escaping to Laos appears to have been minimal, partly because the border region was sparsely populated but also because, in some parts of the north and northeast, the Khmer Rouge had been around since 1970. Although there are some grounds for believing that—in Stung Treng province, for example—the communists were not so zealous in their ill treatment of the *sangha,* it is still the case that oppressive policies began to bite quite early. This meant that many monks had been disrobed well before the general population recognized the potential benefits of escaping to neighboring countries.[76] One informant claimed that he had never heard of any monks trying to escape to Laos during the Pol Pot period,[77] while another had heard reports of monks being captured and executed for attempting to do so.[78] One additional report perhaps further indicates the difficulties involved in monastic escape from the Khmer Rouge–controlled north and northeast. It is a story of a senior monk (*bālăt*) of Wat Phnom, Phnom Stung Treng. The revolutionaries tried to arrest him, but he is said to have used his magical powers to turn into smoke that was blown across the border.[79]

At this point it is worth noting that the situation for Buddhism in Laos during the 1970s, although it appears to have followed much the same general pattern as in communist-controlled Cambodia, was less severe. In the late 1950s the United States was beginning to exercise some political and ideological influence over the Lao *sangha,* but its crude attempts to use Buddhism as part of an anticommunist crusade tended to undermine the credibility of the monastic order (Stuart-Fox 1983, 436), and two separate pro-communist Buddhist monk groups, the Movement of Novices Claiming Their Rights and the Movement of Young Monks against the Thai Thommayut, emerged by the early 1960s.

US propagandists wrongly believed that the Lao communists would be opposed to Buddhism on ideological grounds. But in fact the Lao Patriotic Front saw no major contradiction between Marxism and Buddhism (Lafont 1982, 148–149).[80] All that was required was for Buddhist monks to become citizens impregnated with "the right of collective mastery." Such Marxist monks would be transmogrified into "ideal Buddhists" who could be expected to engage in ritual denunciations of US imperialism when required (Stuart-Fox 1983, 447). In fact, this was not difficult to achieve, for Lao Buddhist pagodas were by then being regularly destroyed by aerial bombardment as part of the US Air Force's "secret war" (Hayashi 2002, 200).

But when the transformation failed to materialize as quickly as the Party had hoped, it went on the attack. Policy certainly differed from place to place, but by 1976 certain monks were being forced to deny their possession of magical power, while those who promoted the Party line were rewarded with a daily ration of rice. The laity were no longer permitted to feed monks, who were now expected to provide their own food. "Malingering" was no longer permissible. Any vestige of monastic independence ended in 1976 when the ceremonial fans of senior ecclesiastics were smashed. The Party now regarded itself as the sole arbiter of truth, and in early 1979 the eighty-seven-year-old former *saṅgharāja* fled across the Mekong to Thailand on a raft of car tires. His complaint was that the communists had abolished the ecclesiastical hierarchy, nationalized monastery assets, prohibited the use of Buddhist texts printed in Thailand, and forced monks to grow their own food. All of this was true, but perhaps rather surprisingly, not all Thai Buddhists found communist policy in Laos inimical to the flourishing of Buddhism. Many modernists, particularly those close to the highly influential Buddhadasa Bhikkhu (1906–1993), argued that this was precisely what was needed to purify Lao Buddhism of false beliefs and superstitions (Lafont 1982, 159).

It might be expected that more Cambodian monks would have crossed the border into Thailand than was the case with either Vietnam or Laos. Those residing in the western provinces had little impediment to doing so before the establishment of Democratic Kampuchea, but it must be remembered that many parts of Koh Kong and Pursat, particularly the areas closest to the border, are mountainous and/or deeply forested and contain few pagodas.

The provinces of the northwest, such as Siem Reap and Battambang, had better lines of communication, were densely populated, and had strong historical and cultural ties with Thailand. Given this context it is not surprising that Ven. Lev Tong, subsequently the *cau adhikār* of Wat Sangke, Battambang, was a member of a small group of local monks who fled to Thailand in early 1975.[81]

There is a long-standing tradition of Cambodian monks visiting Thailand for educational purposes, and it seems likely that those who had already spent time in Thailand were tempted to return when the situation in Cambodia became intolerable. It is impossible to say how many fell into this category, but they likely were mainly older and of a reasonable level of seniority. Thus, when the Khmer Rouge took Battambang city in April 1975, the provincial governor, Sek Sam Iet, decided to make a run for it. In the company of a few senior monks disguised in black revolutionary garb, he drove a car to Pailin and from there they escaped to Thailand.[82]

Although the number of Khmer monks fleeing to Thailand before May 1975 may have been small, escape became almost impossible after the establishment of Democratic Kampuchea, and the border returned to its former porous state only after the founding of the People's Republic of Kampuchea in 1979. From that time on, the numbers of monks attempting to cross into Thailand grew dramatically, the flow becoming so great that in refugee camps along the border many who had been defrocked by the Khmer Rouge were able to resume their monastic careers in temporary monasteries. Significant numbers of young men and women, many of whom had lost family members and had no other means of support, were also attracted to the religious life at that time.[83]

## Defrocking

From the strict perspective of Buddhist monastic discipline (*vinaya*), only a monk found guilty of one of four offenses entailing defeat (*pārājika*)—sexual relations, theft, killing (including encouraging another to die or assisting in a suicide), and boasting of superhuman perfections—may be expelled from the *saṅgha*. In situations where a monk disrobes voluntarily, the expectation is also that he will perform a brief ceremony in which he expresses a firm intention to leave and further asserts that he is not insane, crazed with pain, or possessed. This ceremony must take place in the presence of a rational witness, to whom the monk must issue a clear statement that he wishes to renounce the training (Vajirananavarorasa 1984, 237). The validity of these acts is premised on the understanding that they take place within the monastic order. Disrobing is the affair of fellow monks, not of the secular power.

Under the Khmer Rouge, none of the above procedures applied, and only a very few courageous individuals sought to defend the independent rights of the *saṅgha*. Most monks were hastily and unceremoniously ejected from the monastic order, and that was that. But when institutional Buddhism was eventually reestablished after 1979, these issues became highly relevant, for a monk forcibly disrobed by the Khmer Rouge might argue that he had never formally left the *saṅgha*. This would become a major bone of contention, bearing on questions of monastic seniority and power. Indeed, wrangling over the ramifications of "defrocking" would mar the period of *saṅgha* reconsolidation from 1979 until the end of the 1980s (see chapter 7).

One witness reported the disrobing of between two hundred and three hundred monks who were given a traditional Khmer scarf (*kramā*), black clothes, and a rifle before being transported to the front in two trucks. He subsequently expressed his concern that the ceremony was not legal.[84] But some monks did try to disrobe according to *vinaya*. One was Ven. Uk Mut, who later said he had done this with the help of another monk, Ven. Lach Pin, at the end of 1977.[85] If a witness was not available, however, a monk might disrobe before a statue of the Buddha, a procedure that seems to have appealed to older members of the order.[86]

Those concerned with ritual observation, as well as with piety, were careful to preserve their discarded robes, which were still considered to hold symbolic significance and magical properties. Furthermore, possession of robes maintained the individual's tenuous links with the Buddhist order. The monks of Wat Che Te Yaram in Stung Treng kept their robes safe after disrobing. However, the wife of the collective's chief found some of the robes and urinated on them. The same province's *megan* also kept his belt safe during Democratic Kampuchea.[87]

Similar stories abound. When Ven. Heng Leang Hor, a senior monk and a member of the Tripiṭaka Commission, was forced to defrock, some very poor Khmer Rouge soldiers asked him for his robes so they could use them as bedding materials. He refused but dyed them black so he could continue having them about his body.[88] Ven. Uk Rorn, who was disrobed when he was over fifty years old, had been a monk since the age of fifteen and was very attached to his robes. Throughout Democratic Kampuchea he kept them in his bag and secretly performed devotions every day.[89]

Younger monks who had no choice but to disrobe in order to survive found different strategies to retain something, however tenuous, of their old religious allegiance. Some cut up their orange robes, sewed them into working clothes and dyed them black (Chhang Song 1996, 57). Ven. Uk Mut continued to wear a monastic belt under his work clothes, and he later confirmed that other prominent monks, such as Ven. Thim Pot, did likewise.[90] Another young Battambang-based monk went to live with his parents after he was disrobed in 1976. His mother kept his robe safe, and he retained his belt, although he was too frightened to wear it.[91]

Although the order to defrock was issued by a local official, it usually originated at a higher level of the administration. The normal arrangement appears to have been a letter from the district office telling local authorities to begin disrobing monks, followed by oral instructions from that point on.[92] In Battambang town the order came from regional leader Mut Su, also known as Khach Pan, immediately after 17 April 1975,[93] whereas at Wat Kdol, on the outskirts of town, it was the commune chief, Ta Chuon, who gave the command toward the end of 1976. We know that Ta Chuon had been instructed to do this by someone further up the chain of command, possibly the district chief, Kaim.[94] On the other hand, Ven. Chhun Chim, an old monk who had been a friend of the 1940s anticolonial hero Ven. Hem Chieu, received more personalized treatment. He was the last of some seventy-five residents at Wat Svay Att, Prey Veng province, to be invited to disrobe. Doung Yi, the cadre responsible for Buddhism in the area, personally presented him with civilian clothes.[95]

The disrobing process could take a distinctly bureaucratic turn. At Wat Koh Dach, Muk Kampoul district, the commune chief forced disrobing monks to sign a document saying that they had "awoken" to their parasitical status.[96] On other occasions the procedure might occur in stages, particularly since many rural *wats* contained both "new monks" from Phnom Penh and "base monks" who had been living with the communists, sometimes for a considerable period of time. Soon after being evacuated from Phnom Penh, Ven. Pes Phann was told that monks over the age of fifty would not be disrobed. But some cadres argued that the city monks were traitors, practicing Buddhism during the day but working for Lon Nol at night. Ven. Pes Phann was disrobed at Wat Kompeng, Kiri Vong district, in July 1975. Local base monks were disrobed three months later.[97] Similarly, Ven. Oum Sum was the only new monk—he had also been a member of the Tripiṭaka Commission—living with forty-six base monks at Wat Moha Leap, Koh Sotin district.

When the order to disrobe arrived from the district office, local officials first believed that it applied only to him. But four days later a further directive arrived, and all the other monks were also forced to defrock.[98]

Evidence for forced disrobing can be traced back to the beginning of the civil war, with significant parallels to the situation in which Theravāda monks in Yunnan province found themselves during the Chinese Cultural Revolution (Keyes 1994, 70n27). The earliest occurrence in Cambodia that I have been able to identify dates back to 1970 in the small and relatively scattered Buddhist communities of Ratanakiri province.[99] After the April 1975 victory the policy intensified. Most new monks appear to have been defrocked before the beginning of the rainy season (*vassā*) in July, while base monks were sometimes allowed to observe the whole of the three-month *vassā* retreat before being obliged to leave the order.

Traditionally *vassā* ends with a ceremony, called *kathin,* in which laypeople offer robes and other gifts to the *saṅgha.* But under the Khmer Rouge there were intriguing, though isolated, examples of an inverted *kathin* ritual in 1975, in which selected base monks were presented with revolutionary garb—black trousers, black shirt, and *kramā*—by prostrating communist officials, after which they were invited to leave the monastic order.[100] During such an event at Wat Prey Chuor, Takeo province, seventy base monks reportedly relinquished their previous condition amid floods of tears (DC-Cam 1996b, 56).[101]

As already noted, some isolated and generally elderly monks stayed in robes longer than this. But a few examples exist of entire pagodas functioning long after the country's liberation. At Wat Samraong Knong, Ek Phnom district, Battambang, remaining monks were not ordered to disrobe until September 1976,[102] and a neighboring pagoda continued into April 1976 (Ken Khun 1994, 45–44, 72–73, 84). Meanwhile, in Prey Veng province Ven. Chhim Chhoun, the chief monk of Wat Mang Sala, and his small band of fellows survived largely unmolested until the middle of 1976, although the Khmer Rouge had first arrived in their village in 1971.[103]

Organized defrocking also took place in Sesan district, Stung Treng, where, astonishingly, the monks of Wat Chey Mongkul did not disrobe until 1977.[104] This relative lateness of their disrobing may be explained by Stung Treng's being far from the center and arguably quite unrepresentative of the country as a whole. However, this disrobing was not, technically speaking, the last such act. That occurred in March 1978 when the army of Democratic Kampuchea began its abortive attempt to recover Kampuchea Krom. It appears that monks from around twenty Khmer pagodas in southern Vietnam were kidnapped during the operation, after which they were forcibly disrobed and transported to northern Cambodia (Kiernan 1996, 426).

Despite the strongly intimidating nature of the process, there is not much evidence that those who complied were singled out for ill treatment, and monks who disrobed without protest were sometimes praised for their revolutionary fervor. As already noted, some areas held out until 1976. Indeed, after a few weeks in the forest the few who had fled Wat Norea, Battambang, heard there were no monks left in the whole of Cambodia, so they agreed to disrobe. It was 11 April 1976, and the Khmer Rouge applauded their decision.[105]

Intimidation could take many forms. On the softer side of the continuum, defrocking could be presented as a temporary measure. An old Thommayut monk called Ven. Mao Visothisart, an ex-colleague of Hem Chieu's, was told that he would be able to be reordained once the country was at peace again.[106] Indeed, some Khmer Rouge may have genuinely believed that these measures were only temporary. At the harsher end of the continuum, monastics were tricked or threatened. One stratagem was to roll up a rifle inside a monk's sleeping mat. When it was discovered, the monk had no option but to disrobe.[107] An old monk from Wat Mohamontrei, Phnom Penh, was evacuated to a pagoda whose residents were eventually urged to defrock. He spoke out against the idea, and the cadres and some of his fellow monks "banged the table" to express their disapproval. New monks disrobed soon after the meeting, and base monks a little later. The old monk finally disrobed in January 1976.[108] But the threat of unknown consequences was omnipresent. Ven. Pok Som Ann had been evacuated from Wat Sansam Kosala, Phnom Penh, to Prey Veng. After he was there three months, the district leader gave the order to disrobe, and those present were told that anyone who refused would go to a pagoda "where there were many graves."[109] The residents of Wat Pothi Reangsey, Chhlong district, were similarly threatened with death if they didn't disrobe. Yet when they all complied, the Khmer Rouge tried to persuade them that they had performed the act voluntarily.[110]

Personal connections between monks and officials could have a beneficial influence. Two monks from Pursat province who refused to disrobe were forced to look after pigs and chickens but were not killed.[111] Ven. Uem, vice-chief of Wat Yiey Kab, Krakor district, also refused disrobing but was not harmed, because some senior Khmer Rouge were his relatives. It was made clear to him, however, that no one would now give him alms and he must provide for himself. As a result he disrobed but continued living as a pious layman. Indeed, he was discovered there, starving to death, at the end of Democratic Kampuchea, and he passed away soon after.[112] Such events may not have been uncommon, for this was also the fate of Ven. Van Thone, the chief monk of Wat Prey Koki Duoch, Chan Trea district. The last member of his pagoda to disrobe, he remained nearby and died of starvation.[113]

Organized resistance to the defrocking policy was rare, but it did happen from time to time. In Svay Teap district, Svay Rieng, 234 monks resisted, a very high number. They were "taken away," and the leader of the group, Ven. Sar Peou, disappeared.[114] More often an individual monk had the courage to stand up for the continuation of the country's religious tradition. When the Khmer Rouge first entered Dang Tung district, Kampot, they refused to offer the monks food but were more than willing to discuss "how to fight the *yuon*" with them. Organized disrobing commenced in 1974, and thirty monks from Wat Prey Samnang were recruited into a unit to fight the Vietnamese. They all died in the fighting. However, the pagoda's chief monk, twenty-five-year-old Ven. Mao Kan, refused to be conscripted. He stayed in the *wat* another year, disrobing in 1975 only after he heard that So Prim, the *cau adhikār* of a neighboring *wat,* had been killed. During that time the villagers still brought him food, even though he was accused of being a "petty bourgeois monk."[115] Another young monk, based in Svay Rieng town, moved to the relative safety of Chan Trea district in June 1975. He was still there in early 1976, but the situation was deteriorating. Because he was from the town and refused to disrobe, he was left without food for three days. On the fourth day the Khmer Rouge broke down the door of his *kuṭī,* knocked him out, forcibly removed his robe, and burnt it. He was incarcerated for three months near Me Sa Thngak. It seems that around sixty other disrobed monks were held with him in the same prison.[116]

As already noted, strong-minded or older monastics were more likely to resist the pressure to defrock. Few managed to do this for very long, but the reaction of officials was quite variable.[117] When the order to disrobe was delivered to his pagoda in Chan Trea district, Ven. Uk Rorn challenged it on the grounds that the communists had left Buddhism largely untouched for such a long time. The reply was that no one could ignore an order from above. But he and the *cau adhikār* were nevertheless allowed to remain in robes for another week.[118] Ven. Chong Hieng, the chief monk of Wat Veang Chas, also refused, but he was able to retain his vows a little longer. When he did finally disrobe, he was pressured to marry, but declined. He was not punished for either infraction.[119] Meanwhile, at Wat Kdei Romduol, Battambang district, no monks were killed, and most disrobed "voluntarily." Only two older *saṅgha* members refused; one of them was the *cau adhikār,* Ven. Sam Nuon, who argued that "as Buddhism is two thousand years old why disrobe now?" Sam Nuon finally disrobed in 1976 after being approached by a teen-aged boy with a gun who threatened to make him into fertilizer.[120]

## Forced Marriage

Forced marriage is a common component in the persecution of all celibate religious traditions. It was imposed on Roman Catholic priests in the French revolutionary period and on Buddhist monks during the Chinese Cultural Revolution. In the Cambodian context it was justified largely by the need to enhance the country's economic output by increasing the birth rate. But subsidiary reasons included the desire to humiliate and control, tied to an overriding concern for social conformity.[121]

The policy of forced marriage of monks may not have had the desired effect, for the combined influence of trauma, malnutrition, and overwork seems to have had a deleterious impact on the general level of fertility during the Democratic Kampuchea period. But reports of monks, either individually or en masse, being coerced into taking partners are extraordinarily frequent, and the practice may have been more widespread than evidence suggests. One reason that evidence may be lacking is that many monks who rejoined the order in the PRK period were reluctant to admit to any diminution of celibacy during the Democratic Kampuchea period, for such a revelation would have simultaneously affected their spiritual prestige and their future career prospects within the *saṅgha.*

At Wat Pothi Voan Hanchey Krom in Chhlong district, Kratie province, monks appear to have been given the option of joining the army or getting married. Indeed, a number of pre-1975 novices who made the latter choice still live in the area as householders today.[122] Nevertheless, the proportion of monks who were forced to marry could be quite high. Of the sixty-eight monks residing at nearby Wat Chum Nik before April 1975, forty ended up in forced marriages,[123] and an informant from Wat Pothi Reangsey claimed that most of the pagoda's pre-1975 monks got married and that this was why so few of the surviving contingent of the village's ex-monks were reordained after 1979.[124] This circumstance has a general application throughout the country and is one of the reasons, investigated elsewhere in this book, why one should be suspicious of some of the more inflated statistics for the numbers of monks killed during Democratic Kampuchea.

As was the case with forced work, slight differences can be detected in the ways that older and younger monks were treated when it came to marriage, with the emphasis, for fairly obvious reasons, placed on cajoling the latter group. Younger monks were less accustomed to celibacy and usually had every intention of marrying after a temporary period spent in robes. Thus many found it not too difficult to walk away from the *saṅgha* once the Khmer Rouge arrived on the scene. It is also necessary to note that monkhood was rarely a straightforward matter of vocation. Although it must always be regarded as an unquantifiable ingredient in the decision to enter the order, ordinations have always occurred for a wide variety of other reasons—the need to gain a basic education or to enhance the family's status, for example. Under such circumstances the idea of an officially sanctioned sexual encounter may have been rather appealing.

Older monks, on the other hand, seem more often to have resorted to subterfuge in order to avoid getting married. Ven. Oum Sum, later to become a senior figure in the post–Pol Pot ecclesiastical hierarchy, eked out an existence for himself as a vegetable gardener after he was forced from his pagoda in Phnom Penh. He came under significant pressure to marry, but because he wished to remain true to his monastic vocation, he somehow managed to avoid this fate (Harris 2005a, 180). The current *megaṇ* of Kampot province, Ven. Em Phoeung, was also pressured to wed but refused, apparently without being punished.[125] Ven. Ith Som was more direct in his methods. He successfully dissuaded local officials from going through with a marriage ceremony on the grounds that he was suffering from gonorrhea.[126] Ven. Las Lay, who by the end of the 1990s occupied the third-highest position in the Mahanikay hierarchy, took a similar line by pretending to be sick.[127]

Although there are undoubtedly many more examples, I have been able to find evidence of only one monk executed for refusing the order to marry. He was Achar Thoan Vann, a member of the Tripiṭaka Commission, who was shot dead for objecting to taking a wife (DC-Cam 1996b, 25).[128] But his murder may also have been connected with his elevated status.

## Military Service

Theravāda Buddhism places an enormous emphasis on the concept of noninjury (*ahiṃsā*) and on the related practice of meditation as a means of calming the mind. This might lead one to suppose that it represents an ideal of radical pacifism. But in all regions of the Buddhist world, and Southeast Asia is no exception, the *saṅgha* has periodically been regarded with suspicion by the authorities, for it is made up of significant numbers of young, unattached, and energetic males who could represent a potential a threat to the state.[129] Insurrections led by monks are a well-attested, though sporadic, element in Cambodian history (Harris 2005a, 131–132), and modern attempts at *saṅgha* reform—by the French, for example—need to be interpreted as efforts to render the monkhood into a compliant partner in a central authority's project of governance. On one level the efforts of the Khmer Rouge to conscript able-bodied monks into the army was purely pragmatic. Since Buddhism no longer made sense, *saṅgha* personnel could be redeployed for other purposes. Yet the policy may also be regarded as a more radical approach to an age-old problem. By forcing monks to be soldiers, the communists also addressed the monkhood's capacity as a locus of opposition and subverted its potential to service the needs of the revolution.

Surviving evidence, nevertheless, does not suggest that a national policy to conscript monks existed. Rather, conscription appears to have been a consideration that emerged in different ways in varying regions of the country to suit local conditions. In July 1973 the Patriotic Monks' Association was calling on each monastery in Kampot and Takeo provinces to supply ten monks each to replenish losses in the army (Kiernan 1985, 377). According to a government intelligence report filed in November 1973, Seng Sovan, age twenty-two, had spent two years as a novice at Wat Ang Proleung when the Khmer Rouge arrived in the area. In July 1973 he and fellow monks were disrobed and forced to fight.[130] Kem Tha, age twenty, was a monk in Memot district. He disrobed on 6 February 1973 and became a militiaman at Matak village. Several months later he was sent to join Battalion 118.[131] But no monks were conscripted at Wat Roka Kandal, near Kratie town,[132] and in Zone 25 in 1974, forcible recruitment occurred only among single males. Married men were accepted only as volunteers, and monks were not expected to join up. Nevertheless, some monks appear to have disrobed and entered the army of their own accord.[133]

Recruitment drives seem to have affected small numbers of individuals, but mass conscriptions also occurred from time to time. In June 1973 more than one thousand monks from Banteay Meas, Kampong Trach, and Chhouk districts, Kampot province, were collected, formed into battalions, and almost immediately sent to the front (Hawk 1986). Sometimes individuals were planted in *wats* as agents of inducement. A Khmer Republic telegram tells of a young man who had been propagandizing monks to disrobe and join the army. He was aware that his job would be difficult because many monks were hostile to the revolutionary movement, and others were simply afraid of war. But he claimed to have been successful in establishing small networks of supportive monks in three *wats*.[134] Senior monks could also be quite helpful as recruiting sergeants, and a number held high office in the revolutionary forces well before the fall of the Khmer Republic. Mit Sam, for example, a villager and a former *cau adhikār* of Wat Krapeu in Kampong Thom province, was the commander of Battalion 403, whose headquarters were located at Wat Kdei.[135]

Monks close to the front stood a much greater chance of being mobilized than those residing elsewhere. This was especially so in the eastern and southeastern provinces close to the border with Vietnam. In Dang Tung district, Kampot province, during 1975–1976 monks from nearly all the area's pagodas had to join special monks' units to fight the enemy. Informants assert that virtually none returned, and the assumption is that they must have been killed in the fighting.[136] Casualties among monk soldiers recruited near the front were extremely high. In early 1974 a mass meeting of monks at Sras Thoul was held to the northwest of Peang Lvea Mountain. They were told that it had been decided to transfer them into military service, and each monk present was obliged to agree to this individually in front of those meeting. They were then given black uniforms and sent off to fight. With no military training, many surrendered to government forces at the first sign of danger (*Le Republicain* 1974c, 3, 6). Farther away from conflict, however, there was the possibility of some very basic training. Thus, Sam Tis, age twenty-two, from Kampong Speu province, told his Khmer Republic interrogators that after being disrobed in 1974 he was sent for seven days of military training in Phnom Sruoch district before being enrolled in Battalion 137 and sent to Zone 32.[137] It is possible that in such areas the proportion of monk soldiers surviving Democratic Kampuchea was higher.

# CHAPTER FIVE

# Buddhist Practice and Material Culture under the Khmer Rouge

## Buddhist Rites

The ordination of a monk is arguably the most significant of all Buddhist rituals. It is a two-stage process, starting with the "going forth" (*pabbajjā*) of the novice (*sāmaṇera*) and followed sometime later by a higher-level initiation (*upasampadā*) into the status of the fully ordained monk (*bhikkhu*). Under normal circumstances the novice should be between seven and nineteen years of age, and the *bhikkhu* twenty-one or over. There is reasonable evidence that in some parts of the liberated area the Khmer Rouge did not obstruct novice ordinations before 1975.[1] One informant, for instance, was confident that many young boys in and around the town of Stung Treng continued to be ordained well after 1973 and that local cadres did not seem to mind.[2] Novice ordinations in Svay Rieng were officially prohibited in some locales, but parents could circumvent opposition by having the ceremony conducted in a neighboring commune where things were allowed to proceed in a more relaxed manner.[3] The major ordination of a *bhikkhu,* however, was another matter. These rarely occurred, even in areas where novices could freely enter the order.[4]

The discrepancy in treatment of the two groups had a certain logic. In the liberated areas schools were clearly no longer under government control, and in the absence of paid staff they were forced to close. This meant that the only education available for children was that supplied by the *wat*s (Huy Vannak 2003, 16). By continuing to admit young boys to the novitiate, the

Khmer Rouge could more effectively control the local population and ensure that the minds of the young were exposed to the communist propaganda now beginning to replace the traditional curriculum of pagoda schools. An August 1974 intelligence report from Pursat province confirms this. By opening schools in all the pagodas of the province, the communists controlled a setting where pupils could be urged to hate Buddhism.[5]

One of the best means of spiritual progress as a lay Buddhist is through the feeding of monks. But as we have seen, this practice was discouraged. Ponchaud (1978, 150) reports a particularly chilling order given toward the end of 1975: "If any worker secretly takes rice to the bonzes, we shall set him to planting cabbages. If the cabbages are not full-grown in three days, he will dig his own grave." In this situation, customary links between the *sangha* and the wider community were difficult to sustain, and the economic support structure on which monasteries relied quickly disintegrated. The effect of all of this was to disorient and disaggregate villagers, for the monastery had traditionally functioned as the prime focus of communal life and shared meaning.

The laity are also expected to supply monks with other essentials, most notably lodging, medicine, and clothing. It is established custom to conclude the monks' three-month rainy season retreat (*vassā*) with a ceremony called *kathin,* in which the pious make gifts of robe to the *sangha.* Clearly the ceremony is built on the same conceptual foundations as the practice of alms giving, underlining as it does the otherworldly character of the *sangha* and its dependency on lay supporters. For this reason *kathin* was condemned by the communists. People were not permitted to bring cloth for robes into the liberated zones, and by the middle of 1974 it was rare to hear of a *kathin* ceremony beyond the areas still held by government forces.[6]

In January 1974 around forty Takeo-based monks were defrocked to serve in the army. In May another twenty-five were conscripted. But villagers were still allowed to practice the Buddhist precepts and to hold small donation festivals. In fact kathin was observed that year at both *wat*s, but no robes were offered, just money, and half of the money went to Angkar.[7] Although Angkar did not readily tolerate rites that acted merely to support the *sangha,* it is clear that rituals might continue, particularly when official permission had been granted in advance.[8] An intelligence report from May 1974 mentions a pagoda holding a flower festival (*puny phkā*) in which monks received 100 riels each, while Angkar took the lion's share of 20,000 riels.[9]

By early 1973 the only customary rites still widely observed in the liberated areas were the festival of merit-making for dead ancestors (*bhjuṃ piṇḍ*), Khmer New Year, and funerals.[10] The somber tone of *bhjuṃ piṇḍ* posed few difficulties when set against the background of a continuing war. Yang Sam (1987, 70) witnessed the ceremony being performed by three monks in Phnom Srok district, Battambang province, as late as October 1975. Similarly, both *bhjuṃ piṇḍ* and the New Year rites were held in Kampong Cham province well into 1974, but only if local people were sufficiently persistent in their requests and only when they were prepared to scale back expenditures to a minimum so that savings could be offered as a donation to Angkar. In addition, for every ten monks fed during the event, food had to be donated to around twenty-five soldiers.[11]

In prerevolutionary times the Khmer New Year had been a time to let off steam. Its observance could be rambunctious and provided an opportunity for the release of social tension. The Khmer Rouge were faced with a dilemma over whether to let it continue. Its transgressive character meant that it had the potential to unleash criticism of the new regime, yet to ban it might store up greater resentment. The answer was to hold it in a seriously weakened form. After 1973, dance was outlawed at the event, all elements of conspicuous consumption were eliminated, and the Party determined which songs could be sung.

A slogan that circulated during Democratic Kampuchea maintained that there was no need to bother with rituals associated with the old order, for now "every day is a festival" (*thṅai ṇā gi puṇy*) (Locard 1996, 218). Nevertheless, new ceremonies emerged to promote the revolutionary ideology. Chief among these were Soldiers' Memorial Day[12] and Workers' Day. There are reports from Kampong Cham that Workers' Day was observed in local pagodas, where banners criticizing the Khmer Republic and the United States were prominently displayed.[13]

Evidence for the performance of traditional death rites is patchy. In some of the liberated areas they were permitted,[14] but in others they were not. This particular restriction, where it applied, appears to have made many people angry.[15] The issue of funerary rites may be regarded as a microcosm of official attitudes to Buddhism. The economic ramifications of elaborate funerals offended the revolutionary conscience. In addition to consuming resources that would be better used on the living, death rituals disrupted work routines and could provide an opportunity for the gathering of large groups who might be encouraged to express emotional, religious, or antirevolutionary sentiments. The dead, therefore, were to be disposed of without fuss, and with minimal personal recognition. It occasionally happened that heaps of dead bodies were simply left exposed to the light of day, a practice that traumatized the general population (Mak Phœun 2003, 71–72). In addition, no attempt was made to alleviate the grief of those who had lost a loved one.

The traditional method of disposing of the dead by incineration was hardly practiced under the Khmer Rouge. Burial became the general custom, often in a common grave, although it seems that high officials were sometimes provided with a coffin.[16] It was only through the "exceptional grace" of a local Khmer Rouge official that one memoirist was able to cremate and collect the ashes of his younger brother (Pin Yathay 1980, 124, 142).[17] One assumes that the motive for burial was economic, since wood that would have been used for cremation fires was required for cooking and other more pressing purposes.

But such attitudes did not apply quite across the board. A somewhat more ambivalent attitude toward mortality may be detected among the elites who still existed within Democratic Kampuchea, for as Ernest Gellner once noted, death is always the last bastion of conservatism. Quite elaborate funeral rites for Sihanouk's mother, Queen Kossamak, took place at the Royal Palace in September 1975. Although most definitely not a public occasion, the ceremony was presided over by a number of monks who had come over to the Khmer Rouge in the early 1970s. Khieu Samphan

Funeral of Queen Kossamak, Royal Palace, Phnom Penh, September 1975. (Documentation Center of Cambodia)

and Son Sen also attended (Ponchaud 1978, 149–150). Nuon Chea's mother received a traditional Buddhist funeral at Wat Kor, Battambang, around the same time (Ken Khun 1994, 86),[18] and there are some tantalizing pieces of evidence to suggest that death rituals might have been allowed at lower levels of Angkar. For instance, relatives of high-ranking cadres who had died in Khsach Kandal district reportedly distributed rice to old people as a form of revolutionary merit-making,[19] and Ven. Las Lay claimed that in Koh Sotin district his services as a "president of funerals" were called on when there was a death in the household of a senior official.[20] Old people attended the ceremony that Las Lay oversaw, but there was no chanting. Las Lay was paid with an additional ration of rice, and he may have narrowly escaped execution twice because he performed this function (DC-Cam 1996b, 33).[21]

## Interiorizing Practice

External forms of religion are more fragile and more easily manipulated than those that go on inside a person's heart. This is especially so for Buddhism, a religion that depends so heavily on the activities of its monastic order. As has been noted, a measure as simple as prohibiting the laity from providing food to monks, an action that might not be regarded as being at the harsher end of the repressive spectrum, had major ramifications. Without alms, monks were obliged to break their rules of discipline (*vinaya*), and the *sangha* quite rapidly fell apart as a consequence. But it would be wrong to assume that Buddhist practice and belief entirely died out once its external forms had been dismantled.

Reports of continuing but secret practice during Democratic Kampuchea are widespread. One informant told me that people practiced Buddhism in their minds, but it was difficult to practice externally because children hid under beds and acted as spies.[22] Another reported that he performed his devotions every morning and night and that without these rituals he would not have been able to sleep. But he did not use incense or candles as usual. In the first place they were not available, but, more importantly, he did not wish to draw attention to his actions.[23] Another ex-monk performed a nightly ritual that included a prayer that the Pol Pot regime would come to an end.[24] Clearly activities such as these were rather dangerous. Ven. Hat Saray's secret devotions were uncovered in late 1978, and he has asserted that his name was put on an execution list as a result. He seems to have survived only because this happened just before the Vietnamese invasion of the country.[25]

Although independent practice seems to have been the norm, we also have evidence that groups of the pious cooperated from time to time and when circumstances permitted. The activities of Ven. So Chit, the pre-1975 *cau adhikār* of Wat Kor, Battambang, are a good example. He died in 1982 when he was over eighty years of age, but he is known to have performed a variety of rituals throughout the Democratic Kampuchea period. Indeed, I suspect that he was the monk mentioned above in connection with Nuon Chea's mother, although I have been unable to confirm this. So Chit also provided traditional blessings to the parents of couples forced into marriage by the Khmer Rouge—on one occasion, to the parents of ten couples at the same time—and was invited to houses to sprinkle water.[26]

Ven. Mao Visothisart continued to practice Buddhism in such a way that he did not come to the attention of the Khmer Rouge, but his fellow villagers were aware of his activities and respected him as a consequence.[27] One old man who continued to follow the five Buddhist lay precepts and refused to eat anything after noon was well regarded by neighboring villagers. When he chanted secretly, the people "closed their eyes."[28] Cambodia's most senior post-1979 monk, Ven. Tep Vong, also claims to have led groups of old people in secret acts of worship.[29] On a more sober note, Ven. Nou Song, the current *cau adhikār* of Wat Tep Pranam, near the old capital of Oudong, was in the habit of joining a group of old people to pray, but when the Khmer Rouge found out, they were advised to forget about continuing.[30]

A number of sources suggest that some people kept small images of the Buddha at home and performed their devotions in front of them during the night. The images were then carefully hidden away at daybreak.[31] One man found children playing with some Buddha statues during the Democratic Kampuchea period. Fearing that they would be punished, but also motivated by reverence, he gave the children two bunches of bananas in exchange for the statues and buried the images under a tree.[32] He certainly associated their possession with danger. Ven. Oum Sum was severely reprimanded for picking flowers when he was out working near a lake, his accusers believing that he was going to offer them up to the Buddha.[33] Meanwhile, at a village in Moung Ruessei district a group of ex-monks, ex-nuns, and old laypeople were in the habit of gathering together at night.[34] A painting of the Buddha that was reversed to the wall during the day was turned round as a focus for their worship. But they were reported to the Khmer Rouge and never seen again.[35]

The popular Buddhism of Cambodia tends to consist of a variable blend of mainstream Theravāda practice and indigenous spirit cults. This meant that spirit shrines were also sometimes maintained during the communist period. But frequent population movements severed the link between villagers and their ancestral divinities, and belief in the whole panoply of autochthonous mythological beings, including the tutelary spirits (*anak tā*), began to weaken. Ponchaud (1989, 168) reports of a peasant who came to disbelieve in their power, arguing that since "they didn't do anything against the Khmer Rouge, I don't trust them anymore."[36]

This decline of spirit belief was no doubt aided by the propaganda that the *anak tā* and their related pantheon of godlings were epiphenomena connected with the old regime. In Democratic Kampuchea, Angkar was the only significant power in the land. The message that Angkar was "the master of the water and of the earth" (*aṅgkār mcās' ḍik mcās' ṭī*) (Locard 1996, 34) further demonstrated a clear departure from the customs of the earlier anticolonial Issarak movement that had tried to gain control over villages by "endowing new Neak Ta" (Ponchaud 1989, 169). Angkar, furthermore, claimed possession of cryptosupernatural capabilities. The oft-repeated slogan that "Angkar has the eyes of a pineapple" (*aṅgkār mān bhnaek mnās'*) pointed both to the organization's omniscience and to its quasi-religious character.

But the official line on the *anak tā,* assuming there ever was such a thing, might easily be turned upside down. Wat Prasat Mathar in Kampong Svay district, quite close to the pre-Angkorian site of Sambor Prei Kuk, had two protector spirits, Ta Hang and Lok Yeay. During Democratic Kampuchea both villagers and new people kept up a secret belief in these divinities. Sticks of incense were burnt at the entrance to their shrines, and according to one informant, even the Pol Pot officers participated in the cult. When the daughter of an important cadre became lost in a nearby forest, her father made offerings of a roast pig and wine to Ta Hang and Lok Yeay, and the girl was found (An Rasmey 2004, 14). There are many other examples of similar occurrences, from an official who persisted in practicing traditional medicine (Mak Phœun 2003, 71–72) to a cadre who offered chickens to a demon that was thought to be causing illness in the neighborhood (Ken Khun 1994, 95).

## Wearing White Robes

As has been noted, the precise level of repression differed from place to place and seems to have been largely determined by the character of senior officials. If they had previously been *saṅgha* members or had come from pious backgrounds, they might be reasonably sympathetic to the adverse circumstances in which monks now found themselves. Additionally, they may have been susceptible to the force of the moral, intellectual, or alleged magical attainments of certain Buddhist practitioners. Indeed, it seems that some individuals continued to enjoy a modicum of the respect they had received in prerevolutionary times. This was particularly so when some prior personal relationship existed between local Khmer Rouge officials and the monks, such as being related or having had a student-teacher relationship (Kiernan 1996, 60–61, 205, 338).[37]

The case of the base monk Ven. Srey Ith (b. 1907), the *cau adhikār* of Wat Kork Kak in Kandal province is instructive here. Ignoring the warnings of former students to leave his home monastery, he was forced to disrobe after the 1975 rainy-season retreat (*vassā*). But his authoritative

Contemporary white-robed sage.

status appears to have been acknowledged by local officials, and he was assigned light duties in the agricultural commune to which he was attached. Moreover, after using traditional healing techniques to cure the sick child of a senior cadre, he was allowed to live for a time as a white-robed hermit on a nearby hill, where he was brought alms food.[38] Similar stories concerning charismatic individuals who continued to perform protective rituals for the sick, the malnourished, the bereaved, and the terrified and were protected in consequence, are not uncommon. They seem to suggest that while the communists were clear in their desire to eliminate Buddhism as an institution, the apotropaic dimensions of religion were never entirely extinguished in Democratic Kampuchea.[39]

That some religious aspects remained is most evident in the wearing of white robes during Democratic Kampuchea. The extent of the practice is difficult to quantify, but it is attested in various parts of the country, almost always associated with respected individuals who were generally too old or ill to make any significant contribution in the economic arena. Ven. Chu Kroeng, for example, had been the *cau adhikār* of Wat Kdol, Battambang province. Soon after the Khmer Rouge arrived, he was forced to defrock, but he continued wearing the white robes of a pious Buddhist layman for another two years while he attended to light work duties. It is said that local officials allowed this because some had been his students. But there may have been additional reasons, since it is known that he became mentally ill.[40] Similarly, at Wat Pothi Voan Hanchey Leu an old monk called Hoy Keum survived for a period in white robes, even though his fellows had been forcibly disrobed by 1974.[41] During this period he successfully avoided a forced marriage, openly but occasionally received the formal respects of laypeople, and spent his time making baskets. But lest we imagine that this was some sort of idyllic existence, it is necessary to point out that Hoy Keum died of illness and starvation in 1976.[42]

The case of Ven. Sroy Kun, the *cau adhikār* of Wat Pong Ro, Koh Sotin district, is especially illuminating. He was forcibly disrobed—the date is unknown—but the day after the event, he reappeared in his yellow monk's robes. The villagers thought that the Khmer Rouge would be angry and would execute him. But all they did was to ask him to change into white robes, and he complied with the request. From that point on, he continued to wear white and lived openly in a house in front of his old pagoda. It appears that he was protected by some of his ex-students. The commune chief, who had once been an *achar,* and the official in charge of the subdistrict were also sympathetic. Villagers fed Sroy Kun throughout the Democratic Kampuchea period, and those who knew him are adamant that he kept the ten precepts. He continued to practice his Buddhist devotions, and people sometimes visited him for advice.

Sroy Kun was clearly a courageous individual. On one occasion he predicted to a local cadre that Angkar would not last long, and he also criticized communist policies in public. This certainly annoyed the Khmer Rouge, for they fired their guns in the air in response. But nobody was injured. In fact Ven. Sroy Kun lived to see the demise of Democratic Kampuchea. He died in 1981, at age ninety-nine, still wearing his white robes. His funeral attracted a large gathering that included many newly ordained monks, as well as ex-monks from the early PRK period.[43]

Kampong Cham province had more than its fair share of white-robed worthies. Two old monks, Ta Korn of Wat Khchao and Ta Chea of Wat Kao, both located in Prey Chhor, Mean subdistrict, are good examples.[44] Ta Yun of Ambeng Chas, Lver subdistrict, also wore white through the whole of the Democratic Kampuchea period. It seems that Ta Yun's son, Khean, was the village chief, and the old man lived in a small cottage and had one meal of rice a day, "even if the Khmer Rouge provided him with two." He died in 1998 or 1999.[45] The *cau adhikār* of Wat Moha Leap in Koh Sotin district, Ta Sim, also wore white after being forcibly deprived of his yellow robes. He was around eighty years of age at the time, but there is no evidence that his behavior angered the revolutionaries. He continued to practice Buddhism after he was forced out of the pagoda. He died of starvation in 1981, but not before he had returned to Wat Moha Leap with two other old men, Ta Pao and Ta Khat.[46]

Although not quite as frequent, similar reports are attested in the Battambang and Siem Reap areas. A certain Ven. Sorn residing in Siem Reap town is reported to have survived in robes until well into the PRK period,[47] and a small community of white-robed survivors are said to have lived just across the Sangke River from Wat Norea, Battambang, during at least a part of Democratic Kampuchea.[48] Perhaps most surprising are the occasional stories of nuns, one of whom remained in white robes and continued to shave her head and eyebrows while living in Kok Lun village, Preah Net Preah district. She claimed that in the final months of 1978 she used Buddhist sources to teach a female cadre to read, and the woman subsequently brought a comrade along with her to learn (Wagner 2002, 129–130).

## Pagodas and Material Culture

Bearing in mind that iconoclasm is not in and of itself a sign of absolute hostility to religion, the extent and the specific nature of Khmer Rouge damage to Buddhist material culture are difficult to quantify. Becker (1979, 6), one of the few Western visitors to the country during Democratic Kampuchea, for instance, reported that when she toured Angkor toward the end of the period, she could detect no major damage to the temples beyond that caused by water seepage, fungal growth, and the like. The Khmer Rouge, furthermore, were not the first group to destroy Buddhist material culture in Cambodia. Looking back on an earlier period of Siamese and Vietnamese interference in the country, Ta Meas, a nineteenth-century author and native of Longvek, remarked:

> Novices and priests also suffered because the *vihāra*s had been plundered. Gold and silver buddhas had been removed, and soldiers had set fire to many *vihāra*s. In many places, the remaining *vatt* lacked roofs. Their roofs were sunken down and broken apart, allowing rain to come in on the monks. The monks had been unable to find anyone willing to repair the roofs because one war after another for fifty years had prevented it. . . . [T]here were no scriptures left. Fire and theft had destroyed some. The Siamese took some and the Vietnamese took some, and in the *vatt* where I was ordained as a *bhikkhu,* there remained only ignorant and backward monks. (Quoted in Hansen 2007, 49–50)

### Civil War Damage

Although statistics relevant to most areas of recent Cambodian history are rather unreliable, many monasteries were put out of action or significantly damaged once civil war erupted, as we have seen. According to one source, 997 *wat*s, about one-third of all *wat*s in the country, were disabled between March 1970 and June 1973, with around 70 percent of these meeting their fate in 1972 (Yang Sam 1987, 58–59; Chhang Song 1973, 248–250). Responsibility for the destruction has often been uncritically assigned to the communists, a view no doubt reinforced by the movement's own self-congratulatory claims. But on the ground both Khmer Republic and communist troops found monastery compounds to be ideal military bases.

The compounds could be relatively easily defended, and the communists believed that the notionally Buddhist government in Phnom Penh could be expected to respect religious sites. The Lon Nol regime was, after all, supposed to be fighting a holy war. This must have also been one of the reasons why the Khmer Rouge established themselves in the heavily symbolic area around Angkor at an early point in hostilities. However, their assumption that the government would be reluctant to launch attacks on such locations was misplaced.

The government side had been accumulating considerable quantities of intelligence since the onset of hostilities. Its leaders knew that in late 1971 the Vietcong had weapons and rice stored at Wat Prah Chy Andet, Angkor Borei district. The pagoda's residents had been forced to move out, and local people were prohibited from entry.[49] By November 1973 around 250 armed revolutionaries from Battalion 101 were based at Wat Polyum, Samdech Chuon Nath district,[50] and a local communist commander had his office at Wat Ruessei Srok, Kien Svay district, from where weapons were being siphoned into Sa-ang district.[51] Toward the end of the following year a

Damaged pagoda, location and date unknown. (Documentation Center of Cambodia)

substantial arsenal had been assembled at Wat Vihear Suor, Khsach Kandal district[52] and the Twelfth Division of the Revolutionary Army had been inaugurated at a large ceremony held at Watt Sampan, Koh Thom district (Huy Vannak 2003, 7).

Wat Preah Put Nippean, Kong Pisei district, was aerially bombarded early in the conflict after government forces heard stories of people bringing food to the *wat*. It was thought that they were supplying the communists.[53] The risk of such an action was obviously high. At Wat Kdol in Battambang a large banner in both Khmer and English was placed on the roof, calling on pilots not to drop bombs on the pagoda because it was home to two cabinets of ancient objects that were the "property of the nation." Wat Kdol was, indeed, never bombed.[54] Other monasteries were less fortunate.

In Kampong Thom province, Wat Kreul suffered aerial bombardment during the government's Chenla II campaign in September 1971 (Locard 2004, 12). Wat Sokharam, some sixteen kilometers from Phnom Penh, was badly damaged in December 1971 by a napalm attack in which a young monk was killed and two others injured; the pagoda had been consecrated by Sihanouk only two years earlier. The Khmer Republic government blamed the outrage on the Vietcong, but when Serge Thion interviewed the *cau adhikār* shortly after the incident, he attributed blame to Lon Nol forces.[55] Such incidents occurred throughout the civil war period. Thus a pagoda in Kampong Svay district, with both monks and communist troops in residence, suffered an air attack in 1974, and the resulting fire destroyed many palm-leaf manuscripts (Kobayashi 2005, 507).[56]

We must not forget that from 1965 on, the United States had also been bombarding the country, the action greatly intensifying between autumn 1972 and August 1973. This was undoubtedly another factor contributing to major structural damage in provinces close to the Vietnamese border. Only in recent years has the extent of the US bombardment come to light. During an official visit by Bill Clinton to Vietnam in autumn 2000, the president provided officials with a highly detailed though still incomplete database containing records of the US Air Force bombing of Indochina from 1964 to 1975. The database indicates that over that period the United States dropped 2,756,941 tons of ordnance on Cambodia, in 230,516 sorties at 113,716 sites, most of which remain poorly identified. The tonnage is nearly five times the previously accepted figure, and significantly more than the estimated two million tons dropped by the Allied Powers during the whole of World War II (Owen and Kiernan 2006, 63).

The database also demonstrates the problematic nature of the claim made by former US secretary of state Henry Kissinger that "air operations were subject to rules of engagement that prohibited the use of B-52s against targets closer than one kilometer to friendly forces, villages, hamlets, houses, monuments, temples, pagodas, or holy places" (Kissinger 2003, 479). We know, in any case, that US Intelligence was aware as early as 1970 that many of the communist "training camps" the Lon Nol regime had asked them to strike by air were functioning monasteries (Kiernan 1989, 7). Given the intensity of bombing, it was inevitable that a great number of pagodas in the east of the country were struck. Wat Sang Samei in Chan Trea district was bombed by B-52s over a three-day period in 1970. All of the *kuṭī*s and the dining hall were destroyed, and around thirty-five Khmer and many Vietnamese were killed. However, the monks had left before the attack, setting themselves up at Wat Chras, about seven kilometers away, where they raised a white flag to indicate that the bombers should not attack. This tactic does not seem to have been especially effective, for nearly all the pagodas in the area, including Wat Chras, were destroyed by bombardment soon after.[57] Another monastery in the same district, Wat Botum Reangsei, was pounded by B-52s in the winter of 1972. The *brah vihāra* and associated buildings were hit, but only one monk died. Thirty villagers living nearby were not so fortunate.[58]

## Deliberate Demolition

In the period between October and December 1975 almost all monasteries still remaining active in the country were closed. A Party document, *About the Control and Application of Political Leadership in Accumulating Forces for the National Front and Democracy of the Party,* dated September 1975, stated: "90 to 95% of the monks have disappeared, in the sense that the majority of monks have abandoned religion. Monasteries, which were the pillars for monks, are largely abandoned. The foundation pillars of Buddhism are abandoned. . . . [I]n future they will dissolve further" (quoted in Chantou Boua 1991, 235).

In some regions of the country, the Khmer Rouge dismantled abandoned pagodas to take advantage of recycled building materials. The stupas and *brah vihāra* of the prominent monastery Wat Tep Pranam, near Oudong, were demolished so that bricks could be reused for bridge construction,[59] while Wat Mony Sovannaram in Antong Vien had its iron removed to build a dike at Ou Kantuot.[60] Bunhaeng Ung also gives a firsthand account the dismantling of Wat Phum Andong in Maesor Prachan village, Prey Veng (Stuart-Fox and Bunhaeng Ung 1998, 133).

The Khmer Rouge first arrived at Wat Samraong Meanchey, Kampong Thom, in late 1970. Sometime after this, the monastery was badly damaged in a government offensive. Although it was not totally destroyed, the communists decided that it should be torn down. Despite the danger, villagers who had been ordered to do the work refused, on the grounds that to do so would have been incompatible with their religious convictions. Surprisingly, they were not punished. Indeed, local cadres appear to have been "understanding." But the work had to be done, nevertheless, and laborers were brought in from a nearby village instead.[61]

Assertions that the Khmer Rouge systematically organized the destruction of pagodas surfaced at the 1979 Pol Pot/Ieng Sary trial (Groupe de Juristes Cambodgiens 1990, 218–219). But on the evidence available, it is difficult to determine whether the work of dismantlement was by local initiative or whether orders were formulated at a higher level and, if so, at what level. The most illuminating evidence I have been able to gather concerns the existence of an organized group of pagoda demolition workers

Damaged pagoda, location and date unknown. (Documentation Center of Cambodia)

who certainly did move quite systematically around Khsach Kandal district, Kandal province, during the Democratic Kampuchea period.

The following story gives a good indication of what happened. A young Cham man called Ismael had escaped from his home village in Kampong Siem district but was arrested in Khsach Kandal, where he was held in prison at Prek Ta Moak for twelve days. The prison chief, named So Ny, also supervised a pagoda demolition team, and Ismael was recruited into it directly from prison in early 1978.[62] He remained part of the team for around a year. Because he soon became skilful in his work, he was appointed chief of the unit, comprising two Cham Muslims and twenty-eight Khmer workers.

The workers did not return to the prison every night but generally slept on-site, the working day stretching from six to eleven in the morning and from one to five in the afternoon. They enjoyed adequate food rations, even had dessert with their meals, were supplied with tobacco and clothing, and did not have to work at night. However, their activities were monitored by a high-ranking cadre, and the work was dangerous. Ismael personally suffered a number of serious injuries.[63] Sledgehammers were the main tool, and explosives were never employed. Most team members were Buddhists and therefore were concerned about the consequences of their actions. One continually prayed, "Please, Buddha, do not accuse me; I was ordered to do it." He also lit incense made of reeds.[64]

Ismael's unit dismantled more than twenty pagodas during the period when he was involved. These comprised most of the *wat*s around Khsach Kandal, with the exception of Wat Vihear Suor, which served as a rice storehouse, and Wat Svay Chum, which was being used as a dormitory for artists and performers.[65] The rest were dismantled for their iron girders (usually transported by boat to Phnom Penh), wood, and other building materials. It took approximately fifteen days to demolish a two-story *braḥ vihāra,* and even stupas without iron were dismantled. Sometimes Buddha images still survived intact, but by the time the men were ready to move on, all had to be broken into small pieces. Interestingly the gateways and outer walls of the *wat* precinct were, perhaps for defensive reasons, always left unharmed.

Ismael believed that the work had two basic goals: to provide building materials and to ensure that future generations would never be aware that the Buddhist religion had once flourished in Cambodia. The team never saw monks when they arrived at a new pagoda, because all monks had been disrobed by 1978; and no villagers opposed their work, because when they arrived in a new village, a cadre would explain what they planned to do.

Although Ismael recalled hearing of similar teams at work in other districts, he did not know where they were operating or who was involved.[66]

Reputedly a "cruel man," Prum Preung, also known as So Ny, was the prison chief at Prek Ta Moak and in a 2005 interview was able to confirm most of Ismael's account. Born in 1952, he was a native of Khsach Kandal district. According to him, all orders, including those to demolish pagodas, came from a high level within the Khmer Rouge and were delivered by letter to the district.[67] From that point on, they moved downward in oral form, so he never knew who formulated the policy in the first place. Nevertheless, he did recall that the zone chief, Ta Mith, ordered the destruction of Wats Ta Kut and Me Ban so that their iron could be used to construct a dam at Sanlong Vihear Sour.

## In Phnom Penh

After the establishment of the People's Republic of Kampuchea, it was claimed that the followers of Pol Pot had destroyed most of Phnom Penh's monasteries. This is not credible, however. Vickery (1988, 71), for one, has noted that "most of the city's old *wats* survived intact except for minor damage and deterioration." He is also critical of the PRK's official estimate of forty-seven city *wats* destroyed, when, according to Migozzi (1973), only twenty-four such structures existed in the first place.[68] In actuality, the evacuation of

Communist grenade-throwing practice on the grounds of an unidentified *wat*, 1970 or 1971.
(From National United Front of Cambodia 1971a, 10)

the city in the days after 17 April 1975 massively reduced its population, and the end of fighting ensured that post–civil war damage was fairly minimal.

Reasonably good evidence indicates that Phnom Penh's Buddhist monasteries did not suffer unduly. One witness who visited the city in 1976 reported, "[It] was very well maintained, cleaned up and beautiful, bustling with workers, although there were no little children. *Wats* . . . were particularly well-maintained, squeaky clean."[69] This is something of an exaggeration, but my own suspicion is that reports of monastery devastation on a grand scale in the city may have been extrapolated from stories about the fate of the Catholic cathedral. The cathedral was most certainly destroyed, its stones being used to reinforce dams for paddy farming. This happened a year after liberation and appears to have been undertaken by a special forces battalion on orders from above.[70] Nevertheless, the grounds of Wat Saravan were turned into a vegetable garden, and by 1979 almost all of its more than one hundred stupas had been broken.[71] Soldiers from the 704th Special Forces Battalion trained in martial arts and bayonet practice in the compound of Wat Langka (Huy Vannak 2003, 58), and Wat Mangalavan, close to Phnom Penh's central railway station, was used as a car repair factory.[72] Farther out from the center of the city, Wat Sansam Kosala appears to have doubled as a location for rearing livestock and as a child care unit.[73]

## Reusing Pagodas

Quite good sources of information are available about the use to which pagodas were put once monks had been disrobed. In his evidence presented at the 1979 Pol Pot/Ieng Sary trial, Ven. Tep Vong gave an overall description of what happened to the nine pagodas of Siem Reap town. They were variously transformed into premises for the regional security service (Wat Thommayut), arm depots, a school for officer training (Wat Preah Prum Roth) and vehicle repair workshops (Wat Svay). Wats Monisovan, Por, Enkosa, and Enkosey, on the other hand, were abandoned to the growth of wild grass (Groupe de Juristes 1990, 89–90).[74] The 1986 Indochina Studies Program Project of the US Social Science Research Council [75] provided additional helpful insights into the circumstances of ten monasteries in Battambang,[76] twenty-one in Takeo,[77] fifteen in Kampong Cham,[78] and a reasonable cross section of pagodas in Preah Vihear province.[79]

An Rasmey's (2004) dissertation on Wat Prasat Mathar is the only work available giving a detailed account of a specific pagoda under Khmer

Rouge control. It seems that once the monkhood had been disbanded, the *brah vihāra* was first used to store kapok fruit and later became a textile storehouse. Meanwhile a hospital was located in the house of the old *cau adhikār* (ibid., 1, 34–36). The conversion of sections of other pagodas into basic medical facilities is well attested throughout the country. Wats Lver and Moha Leap in Koh Sotin district[80] and Wat Kok Thouch in Battambang province[81] are specific examples.

The raising of animals and the cultivation of fruit and vegetables were also common. Wat Roka Kandal, on the eastern bank of the Mekong to the south of Kratie town, was used for raising pigs. The villagers felt this to be sacrilege, but they were afraid to speak out.[82] Wat Veal Sbov, a little to the south of Phnom Penh, was dismantled under the leadership of section chairman Saruon, in order to convert it into a pig-raising facility.[83] Pig husbandry also occurred at Wat Me Ban, Khsach Kandal district, a pagoda largely occupied by disabled people.[84] Wat Phnom Sampeou, a previously important pilgrimage center to the west of Battambang town, on the other hand, was completely flattened and turned into a banana plantation.[85]

The use of pagodas for various bureaucratic functions has already been mentioned. Some became local economic bureaus (*mandīr seṭṭhakicc*). Others were district offices. Wats Ta Kut and Sunlong, both in Khsach Kandal district, are good examples of the latter,[86] as was Wat Kratie in Kratie town. It seems that the Khmer Rouge hoarded gold in the Wat Kratie pagoda, telling the local populace that it would be used to buy tractors so that they would not have to work so hard. The *brah vihāra,* however, doubled as a prison and a place for storing salt.[87]

Monastery compounds made both good barracks and good prisons. The important study by Henri Locard (2004, 1) of the Khmer Rouge prison system in Kampong Thom and Siem Reap observes that "in Kampong Thom province twenty-four more or less permanent prisons have been identified, out of which sixteen were in pagodas."[88] In the Southwestern Zone, fifteen of the twenty-one district "reeducation centers" were housed in pagodas (Ea 2005, 59). Some of these were general prisons, but others had more specific functions. Wat Chres in Svay Rieng province, for example, was used to hold Eastern Zone soldiers and cadres who had been accused of collaborating with the Vietnamese army after the zone's defensive lines were broken during a particularly severe attack in 1978 (Huy Vannak 2003, 114). After April 1975, Lolei pagoda, next to the famous pre-Angkorian temple (*prāsād*), was used to incarcerate Khmer Republican military evacuated from Siem Reap, and Wat Preah Dak, next to Pre Rup, served as a commune prison housing two hundred to three hundred mostly "17 April" inmates, who were tied with ropes (Locard 2004, 38, 49).

Monasteries were also employed for more sinister purposes, their widespread use as workshops of torture and execution chillingly reinforcing the traditional association of Buddhism and death. The *brah vihāra* of Wat Kesararam in Siem Reap had been used as a prison, and when monks finally returned after the end of Democratic Kampuchea, they found a number of dead victims still held in wooden shackles (*khnoh*) and about one hundred other bodies buried on the grounds.[89] Wat Kaich Roteh, Moung Ruessei district, was a holding place for intellectuals. It is claimed that after they were executed, their bodies were burnt and people were forced to use the ashes as fertilizer.[90]

The numbers of individuals who passed through or were executed at these sites have been notoriously difficult to quantify or corroborate. Nevertheless, some figures circulate in the public domain: 21,151 people are said to have been executed at Wat Kampong Tralach, Kampot district; 17,000 at Wat Preah Theat, Kirivong district; and many more at Wat Champukaek,

Shrine of skulls, Wat Kakok, with damaged *brah vihāra* in background, early 1980s.
(Documentation Center of Cambodia)

Kien Svay district (Ea 2005, 59). At the 1979 trial of Pol Pot and Ieng Sary, evidence was given that at Wat Champukaek around two hundred monks who had been ejected from Phnom Penh immediately after liberation were individually escorted to the central sanctuary and asked to appeal to the main Buddha image for help before being executed with a swift blow of an iron bar on the nape of the neck (Groupe de Juristes Cambodgiens 1990, 218–219).

The list is sickening in its extent. Wat Norea, Battambang, was the prison and killing field for District 41, Zone 4 (Huot Robiep 2004). Wat Vihear Ton Tem had the same function in Tbong Khmum district. An eyewitness claimed to have seen graves overflowing with bodies there during Democratic Kampuchea.[91] In September 1980, mass graves indicating in excess of five thousand deaths were discovered at Wat Ampe Phnom, Kampong Speu. A torture room and further bodies were found in a compartment under the floor of its *brah vihāra* (Hinton 1997, 27–28). Oddly enough, Buddhist ritual sites associated with mountains and caves exercised a special fascination for those engaged in mass murder. The pagoda on Phnom Bros, close to Kampong Cham town, was a prominent execution center, as were the temples and caves in and around the previously mentioned site of Phnom Sampeou.

## Images of the Buddha

Damage to or removal of Buddha images and other sacred objects from pagodas occurred frequently, but the motivation was complex and it seems unlikely that there was a general directive to this effect. Naturally some images had a significant monetary value. Ven. Tep Vong has asserted that a number of golden Buddha images went missing from his home monastery, the relatively prosperous Wat Bo in Siem Reap town, but who took them is uncertain.[92] Similarly, many precious Buddha images at Wat Toul Tompoung in Phnom Penh had disappeared by the early 1980s.[93] We are on somewhat firmer ground when we come to the case of Wat Kdol in Battambang. The Khmer Rouge arrived in April 1975, and the following year they removed all of the statues that were made of gold. Cement statues were simply destroyed.[94]

Statues, stupas, and other sacred objects made of the traditional threefold mixture of sticky rice, lime, and cow dung were not demolished, because they had minimal recycling potential.[95] But a well-attested slogan of the period did advise, "If you demolish a statue of the Buddha, you will gain a sack of cement (*kaṃtec brah muoy aṅg caṃneñ sīmaṅ muoy pāv*)" (Locard 1996, 152). But the emphasis on recycling seems rather unconvincing, for the effort involved in rendering a statue back to its constituent parts would have far outweighed the value of the finished product.

At some point in January 1975 a cadre called Ham was overheard ordering a subordinate to smash a statue of the Buddha at Wat Po Prek Sleng in Kandal province. The latter replied, "Why do you want to smash it[?] . . . [T]he statue has no feelings, it's made of cement." He was arrested, paradoxically accused of being a materialist and of verbally attacking Angkar, and taken to Tuol Speu, where he was held in chains and beaten for three days. Then he was transferred to the Sa-ang district reeducation center (*mandīr* no. 8) on Koh Kor, where he remained until the arrival of the Vietnamese liberation forces.[96]

It has been alleged that considerable efforts were sometimes made to destroy particular images, suggesting that a desire to eliminate a potential site of veneration might have been foremost in the minds of the revolutionaries. According to the evidence given by Ven. Tep Vong at the 1979 trial of Pol Pot and Ieng Sary, two especially celebrated and powerful Buddha

Brah Aṅg Chek and Brah Aṅg Chom, Siem Reap.

statues from the Siem Reap region—Braḥ Aṅg Chek and Braḥ Aṅg Chom—
were deliberately destroyed, along with several other highly venerated
images at Angkor Thom and Angkor Wat (de Nike et al. 2000, 149, document 2.1.2.03). But I do not think that this is quite accurate. More likely,
particularly in the light of their continued cult today, Braḥ Aṅg Chek and
Braḥ Aṅg Chom were thrown into a pond.[97]

At Wat Preah Ang Thom, on the riverfront in Stung Treng town, the
Khmer Rouge used a chain attached to a truck to pull down the head of the
pagoda's colossal Buddha image. It was then flung into the water, where
it remained until it was retrieved and stuck back on to the surviving body
in 1980.[98] One of the Buddha statues at Wat Sangke in Battambang was so
large and strongly constructed that land mines were used to destroy it.[99] In
the same province, sacred images were removed from Wat Saat and deliberately placed under a bridge so that people would be forced to commit
sacrilege when crossing over.[100] When the Buddha images of Wat Veal Sbov
were smashed and dumped in the road, some villagers were asked to participate, but they were too afraid of the consequences of desecration. A cadre
attempted to reassure them by arguing that neither souls nor good or bad
deeds existed. One of his audience was so horrified at these impieties that he
secretly burnt incense to cleanse the area.[101] But not all officials were willing iconoclasts. Ta Phon, a commune chief at Kaoh Sampeay, Stung Treng
province, was renowned for his kindness. Instead of destroying Wat Sokha
Phi La Lam's Buddha images presumably on orders from above, he had
them gently placed in the river so that they could be retrieved easily when
circumstances allowed.[102]

Stories also abound of sacred images that were preserved by miraculous
forces. The statue of Yiey Deb had originally stood at Wat Khnat Reangsei
near the Western Baray at Angkor. According to popular belief, the communists, try as they might, were incapable of transporting the statue far from its
original site, nor could it be completely destroyed. The reason for this, it was
argued at the time, was that the statue was the abode of a protective spirit
(*pāramī*). In 1985 the pieces of Yiey Deb, minus the original head, were
reassembled and reestablished in a shrine in central Siem Reap (Hang Chan
Sophea 2004, 116). It is also said that at the ancient Angkorian site of Wat
Nokor Bachey Ba-Ar, on the outskirts of Kampong Cham town, local Khmer
Rouge were ordered to destroy some statues, but they were too frightened
to do so, because they had heard that the statues were protected by serpents'
spirits (*nāg*) living in a secret cave nearby.[103] A similar story is told of Wat

Phnom Sia, between Kampot and Kep. According to local inhabitants, when Khmer Rouge forces came to blow up the *wat,* huge snakes appeared from the temple mound and killed them. Subsequent units were too terrified to repeat the actions of their comrades, so the monastery remained undamaged (Brown 1993).

But most of the desecration was routine and low-key. At Wat Pothi Reangsey in Chhlong district, Buddha statues were thrown into the river and deposited in a toilet. Many of these were recovered and rededicated after Democratic Kampuchea.[104] At Wat Chum Nik, Krouch Chmar district, a sacred racing canoe was cut into firewood by a mobile youth team.[105] The same thing happened at Wat Phum Tmey, Khsach Andet commune, Chhlong district. But attempts were made to preserve at least some items of religious and cultic significance. This was difficult for large statues that could not easily be hidden, but at Wat Pothi Preuk, Chhlong district, for example, villagers did manage to hide the contents of a cabinet containing more than ninety small statues, including some of gold.[106]

Few of Cambodia's pre-1975 Buddhist murals, mostly executed on the interior walls of a pagoda's central sanctuary (*braḥ vihāra*), were very old.[107] But many fine examples dating from the last years of the nineteenth century and the early decades of the twentieth century did exist. Obviously, when a

Damaged mural, Wat Saravan, Phnom Penh.

*brah vihāra* was demolished, destroyed by shell fire, or given over to some other purpose, its murals perished. What happened at Wat Preah Dak, near the famous Pre Rup temple, is a good example. Its paintings were obliterated when a bulldozer leveled its central sanctuary in 1978, leaving only some foundation stones and a few old Buddha statues (Locard 2004, 49). But most murals simply deteriorated through neglect, and few that survive appear to have been deliberately mutilated. One example from Wat Saravan in Phnom Penh does spring to mind, but local informants have attributed its damage to Vietnamese troops who were barracked there after the overthrown of Pol Pot.

The widespread practice of overpainting meant that even those murals that did survive Democratic Kampuchea were unlikely to remain unscathed. But there are exceptions. Among the best in terms of their artistic merit are a unique sequence illustrating the *Rāmakīrti* (a Khmer version of the Indian *Rāmāyaṇa*) at Wat Bo, Siem Reap (Harris 2005a, 90–91), and the remarkably well-preserved interior of the *brah vihāra* at Wat Sisowath Ratanaram, on the eastern banks of the Bassac River some way south of the capital. I have been unable to discover how or why they survived, but in some other locations monks or villagers did have the forethought to protect artworks for future generations. Ven. Chan Chhet, the *cau adhikār* of Wat Prasat Mathar, for example, was ordered to scrape off his pagoda's murals, but as this seemed a lot of work, he persuaded officials that he should paint the walls black instead. Rice porridge mixed with charcoal was used for this purpose, a material that could easily be cleaned off at a later date (An Rasmey 2004, 34). A good cluster of further examples survive in Koh Sotin district, an area especially rich in fine Buddhist architecture and painting. The one-hundred-year-old decorated columns at Wat Moha Leap were apparently smeared with mud before the building was converted into a dormitory for the region's medical staff,[108] and something similar happened at nearby Wat Sokunthearam Pong Ro.[109] Both pagodas were washed clean and their artworks reexposed in 1979.

## Religious Literature

The deliberate burning of books certainly happened under the Khmer Rouge, but it is difficult to determine whether specific directives to do this were issued. Incidents at the Catholic cathedral in Phnom Penh (Ponchaud 1978, 32) and the "pathetic *auto da fé*" (Bizot 2000, 221–222) at the École

Française d'Extrême-Orient, both in Phnom Penh, were more likely the result of poor discipline among troops celebrating the capital's fall than part of a concerted policy.[110] Indeed, such behavior was condemned by one senior revolutionary, Thiounn Mumm, a cofounder of the Parisian Cercle Marxiste who appears to have fallen out with Pol Pot over the issue.

As far as specifically Buddhist literature is concerned, however, we have reliable evidence for its destruction at a few locations. Old palm-leaf manuscripts stored in two big cupboards at Wat Prasat Mathar were burnt by the Khmer Rouge soon after their arrival in the area (An Rasmey 2004, 23). Similarly, at Wat Mang Sala, a Thommayut pagoda in Prey Veng, all Buddhist books were burnt over a period of three nights. Strangely, it was only after this event that the monks realized that the previously friendly revolutionaries, who had been in the area for around a year, were fervently anti-Buddhist.[111] In early 1971 monks at Wat Pothi Reangsey, Chhlong district, were forced to work on roads and were subsequently threatened with death if they refused to disrobe. Around the same time, all the pagoda's documents were collected and taken away. No one knew where.[112] Buddhist writings sometimes do seem to have been stored—Moung Ruessei district, for instance, had a Khmer Rouge "culture office" where scriptures were accumulated[113]—but for what purpose I have been unable to establish. More often they must simply have been destroyed. But the oft-repeated assertion that Buddhist palm-leaf manuscripts were used for rolling tobacco is rather obvious propaganda, for the resulting cigarette would have been virtually impossible to smoke.[114]

Learned monks seem to have been aware of this threat to Cambodia's cultural and religious patrimony, and occasional attempts were made to save important documents for future generations. The magical and protective character ascribed to Buddhist writings, especially those inscribed in the traditional manner on palm leaves, may have been an additional reason for seeking their preservation.[115] At Wat Chum Nik, Krouch Chmar district, a certain Achar Suong is said to have collected and hid manuscripts,[116] while another report describes the disinterring of scriptures hidden underground at an unidentified *wat* in 1979.[117]

Regretfully, hiding manuscripts underground as a manner of preservation was not always successful, especially given Cambodia's monsoon climate. Achar Keo Sophol claimed that he had given sacred writings into the safekeeping of laypeople, but when he discovered that the documents were not being looked after properly, he decided to bury another cache at

Wat Sokan, Pursat province. Unfortunately, when they were dug up in the early PRK period, they had become moldy.[118] It also seems that in 1974 an elderly monk from Kien Svay district deposited seventy-four volumes of the *Tripiṭaka* at the Australian Embassy in Phnom Penh. Shortly before the Khmer Rouge victory, they were transferred to the National Library in Canberra, and in September 1992 they were ceremonially returned to King Sihanouk by Prime Minister Paul Keating when he made an official visit to Phnom Penh (Dobbs 1992).[119]

The extent of deliberate book and document destruction is difficult to determine, but it may have been less than was assumed, often for ideological purposes, immediately after the fall of Pol Pot. In 1979 the director of the National Library of Cambodia reported that only 20 percent of the pre-1975 collection had survived Democratic Kampuchea. More recent estimates suggest a vastly higher survival rate (Jarvis n.d., 108). It had also been claimed that virtually the entire library of the Buddhist Institute in Phnom Penh, comprising around thirty thousand titles and four thousand documents, had disappeared. It is odd, then, that the collection was still intact when visited by a Ministry of Education official in the early months of 1979 (de Bernon 1997, 44n33). By far the most likely explanation for these discrepancies is that while some writings were consigned to the flames by zealous revolutionaries, and others moldered away through simple neglect, the rest—and this may apply to the Phnom Penh collections mentioned above—disappeared as a result of simple foraging during the well-attested paper shortages of the early PRK period.

One scholar has estimated that 95 percent of the literary patrimony of Cambodia inscribed on palm leaves or traditional paper was destroyed in the holocaust (de Bernon 1998b, 873). But this estimate may be rather high. In mid-1979 a Vietnamese newspaper reported that a visitor from the National Library of Vietnam had discovered "an underground room with thousands of books written on palm leaves" in a ruined pagoda (Jarvis n.d., 110). Further reports suggested that manuscripts had survived in quantity in four Phnom Penh monasteries—Wat Neak Voan, Wat Sansam Kosala, Wat Chak Angre Kraom, and Wat Stung Meanchey (de Bernon 1992, 245)—and new discoveries have since been made. Ven. Ken Vong (d. 1994), the *cau adhikār* of Wat Saravan in Phnom Penh and one of the original group of seven monks officially reordained in September 1979, also managed to make a collection of around 3,400 manuscripts after 1979,[120] and a library at Wat Thmei, Kang

Meas, Kampong Cham province, was discovered in the late 1990s. It appears that in 1975 the *cau adhikār* had distributed texts to pious villagers who were urged to hide them until things died down.

## Concluding Remarks

This chapter has focused on the manner in which Buddhist practice was restricted and finally extinguished by the Khmer Rouge. Although it seems reasonable to assert some underlying strategy, this idea is somewhat undermined by the knowledge that when it comes to specific restrictions—be they on ordination, the feeding of monks, the celebration of annual festivals, or funerary customs—only rarely has it been possible to establish that local initiatives emanated from the center. The same applies to the treatment of pagodas, Buddha images, sacred texts, and other forms of material culture. The chaotic nature of the regime largely explains the apparent lack of a central strategy. But other factors complicate the picture. At the local level, policies were implemented in one of two ways, either dogmatically and with ill-considered fervor or in ways that still left scope for determined individuals, sometimes with the connivance of sympathetic officials, to maintain a minimal level of religiosity. In the case of a very limited number of courageous elderly monks and laypeople, living the life of a white-robed ascetic became an option, if only for a short period. A slightly larger group resolutely confronted their terrors and performed devotions in secret. But by far and away the largest proportion of previously active Buddhists rapidly and completely abandoned any semblance of the religious life. A decision born of rationality and fear in equal measure, it certainly increased one's chances of survival.

# CHAPTER SIX

# Monk Mortality and the Destruction of Institutional Buddhism

## Monks and Class Analysis

In the 1950s the Khmer Workers' Party still reflected its connections with the *saṅgha* by describing significant segments of the Buddhist monastic order as possessing a "patriotic, progressive and national outlook" (Sher 2004, 70). Many of these monks were close enough to the land to have some "peasant-like characteristics," according to the KWP, while others manifested "good political standpoints." However, by the time of Democratic Kampuchea this preexisting yet rough-and-ready division between rural and urban monks had crystallized into a fairly solid distinction between "base monks" (*saṅgh mūlaṭṭhān*) and "new monks" (*saṅgh thmī*). While the former were deemed "proper and revolutionary," the latter were now described as "imperialists" or as "April 17 monks" (*saṅgh ṭap' prāṃ bīr mesā*). Nuon Chea (1987) made a similar distinction in a speech to delegates of the Danish Communist Workers' Party visiting Cambodia in July 1978. In the talk, he contrasted "rank and file monks . . . [who were] not so reactionary" with those who occupied a high rank in the ecclesiastical hierarchy.

After the emptying of the cities, April 17 monks were forced to live side by side with base monks. Often the base monks had lived under communist control for a number of years, for monasteries in base areas unaffected by large-scale fighting generally appear to have been in good to fair physical order until well after the fall of Phnom Penh. But the two groups were not treated equally. They were often not allowed to mix socially, and

the former group underwent more rapid laicization. Thus there were virtually no April 17 monks remaining in robes by the beginning of the 1975
rainy-season retreat (*vassā*), which lasted from July to September, but there
is evidence that plenty of base monks were allowed to observe the whole
of *vassā* before being obliged to disrobe (DC-Cam 1996b, 56–58). From
late September 1975, however, earlier distinctions ceased to operate, and
all remaining Buddhist monks were now assigned to a "special" or "separate" class that stood alongside the feudalists, the bourgeoisie, the peasants,
and the workers.[1] This "special class" (*vaṇṇaḥ bises*) also included intellectuals (*anak ceḥ diṅ*),[2] soldiers of the Khmer Republic, the police, and all
national minorities. All were regarded as possessing no "practical awareness" (Ly Sophal 2002, 17), in the sense that they were unaccustomed to the
performance of productive labor.

Early in Democratic Kampuchea, "Khmer Republic military officers
and enlisted men, Khmer Republic civil servants, 'new people,' Buddhist
monks, the Cham, Vietnamese and people of Vietnamese ancestry, and
Chinese and people of Chinese ancestry" (Heder 2005, 382) were redefined
as real or potential enemies (*khmāṃṅ*). The first wave in the elimination of
such individuals largely focused on high-ranking military officers and civil
servants. Senior monastics occupying positions in the national ecclesiastical hierarchy fell into this category, and they were smashed for much the
same reasons as the highest level of the Phnom Penh–based Cham religious hierarchy were. The policy was soon expanded to cover most commissioned officers in the previous regime's military and police forces, plus
civil servants of equivalent rank (*paṇṭāsǎkti*) (ibid., 384). It would not be
long before monks further down the hierarchy, especially at the provincial
level, were in the firing line.[3]

The origins of this policy can be traced back to a conference held on
20–25 May 1975 in which Pol Pot and Nuon Chea announced an eight-point
program, the fourth element of which was to "defrock all Buddhist monks
and put them to work growing rice." The conference also called for the
complete disbanding (*lup paṃpāt'*) of the *saṅgha*,[4] while a follow-up document, *On Grasping and Implementing the Party's Political Line of Gathering
National-Democratic Front Forces*, dated 22 September 1975, stated that the
goal was to ensure that "monks were gone . . . in the sense that they . . . gave
up their religion" and were "dissolved" into "collectively organized peasants" (quoted in Heder and Tittemore 2004, 37n119). Yet neither statement
can be legitimately construed as a plan to exterminate monks.

## Killing Monks

It is difficult to identify many rank-and-file ecclesiastics and laypersons who were killed simply because they practiced Buddhism. A story told to me by Chhorn Iem, currently one of the two secretaries of state at the Ministry of Cults and Religions, illustrates the challenges involved. In the pre-1975 period he had worked at a pedagogical institute in the capital, but by 1977 he was in the Pursat countryside. For reasons of safety he had changed his name to Chhom Ieng, but someone in the vicinity had found a school text-book written by Chhorn Iem. He came under suspicion of being the author—indeed, he was—and feared that he would be executed for being an official of the former regime. However, the village chief, previously a monk at Wat Keo Preah Phloeung, Phnom Penh, came to his rescue. The two individuals had become friendly and occasionally talked about Buddhism, and the chief persuaded his superiors that someone who knew Pāli was not the kind of person to have written a school textbook in Khmer. Buddhist knowledge, then, was no cause for concern, the chief said, and Chhorn Iem's life was saved.

Chhorn Iem's story shares some important features with the fate of Cambodia's small community of Brahmanical priests (*pāragū*). In April 1975 ten of these court functionaries were living at the Royal Palace. After Phnom Penh was evacuated, most of them managed to return to their home villages. Survivor evidence shows that when their biographies were collected, they were treated just like everyone else, even though some of them openly confessed to having been *pāragū*.[5] With this in mind, a comment made by Hinton (2005, 154) that Angkar did not seek out former or serving monks merely because of their religious affiliation appears correct. If they were executed, it was for refusing to obey orders, such as the invitation to disrobe, marry, or raise animals or for "any effort to revive Buddhist practices among the populace" (Heder 2005, 397). With regard to the handling of Cambodia's Cham Muslim minority, however, we notice a clear difference. The Party made few attempts to systematically break up the community until after the first manifestation of Cham unrest in September 1975 (Ysa 2006), but then they were singled out for the sort of coordinated persecution not accorded to the majority Buddhist population.[6]

Nevertheless, from the outset of the conflict, some communists felt little compunction about murdering individual monks. In May 1971 two monks from Wat Kdey Daung, Kampong Svay district, were arrested and stripped of their money and possessions. After attempting to flee, one of them,

Ven. Im Son Kai, was forced to dig his own grave before being executed by a burst of automatic arms fire. Several months later three men—including sixty-five-year-old Ven. Ek San, the *cau adhikār* of Wat Krangok Meas Leu in Kampong Chhnang—had gone to a nearby village to negotiate with the Vietcong and North Vietnamese forces over the capture of two fellow villagers. The bodies of the three searchers were found floating in the river on 28 August. Ven. Ek San had been garroted and his body weighed down with a stone (Ministère de l'Information 1971, 47–49).

Some executions, such as the savage stabbing of Ven. Thaing Chhien, the *cau adhikār* of Wat Phnom Krom, Siem Reap province, on 10 July 1973, resulted when monks tried to prevent the desecration of their pagodas (*Cambodge Nouveau* 1973b, 48). Some occurred as monks were trying to evade capture. In March 1974 thirteen monks from Wat Sovann Kiri, Batheay district, had done precisely that. But five were recaptured and killed, along with the *anugaṇ* of Stung Trang district, Ven. Chhut, who was accused of masterminding the escape attempt.[7] Other killings were quite random. Ven. Om Kai had been the abbot of Wat Tep Pranam, an important monastery in Ponhea Leu district.[8] He was killed with his nephew and several other monks and laypeople in 1975 when they were stopped at a checkpoint on the way to Phnom Penh. The Khmer Rouge claimed that the group possessed a gun.[9]

The customary mode of execution was either striking a blow to the back of the neck with an iron bar or shooting, but there is no shortage of reports describing alternative methods. One high-ranking monk from Wat Balei Chas, Takeo province, is said to have had his eyeballs gouged out before being killed (Yang Sam 1987, 63), and the *cau adhikār* of Wat Pothi Preuk, Chhlong district, Ven. Thach Ty, a former resident of Kampuchea Krom, was tied to a stone and drowned in the river. It seems that some local Khmer Rouge cadres had been his former students, and they were aware that he opposed their movement.[10] Achar Sang, chief monk of Wat Kam Pheng, Battambang, was killed and his body thrown in the river.[11] Another report concerns around fifty monks from Wat Ba Nan who were forcibly disrobed and made to work in a nearby forest. Poor food, illness, and overwork caused them to be severely debilitated, and when the pagoda's chief monk fell unconscious one day, he was clubbed to death. The survivors were told that when their number diminished below ten, the work program would no longer be viable. Several weeks later only nine reported for work. They were gathered together and suffocated with plastic bags (Debré 1976, 18–19).

Ven. Sau, the chief monk of Wat Roka, Omal commune, was rumored to be invulnerable, and it was popularly believed that bullets could not kill him. In October 1976 a rope was tied around his neck, and he was dragged along the road by a car before being run over a number of times. Many people were forced to witness the execution.[12] Although there was no widespread pattern of killing monks supposedly possessing supernatural abilities, similar stories have cropped up from time to time. One informant, for example, claimed to have heard of a Battambang-based monk who was buried alive because of his putative magical powers.[13]

## Spies

The Khmer Rouge accused many monks of spying for foreign powers. Given the prevalence of the accusation, it is likely that most of those accused were innocent. Ven. San Huon, the *cau adhikār* of Wat Preah Put Nippean in Kong Pisei district, a pagoda of great beauty before the onset of conflict, was accused of being a CIA agent. He was taken to a nearby village and not seen again.[14] Another monk, Ven. Hong Peng, had been the *megan* of Kratie province and the *cau adhikār* of Wat Kratie for around thirty years. It seems that in 1976 he had used a megaphone to speak out against executions. After he refused to disrobe, the communists accused him of belonging to the CIA, and he was taken to Kantuot, where he was forced to dig his own grave because the Khmer Rouge "will only dig to plant a banana tree." He then shared a cigarette with a soldier before receiving a blow on the back of the head from a mattock.[15]

The notion that rural monks were acting for US intelligence services is, with one or two possible exceptions, absurd. But there is more reason to believe that some did spy for the Lon Nol government, even though many accused of this were clearly quite innocent. Ven. Peou Sam Ang of Wat Thbeng Meanchey, Preah Vihear province, was summarily executed in December 1970 on the grounds that he had been working for the Khmer Republic intelligence services (Ministère de l'Information 1971, 47); the *cau adhikār* at Wat Sambok, Kratie province, was killed, probably in late 1973, after he was accused of communicating with a plane that had been flying close by;[16] and in June 1974 the chief monk of Wat Punlei in Phnom Srok was killed after he was accused of possessing a pistol and holding the rank of lieutenant in the National Army.[17]

The communists' suspicion about Buddhist monks with connections to the Lon Nol military may not have been without substance in some instances, as is demonstrated by the case of Ven. Chan Dy, a monk from Wat Keo in Sangke district. In December 1972 he was commissioned to gather intelligence in the pagodas of the liberated areas of Battambang province, for Lon Nol government documents testifying to this fact are still extant.[18] His activities were finally discovered by local Khmer Rouge, some of whom had been his students. In 1973 or 1974 they invited him to their base, where he was executed.[19]

## Refusal to Disrobe

The vast majority of Cambodia's monks acquiesced when ordered to defrock, and most of the country's pagodas were emptied with minimal violence. Examples are too numerous to list in detail, but a few reports give a flavor. At Wat Chantekriem in Battambang district no one was killed, although the *cau adhikār,* Ven. Kun Tung, was "forced to marry immediately."[20] Everyone also agreed to disrobe and there were no killings at Wat Phum Prek Thmey, Kien Svay district;[21] Wat Pothi Reangsey, Chhlong district;[22] or the ancient pagoda of Wat Nokor Bachey Ba-Ar, on the outskirts of Kampong Cham.[23] The same was true for Wat Sovann Kiri, Batheay district, although one of its senior residents, Ven. Paen Sen, was among a handful of monks who managed to remain in robes throughout the Democratic Kampuchea period.[24] Nonviolent defrocking also occurred in a number of pagodas in Kampong Thom province (Locard 2004, 19, 35, 36).

Nevertheless, it appears that by far the most common cause of violent death in the *saṅgha* was a refusal to disrobe. The harsh treatment of one individual often set an example and was usually sufficient to achieve the desired aim. Indeed, there are many cases in which one monk, usually an uncooperative senior figure, was singled out for execution.[25] Ven. So from Kong Pisei district spoke out against forcible defrocking and was killed immediately. People later reported seeing his robes "at the hill."[26] In Takeo the province's chief monk, Ven. Son Sum, was forced to dig a canal as punishment after resisting the order to disrobe. Ten days later he was too sick to continue digging, and he was executed at a public meeting. After that, no other monk in the province refused.[27] Ven. Chea Oun, the chief monk of Wat Borseth, Takeo province, was likewise killed in July 1973 as an example to other monks that they should disrobe and join the military.[28]

There are occasional reports of monks being executed by people they had known quite well in more peaceful times. Ven. Chhem, the *cau adhikār* of Wat Chaom Leu in Prasat Sambour district, for example, was killed for refusing the request of one of his ex-students to disrobe.[29] The same fate befell Svay Rieng's provincial chief, Ven. Sar Peou. Warned that he would be shot if he refused to disrobe, he replied, "OK, go ahead." Ordered to eat pig swill, he again declined and was shot while still wearing his robe. This happened at Wat Chambak, Svay Rieng province.[30]

Although in some cases monks were executed while still performing their monastic functions, it is possible to discern some reluctance to desecrate the orange robe, an object that had traditionally been the locus of both respect and occult power. The abbot of Wat Vihear Khpo near Oudong failed to obey an order to return to lay life and was imprisoned without food for around a week. But he still refused. Following torture, he dressed in black clothes before being transported to Phnom Baset, where he was killed.[31] A similar pattern was apparent in Dang Tung district, where Ven. So Prim, the *cau adhikār* of Wat Thao Kon, was executed in 1976 after refusing to disrobe. The revolutionaries also removed his robes and gave him alternative clothing before killing him on a nearby mountain.[32] More explicitly magical elements have become associated with the stories of some monk executions. For instance, Ven. Nou Sin, the *anugaṇ* of Wat Kandal in Stung Treng district, was killed for his refusal to disrobe, but nearby villagers were unable to accept the reality of his death and claimed that he had used his magical powers to escape to Laos.[33]

## Senior Ecclesiastics

Ven. Tep Loeung, who had ascended to the rank of chief monk of the Thommayut in 1970, was fortunate not to fall into the hands of the communists. He died of natural causes at his Phnom Penh pagoda, Wat Botum Vaddei, on 15 April 1975, two days before the city fell. He was ninety-three years old. Others were not so lucky. After the Khmer Rouge had taken the Information Ministry in Phnom Penh at around 11:30 a.m. on 17 April 1975, Ven. Huot Tat, the Mahanikay *saṅgharāja,* made a radio broadcast appealing for a cease-fire. He also called on the communist commanders to meet with the ousted military high command, saying, "Now we have peace: put down your guns" (Kiernan 1996, 36–37). Huot Tat is then thought to have returned to Wat Unnalom, where sometime later he was interrogated. It is more than likely that his questioners treated him roughly and accused him of having a wife and children in Paris.

Evidence brought before the August 1979 trial of Pol Pot and Ieng Sary suggests that Huot Tat was executed at his home pagoda of Wat Prang[34] in the old capital of Oudong the day following his interrogation (de Nike et al. 2000, 361, document 2.4.09). But it is difficult to be precise about what happened to him or to fellow members of the national ecclesiastical hierarchy. A common rumor is that Huot Tat was executed in a particularly brutal fashion—by being flattened by a heavy vehicle. He had, after all, regularly spoken out against the communists on national radio.[35] But we do not know whether this rumor is true, and competing testimonies raise uncertainties about the account.

The current *megan* of Kampot province told me that around twenty senior monks were captured and held "as shields" by the Khmer Rouge and were never seen again. He believed that, besides Huot Tat, the group included So Hay, Kem To, and Sek Neang.[36] I also found a witness who asserted that he himself left Wat Unnalom on 19 April in a party that included Huot Tat, Kem To, So Hay, and Pang Khat. Apparently they even had the time to stop for lunch at the old US Embassy. But as they passed through the outskirts of the city the four senior monks were identified and ordered back to Wat Phnom, the old stupa at the center of the capital.[37] Perhaps shortly after this, they were driven out of Phnom Penh in a southerly direction—in other words, in the opposite direction from Oudong—in two cars.[38]

But here the available evidence becomes confusing, for another person has stated that ten of the twelve members of the influential Tripiṭaka Commission were identified and executed in the first three days after Phnom Penh fell.[39] It certainly seems that the previously mentioned Ven. So Hay,

Ven. So Hay.

Ven. Sek Neang.

Ven. Pang Khat.

who had acted as the commission's chairman, died in Phnom Penh, for a reliable report maintains that he was imprisoned in a cellar at the Ministry of Industry before being hung on a railing at a neighboring private house with two other victims, one of whom was a woman. Furthermore, in 1979 a nearby grave was excavated, and one of the bodies still wore a monastic belt. To one of his close students, its jawbone seemed to be that of So Hay.[40]

A few of the country's most senior monks were outside Phnom Penh at this time. Pon Sompheach,[41] who with So Hay and Kem To was a member of the first rank of the national hierarchy immediately below Huot Tat, was the chief monk of Battambang province. It seems that he had approved the call of college students to surrender Battambang city to the National United Front of Kampuchea and allow Sihanouk to return shortly before the fall of Phnom Penh (Corfield 1994, 219). On 24 April he and his assistant were taken to Battambang airport and told that they were to fly to Phnom Penh to greet Sihanouk. But this was a ruse. They were executed at the airport because they had "too much influence over the people" (Ponchaud 1978, 148).

Another important target was Ven. Khieu Chum, a leading theoretician of the republican regime and a personal friend of Lon Nol and Son Ngoc Thanh—in communist eyes, two of the seven "fascist and corrupt traitors . . . guilty of monstrous crimes unprecedented in Cambodian history" (Khieu Samphan 1975, 2). A few days after 17 April 1975, troops opened fire on *kuṭī* number 33 at Wat Langka. This was Khieu Chum's residence, but he was not there. It appears likely that he was arrested a little later at Calmette Hospital, where he had been a patient for around a month. No one

Ven. Pon Sompheach.

knows what happened to him after that. Corfield's (1991, 5) claim that he was hunted down and killed in Kampong Chhnang province within the first few weeks of the fall of Phnom Penh is impossible to verify.[42]

The elimination of leading monks continued as the year progressed, a policy that was also extended to Cambodia's Muslim population. Two of the country's highest Muslim dignitaries, the grand mufti and the hakim of Noor Alihsan mosque, were executed in July or August, suggesting the regime's evenhanded hostility toward the higher functionaries of all forms of organized religion. But we have now had the opportunity to observe three phases in the subjugation of Buddhism that can be dimly discerned amidst the chaos of 1970s Cambodia. The establishment of a separate revolutionary form of administration, with its associated differentiation of monks into two camps—"base" and "new"—might be said to constitute the bureaucratic phase. The next involved the harassment of monks, both individually and en masse, through dissolution of the traditional monastic economy combined with attempts at forced marriage and military conscription. As we have seen, one of the distinctive features of this phase is that few monks resisted these pressures for long, no doubt in part because Buddhism does not appear to value martyrdom as highly as the Christian and Islamic traditions do. Some, mainly older members of the order did stand firm against intimidation, however. Their elimination along with senior figures from the ecclesiastical hierarchy and assorted "spies" constituted the final act in the tragedy of Buddhism under the Khmer Rouge. The following section attempts to determine how many were murdered.

## Quantifying Monk Mortality

From the beginning of the civil war that marked Lon Nol's overthrow of Sihanouk in 1970, Buddhist monks shared the sufferings of their fellow compatriots. In addition, the frequent use of pagodas for military purposes and the massive US bombardment of Cambodia's eastern provinces exacerbated the situation. However, despite the heavy mortality rate sustained by the population at large, there does not appear to have been a policy for the systematic liquidation of Buddhist monks in Democratic Kampuchea.

While I do not wish in any way to minimize the horrific monastic death toll and the collateral damage to Buddhist spiritual, intellectual, and material culture, ample evidence suggests that the Khmer Rouge worldview was heavily influenced by Buddhist categories and that this may well have been a mitigating factor. That said, senior monk members of both the national and the provincial ecclesiastical hierarchies were regarded as functionaries of the previous regime or were occasionally accused of being enemy agents. For either reason they could be summarily executed. Monks also died for refusing to obey orders. However, it was generally only after they had been disrobed and returned to lay life, where they were indistinguishable from the rest of the population, that ex-monks suffered death from famine, overwork, absence of adequate health care, migration to hostile epidemiological environments, and all of the other basic indignities associated with the Pol Pot period. Violent death through war or deliberate execution during 1975–1979 is known to have had a disproportionate impact on adult males, and it had a significant influence on the number of ex-monks who eventually perished.

With the overthrow of Pol Pot and the establishment of relative security under the People's Republic of Kampuchea (PRK), attempts were made, both in Cambodia and abroad, to quantify the damage to institutional Buddhism. These efforts culminated in a PRK-period estimate of 25,168 Buddhist monk deaths and 1,968 pagodas destroyed or used for alternative purposes (Min Khin 1983). But such calculations took place in a strongly ideological environment and, even when made in good faith, may not always have followed entirely coherent methodologies. The following discussion comments on these early attempts at quantification and seeks to situate them within the PRK's own ambiguous policy on the restoration of Buddhism after its virtual disappearance from Cambodian soil. It also attempts to better delineate the kind of monk most likely to have been executed by the regime.

## Civil War Death and Destruction: Attributing Blame

We have already seen that a letter circulated by Leang Hap An near the beginning of the civil war condemned the destruction of sacred literature and of Buddhist monasteries by the Vietcong and North Vietnamese forces, in the strongest terms. It also provided a comprehensive a list of those monks who has succumbed to a violent end (Cambodge Nouveau 1970a). This was supplemented by Bunchhan Mul, who in his capacity as minister of religions and cults and chairman of the Buddhist Association of Cambodia, had authored the *Appeal Made by the Buddhist Association of Cambodia Concerning the Aggression Committed by Vietcong–North*

*Vietnamese Forces against Peaceful and Neutral Cambodia* a few days later (Buddhist Association of Cambodia 1970). Indeed, the government continued to publish statistics as the conflict intensified, one source claiming that 997 monasteries, around one-third of the country's total—mainly in the east and southwest—had been significantly damaged by fighting between March 1970 and June 1973. It was also suggested that 114 monks had been assassinated, 1,153 wounded, and 360 arrested by the Vietcong or the Khmer Rouge, while 1,186 rural monks had been displaced and forced to settle in urban *wat*s (Chhang Song 1973, 248–250).[43]

But the figures contained in pro-government publications, even if accurate, are problematic. We know that both sides in the conflict occupied pagodas for military purposes, and the responsibility for casualties cannot be easily attributed solely to one side or the other. A case in point relates to events of late August 1972, when three units of the National Army under the command of Brigadier General Dien Del, the governor of Kandal province, drove the enemy out of Siem Reap commune. Thirteen villages were liberated in the action, but some monks fleeing from the area reported that the enemy forces were well armed and that enemy fire had damaged Wat Chambok Bitmeas, a location previously used as a base for government troops (*Koḥ Santibhāb* 1972c).[44] In a counteroffensive a few days later, the National Army took nearby Wat Khleang Moeung, which was almost completely destroyed in consequence (*Koḥ Santibhāb* 1972a).

Meanwhile Cambodia's eastern provinces were suffering from devastating American bombardment. The enormous scale of this activity has been recognized for many years, but as noted in the last chapter, a compilation of US Air Force bombing data donated to the Vietnamese government by President Bill Clinton in 2000 reveals that the scale was five times greater and significantly longer in terms of its duration than had previously been accepted (Owen and Kiernan 2006). Previous estimates had suggested that between 50,000 and 150,000 fatalities resulted from the carpet bombing initiated on 18 March 1970, when the Menu campaign started. That many locations were bombed repeatedly over short periods of time must be kept in mind, but the new bombing data require that previous estimates of the damage to institutional Buddhism must be recalculated. Even if the mean of the former range of estimated fatalities (100,000) is simply doubled—and assuming a figure of 1.1 percent as the proportion of the general population in robes—then 2,200 monks may have perished in the bombing.

## Khmer Rouge Responsibility for Monk Mortality

I believe that Martin (1994, 183) is correct in her belief that, despite the significant losses sustained by Cambodia's population, including disrobed monastics, there was no policy for the systematic liquidation of Buddhist monks in Democratic Kampuchea. But as we have seen, uncooperative monks might be accused of being enemy agents and summarily executed. In 1986 Ven. Tep Vong reported that a group of 57 monks who had come to Siem Reap from the liberated zones were singled out and taken away within days of the arrival of the Khmer Rouge in the town. They were never seen again.[45] This incident seems to be the basis of an earlier United Nations document that mentions the massacre of 57 monks in Ok forest near Chanta Sor, Siem Reap province (United Nations 1979). The same source also mentions the execution of more than 200 Phnom Penh–based monks at Wat Champukaek, several kilometers to the south of the city. No date is given for either event. My own research has failed to uncover evidence for comparably sized events, and I think we must conclude that monk executions on such a scale were not the norm.

Nevertheless, we know that a significant proportion of the national and provincial ecclesiastical hierarchies were "routinely liquidated" (Gyallay-Pap 2002, 109) following the communists' final victory on 17 April 1975. Senior Buddhist monks were now regarded as belonging to a "special" or "separate" class, largely because they were lumped together with other officials of the hated Khmer Republic regime. These monks were smashed for much the same reasons that senior military personnel, civil servants, and the highest levels of the Cham Muslim religious hierarchy were.

The national Buddhist ecclesiastical hierarchy in the form that it existed in Cambodia before 1975 was, in fact, a relatively modern development that had its origins in Thailand, although this structure was subsequently modified during the period of French colonial rule. As such, it was intricately linked to a modernist model of the nation-state that evoked extremely negative reactions in the hearts of the communist leadership. As far as the national rankings were concerned, the larger Mahanikay order had 36 placeholders while the Thommayut, reflecting its smaller size, had only 22 (Harris 2005a, 236–238). As was previously noted, only 2 members of the prestigious 12-strong Tripiṭaka Commission survived Democratic Kampuchea. It is impossible to say whether the remainder suffered violent deaths, but if we take this survival rate of approximately 17 percent as a rough index for senior ecclesiastics, perhaps 10 of the 58 members of the national hierarchy may have survived the initial onslaught.

Turning now to the provincial level, we would not expect more than ten monks per province to have the sort of profile necessary for them to draw adverse attention by virtue of their position alone. Given 19 provinces, including Phnom Penh itself, and applying the same survival rate as before, we might expect 32 of the total of 190 senior monks also to have survived the initial onslaught. Naturally the number of senior monks in the country as a whole was quite small, but by adding up potential violent deaths at both national and provincial levels, we can see that around 206 individuals may have perished in violent circumstances. It must be noted, however, that their deaths were primarily due, not to their commitment to the Buddhist religion, but to the perception that they were enemies from higher echelons of the previous regime.

When we move down to the lowest level of *saṅgha* organization, the individual *wat,* what can we say about the fate of abbots (*cau adhikār*) and their right-hand (*stāṃ*) and left-hand (*chveṅ*) assistants (*grū sūtr stāṃ* and *grū sūtr chveṅ*)? My own research strongly suggests that such individuals were rarely executed by virtue of their seniority alone. As already discussed, we certainly know of examples of courageous individuals who, when ordered to disrobe, refused to obey, and such a decision may well have resulted in summary execution. But Theravāda Buddhism does not possess a cult of martyrdom, and most *cau adhikār* simply accepted the changed circumstances and bent themselves to the will of their new masters with a heavy heart.

According to Ministry of Cults and Religions statistics, 3,369 *wat*s were active in Cambodia in 1969.[46] This number remained largely unchanged into the initial stages of the country's civil war. So even if we admit that one in five *cau adhikār* were executed for some infringement of revolutionary discipline—a proportion that seems to me to be far too high—then, at most, 674 violent deaths would have occurred. Adding this to our calculation of 206 for deaths of high-profile monks, we reach an estimated mortality total of 880 for senior monks throughout the country.

## Computing Monk Deaths

Soon after the overthrow of the Pol Pot regime, the National Front for the Salvation of Kampuchea established a research committee under the directorship of Min Khin. The committee engaged in the first detailed analysis of the numbers of monks killed and pagodas destroyed by "Beijing and their servants: Pol Pot, Ieng Sary, Khieu Samphan on the Cambodian people during 1975–1978." The committee's brief alone indicates that we are entering ideological territory. Indeed, soon after the report was published, a conference of some three hundred intellectuals and member of the *saṅgha* was convened on 12 September 1983 to discuss the committee's findings. Among other measures, the conference decided to institute an annual national Day of Anger to be held annually on 20 May (Fawthrop and Jarvis 2004, 73–74).[47]

In terms of methodology, Min Khin's estimates were based on the analysis of reports received from nineteen provinces and towns, supplemented by investigation of "all kinds of [unspecified] documents." One could certainly point to individual inconsistencies in the estimates (table 6.1). The figure of 20 deaths in Siem Reap/Oddar Meanchey, for example, looks quite out of

**TABLE 6.1** Min Khin's statistics on monk deaths and pagoda destruction

| Province | Number of monks killed, 1975–1978 | Number of pagodas* | Average monk deaths/pagoda |
|---|---|---|---|
| Battambang | 1,525 | 252 | 6.05 |
| Kratie | 288 | 68 | 4.24 |
| Stung Treng | 31 | 21 | 1.48 |
| Prey Veng | 2,572 | 387 | 6.65 |
| Kampong Speu | 4,031 | 152 | 26.52 |
| Preah Vihear | 172 | 10 | 17.20 |
| Siem Reap/Oddar Meanchey | 20 | – | – |
| Kampong Cham | 3,960 | 462 | 8.57 |
| Pursat | 374 | 96 | 3.90 |
| Kampong Chhnang | 925 | 167 | 5.54 |
| Kampong Som | 115 | – | – |
| Phnom Penh | 1,798 | 76 | 23.66 |
| Takeo | 5,673 | 276 | 20.55 |
| Kampot | 552 | 172 | 3.21 |
| Mondulkiri | 160 | 3 | 53.33 |
| Koh Kong | 882 | 24 | 36.76 |
| Kampong Thom | 1,819 | 179 | 10.16 |
| Svay Rieng | 234 | 192 | 1.22 |
| Kandal | 429 | 350 | 1.23 |
| Total for country | 25,168 | 3,202 | 7.86 |

*According to Miwa 2000, 468.

line with the sums for comparably populated provinces, while the figure of 5,673 for Takeo, with a total population of around 566,000 in 1971, would comprise almost all of that province's pre-1975 monks. Nevertheless, the strong regional variations certainly seem to suggest the absence of any centralized policy for the smashing of the monastic order as a whole.

Min Khin found that 1,968 of the country's pagodas had been either destroyed or reemployed as fertilizer warehouses, prisons, and so on.[48] But these figures are also problematic, for a separate source informs us that in 1984 a total of 1,895 of the still-existing 3,078 "religious buildings" were being used for religious purposes (Löschmann 2005, 54n13).[49] The number 1,895 tallies exactly with the figure for active pagodas published by the Ministry of Cults and Religions (Centre for Advanced Studies and the Ministry of Cults and Religious Affairs 1996), so it is clear that when Löschmann uses the term "religious buildings," she actually means "*wat*." Since her figure for active *wat*s appears sound, there is good reason to assume that the same holds true for her citation of 3,078 religious structures still extant. If that figure is indeed accurate, we must conclude that, of the 3,369 apparently active in 1969, only 291 had been entirely destroyed, although we must allow that many of the remainder would have been in poor structural condition.

But I shall confine my main comments to the overall methodology of the Min Khin exercise itself. Vickery (1988, 70–71) noted long ago that PRK population figures and estimates of deaths during Democratic Kampuchea were based on a 1982–1983 house-to-house count that was highly problematic, even though this survey may have been conducted scrupulously. A false assumption entertained at the time was that anyone not present at the count had been killed by the Khmer Rouge. It seems that the statistical returns on which Min Khin and his team relied were premised on similar grounds, for they were based not on eyewitness reports of executions but on the number of monks who had simply not returned to their home pagodas or villages after the fall of Pol Pot. Although a significant proportion of this figure will have met their deaths in a variety of manners, we do not know which of those deaths may have occurred violently. We are also entirely in the dark about the motives underlying putative executions. Were these monks killed by virtue of their membership of the monastic order or for some other reason?

The failure of surviving ex-monks to seek reordination after January 1979 can be attributed to a variety factors. As previously discussed, large numbers of disrobed monks were forced into marriage, and many of these unions endured into the PRK. This situation would have been a powerful disincentive for such individuals to reestablish contact with their former monasteries. But a substantial proportion of the population had also been severely dislocated by forced removal to other parts of the country, and given the appalling economic conditions in the aftermath of so much upheaval, it is quite unlikely that ex-monks located far from their natal district would have been able to reestablish communication with home. Emigration to neighboring countries, especially to Kampuchea Krom, was a less significant factor, with one report asserting that fewer than 100 monks escaped to Thailand or Vietnam during DK (Gyallay-Pap 2002, 109). But we should also bear in mind that although the *sangha* had been reestablished under strict Party control in the early PRK period, it was now a shadow of its former self, since the economic underpinnings that under normal conditions would ensure its reasonable functioning were simply not in place. In the past, religious vocation was a relatively rare phenomenon. The motivating factors behind ordination were more likely to be connected with merit-making, questions of family prestige, or the desire to obtain a basic education, and the social foundations for most of these incentives had been undermined in the immediate post–Democratic Kampuchea period. Additionally, the traumas associated with an extended period of violence and upheaval encouraged a highly generalized diminution of faith in the merits of Buddhism. For these and other reasons, the motivation to rejoin the *sangha* was not operative when Min Khin's team was doing their research.

But there is another criticism we can make of the methodology. Even if we accept the statistics at face value, we simply do not know when the "deaths" occurred. The team's ideologically driven assumption was that the deaths took place during Democratic Kampuchea. But we have already seen that violent deaths occurred throughout the 1970s, and those associated with the civil war and US bombing must be factored in.

Heuveline (1998, 49) has noted that historical records on their own are insufficient to give an accurate estimate of the number of deaths during Cambodia's period of upheaval. Previous estimates of "excess mortality" vary from the communists' own figures of 20,000 to 3 million, a calculation made by the Vietnamese immediately after they seized the country from Pol Pot. Extrapolations of excess deaths made from sample materials, such as the number of bodies discovered at grave sites, have tended to yield very high values. But this method furnishes results that cannot easily be verified, for two reasons. First, the dates of death cannot be ascertained, and, second, accurate information on the sample population is not available.

Nevertheless, this was the method adopted by Kiernan (1996) and Sliwinski (1995), who both arrived at an overall estimate of around 1.5 to 2 million. Demographic accounting is an alternative method, and the one adopted by Heuveline (1998). It has tended to yield lower figures.

Now, it is clear that "excess mortality" during Democratic Kampuchea resulted from a variety of factors, including armed conflict, lack of food, overwork, poor health care, and the like. These need to be clearly distinguished from mortality caused by deliberate execution. Heuveline (ibid.), who appears to have made the most rigorous contribution to this debate, concludes that between 600,000 and 2 million "violent deaths," or 1.1 million as a middle figure, occurred.

If we now use our rough figure of 1.1 percent for the proportion of the population consisting of monks around the beginning of the civil war period, and assuming that monks perished at roughly the same proportion as the rest of the population, then we would expect around 12,100 violent *saṅgha* deaths. But we know that excess mortality through deliberate execution was likely to have had a disproportionate impact on adult males and that this is precisely the group represented by the Buddhist *saṅgha*. Nevertheless, the figure of 25,168 deaths reported by Min Khin, representing 38.7 percent of the 1969 *saṅgha* population of 65,062 (see table 6.2), does seem rather inflated.

Kiernan (2003), however, appears to be the most reliable source on statistics relating to Cambodia's Cham minority. He has estimated that more than 36 percent of the 1975 Cham Muslim population suffered excess death during DK, a loss of more than 87,000 (ibid., 588). Furthermore, it is generally agreed that the Cham were at a significantly greater risk of dying than were the majority Buddhist population (de Walque 2005, 361). Kiernan (2003) computes the Buddhist death rate over the same period as 18.7 percent. If this estimated percentage were applied naively to the Buddhist population before the beginning of hostilities, we would be calculating a total of around 1.2 million fatalities. But the monastic order represents a relatively small proportion of the country's overall number of Buddhists (say, 1.1 percent), yielding a figure around half that generated by Min Khin's team and corresponding quite well with the value I derive from Heuveline's estimates.

Chantou Boua (1991), in the first quantitative study by a Western-trained scholar, admitted that it "is hard to determine how many monks died during the time of Pol Pot." Nevertheless, she concluded that "fewer than 2,000 monks may have survived Democratic Kampuchea out of the previous total of 65,000" (ibid., 237–239). Keyes (1994, 60), on the other hand, claims a figure of 100 monastic survivors, the majority in Vietnamese exile, while some official sources give a much lower figure of 12 monks to have remained in robes until the end of the Democratic Kampuchea period (table 6.2).

Min Khin's figures for monk deaths do not tally with PRK estimates made in 1980, which suggested that about 63 percent of monks died or were executed by the Pol Pot regime;[50] a figure that, interestingly, is quite congruent with Ven. Tep Vong's own 1986 observation that of the 60 monks who left his home pagoda of Wat Bo in Siem Reap in 1975, only 20 (i.e., 33 percent) were still alive.[51] In April 1981 Tep Vong had reported the existence of around 3,000 monks in the country. He described 800 of these (26.7 percent) as having been in robes before 1975 (Gyallay-Pap 2002, 109–110). For the reasons already given, we would be naive to conclude that the figure of 800 represents the sum total of monastic survivors. Indeed, Tep Vong also said that of the 20 monastic survivors from his own pagoda, only 3 (i.e., 15 percent) had been reordained after 1979, for most had been forced to marry during DK.[52]

But there are further reasons why we should continue to raise questions about the veracity of these statistics. Even if Tep Vong's overall impressions (3 survivors out of 20 monks) are "correct" from the official perspective, it is well known that an unquantifiable but very substantial number of surviving monks spontaneously took robes again after the defeat of Pol Pot. But many

| TABLE 6.2 Official statistics on active *wats* and numbers of monks | | |
|---|---|---|
| Year | Active *wats* | Number of monks |
| 1969 | 3,369 | 65,062 |
| 1979 | – | 12 |
| 1980 | – | 770 |
| 1984 | 1,895 | 3,200 |
| 1989 | 2,800 | Ca. 10,000 |
| 1992 | 3,089 | 26,257 |
| 1995 | 3,371 Mahanikay | 40,916 Mahanikay—of which 23,630 were novices |
| | 81 Thommayut | 1,095 Thommayut—of which 522 were novices |

*Source:* Centre for Advanced Studies and the Ministry of Cults and Religious Affairs 1996.

of these monks were subsequently deemed "illegal" by the PRK and were forced to disrobe or remain in a clandestine state for many years, a situation that is discussed in more detail in the next chapter.

## Concluding Remarks

Min Khin's calculation of the number of monks killed during Democratic Kampuchea cannot, for the reasons outlined, be correct. As I have intimated, his team's computation for pagodas destroyed appears to be massively inflated, but insofar as it is possible to speak with any precision about violent deaths in the *sangha,* I would suggest that his figure be roughly halved, to about 12,500, and that this number should be regarded as the total number of monks killed from the beginning of hostilities in March 1970 until the effective end of the Pol Pot regime in January 1979. Furthermore, if we accept figures of about 2,200 for fatalities resulting from US bombardment and about 900 for senior members of the *sangha* executed on or around 17 April 1975, we are left with approximately 9,400 monks who suffered violent death in robes over the entire period. It is not possible to specify what proportions of the latter figure can be attributed to the civil war period (1970–April 1975) or the Democratic Kampuchea period (April 1975–January 1979). All other monastic casualties, possibly up to as many as the total computed by Min Khin, must be assumed to have occurred after disrobing. These cannot easily be attributed to individuals' specific associations with Buddhism and most likely resulted from other causes.

This topic is clearly fraught with major difficulties, making any accurate quantification of monk deaths deeply problematic. I have endeavored here to refrain from impugning the motives of previous commentators. I am neither a demographer nor a statistician, but my own investigations suggest that a much smaller proportion of monks met their end than has often been assumed and that overestimates may be linked in some way to the manner in which Buddhist concepts and categories pervaded the ideology and practice of the revolutionaries.

We do know that many senior members of the ecclesiastical hierarchy, at both the national and provincial levels, were executed within a few days of the fall of Phnom Penh on 17 April 1975, but they met their fate primarily as high functionaries of the Lon Nol regime, not as members of a despised religious group. Many more monks died because they refused to obey orders to disrobe, but these courageous individuals remained very much the exception rather than the rule. Almost all of Cambodia's Buddhist monks had been disrobed by the end of 1976. Along with the rest of the population, these ex-monks encountered death largely as the consequence of war, the criminal mismanagement of the agricultural and health sectors, and extreme state violence. Few after this point died because of their prior religious commitment.

# CHAPTER SEVEN

# Aftermath
## Rebuilding the *Saṅgha* under Socialism

### Setting the Scene

During the Khmer Republic period, prophecies circulated predicting the demise of Buddhism. As the Khmer Rouge grip on the country tightened, they seemed to be coming true. By 1978 Yun Yat, the minister of culture, information, and propaganda, told a Yugoslav reporter that "Buddhism is dead and the ground has been cleared for the foundations of a new revolutionary culture" (Stanic 1978). Yet an ex-monk who was present at the time rather courageously took issue with her, on the grounds that, for him at least, Buddhism and communism were compatible. His fate is unknown, but the story suggests, as I have tried to demonstrate in earlier chapters of this book, that some elements of Buddhist belief and practice were subsumed into the Khmer Rouge worldview. Other, more tangible forms of evidence suggest that although Buddhism was in mortal danger during Democratic Kampuchea, it was never totally extinguished, despite the claims of Angkar to the contrary.

### Monks in Robes

We have seen that the Theravāda code of monastic discipline (*vinaya*) allows for the disrobing of a fully ordained a monk only after he has admitted to having committed one of four offenses entailing defeat (*pārājika*)—sexual relations, theft, killing (including encouraging another to die or assisting in a suicide), and boasting of superhuman perfections. His exit from the *saṅgha,* moreover, is deemed valid only after the performance of a formal ritual at which he announces a wish to renounce the training. It is perfectly clear that such disrobing was a very rare occurrence during the period covered in this book, and many reports talk of specific monks continuing to follow Buddhist precepts even though they had been compelled to shed their robes. From the *vinaya* perspective such individuals might quite legitimately claim that they never sullied their monkhood, regardless of whether they were forced to wear civilian clothes or the white robes discussed in chapter 5. However, a handful of witnesses claim that they knew of monks who survived the entire Democratic Kampuchea period without disrobing. I consider two of these remarkable figures now, with discussion of another, Ven. Kaet Vay, held over for a later section of the chapter dealing with the first "official" ordinations in Cambodia after the fall of the Khmer Rouge.

Let us turn our attention to the story of Ven. Paen Sen (1896–1989). When he was twelve years old, Paen Sen became a novice at Wat Tang Sre, Cheung Prey district, under that pagoda's *cau adhikār,* Ven. Sovann Botum Kol. Unusually, this was a Thommayut monastery with well-established links to Siam, so after Paen Sen had undergone full ordination at the age of twenty-one, he transferred to Wat Bowanniwet, the order's Bangkok headquarters, for eight further years of higher study, in line with established Thommayut custom. He returned to Cambodia when his teacher died, and he was soon invited to become the *cau adhikār* of Wat Sovann Kiri in nearby Cheung Chhnok.

The Khmer Rouge had controlled this area well before 1975, and monks were forced to work in the rice fields or to supply soldiers at the front. After 17 April some revolutionary monks arrived with guns. Their leader, Yeum, was often drunk and carried a gun in his bag, so it was assumed that he was only pretending to be a monk.[1] He preached communist ideology but also claimed that if anyone captured members of the despised Lon Nol regime, they would be reborn in paradise.

According to his biographer, most of the local senior Khmer Rouge respected Paen Sen (Hong Dy 1989). Indeed, one of his relatives was an official based at Batheay district headquarters. So he was allowed to move to a small house on the nearby hillside; it was equipped with many books and some Buddha images. His cousin and a young local boy looked after him, he had enough food most of the time, and he was even able to listen to Voice of America and various Thai radio stations.[2]

In the middle of 1976 the region's monkhood was ordered to disrobe. Paen Sen was given the customary black clothes to change into, but he just hung them up in his cottage. From that time on, he wore a white undergarment covered by the traditional orange top robe of a Theravāda monk. It seems that the district chief, Ta Hoy, had been impressed by Paen Sen's preaching many years earlier when he himself had been a novice in Takeo.[3] Because of this, Hoy continued to protect Paen Sen even after many local officials had been purged and replaced by the far more severe rule of Khmer Rouge from the southwest (Hong Dy 1989).

Many people visited Paen Sen, both local villagers and cadres. Indeed, when Ta Ros,[4] a commune chief and a notorious killer, came to pay his respects, Paen Sen condemned his behavior. Yet, oddly, he was not punished

Ven. Paen Sen.

for this. Another official, Hieng, and his wife fed Paen Sen after the death of their child, and people who had been forced to marry also called on him for blessings. The situation in this village is noteworthy. No monks were killed, and, with the exception of Paen Sen, they all disrobed when requested. There was enough food in the area, and many villagers continued to practice some form of Buddhist piety. Even Ta Ros appears to have had a picture of the Buddha in his house, although this does not seem to have prevented him from displaying some hostility toward Buddhism.[5]

Paen Sen survived Democratic Kampuchea. As a member of the Thommayut, he continued to practice according to that order's principles and rituals after 1979, and he ordained monks in this tradition in 1980.[6] Indeed, local people unsuccessfully petitioned the authorities to keep the Thommayut after the PRK's attempt to disband the old monastic orders and create a unified *saṅgha* (*brah saṅgh raṇasirsa*). One imagines that, given Paen Sen's experiences during Democratic Kampuchea, the coercive power of the new government could hardly have been a major deterrent as far as he was concerned. He died on 11 May 1989, at age ninety-four.[7]

The story of Ven. Nut (ca. 1900–1986), a monk with some connection to Paen Sen, has been difficult to verify, for I have heard it in a variety of quite different versions. Nevertheless, it is clear that Nut spent at least some period in robes after the order to disrobe and that he was supported in this endeavor by courageous and pious Buddhist villagers.

Nut was a Thommayut monk who originally came from Wat Thommayut in Koh Sotin district. His given name appears to have been Khong Thanang. After various peregrinations forced on him by the post-1970 conflict, he arrived in Kratie province, where he was appointed to the post of teacher at the Pāli High School in the provincial town. He also became the *cau adhikār* of Wat P'chaa. As the situation worsened and at some unspecified date, probably after 17 April 1975, Ven. Nut removed himself to the more remote area around Phnom Kantuot, eventually finding sanctuary at Wat Antong Vien, where he was able to escape being forced into agricultural work or dam building.[8] Nut was protected by some members of the Kuoy tribal people, who inhabit the region. It is unclear whether the Khmer Rouge knew of Nut's presence at Antong Vien, but during the day, fearful that he would be discovered, he remained hidden in a large coffin (*ktār majhus*). Every night around ten o'clock Kuoy villagers brought him food, announcing their arrival by either knocking on the coffin or crawling under the building and banging on the floor. As a monk determined to maintain his discipline, Nut naturally reserved this food until morning had dawned. Strangely, given the great danger to which the villagers were exposing themselves, Nut does not seem to have performed any Buddhist rituals on their behalf.[9]

We know some of these details from an old *achar* who, in 1980, was so impressed by the stories of Nut's fortitude that he invited the monk to leave Antong Vien and take up residence at Wat Prek A Chi in Krouch Chhmar district. The *achar* is insistent that Nut kept his Buddhist robes and ordination certificate (*chāyā*) throughout Democratic Kampuchea and that, like Ven. Paen Sen, he maintained Thommayut traditions throughout the early PRK period.[10]

## Formation of the Front

A Khmer Rouge telegram dated 11 May 1978 observed that, despite over three years of extreme communist rule throughout the country, some "subversive" people still wanted to reestablish Buddhism, markets, money, and the monarchy.[11] The identity of the group is uncertain, but in the same month Heng Samrin, who had previously been a military commander and number five in the Khmer Rouge Eastern Zone hierarchy, gave a speech calling on "all patriotic forces regardless of political and religious tendencies," including "Buddhist monks and nuns," to join a united front to help "topple the reactionary and nepotistic Pol Pot–Ieng Sary gang" (quoted in Heder 1999, 10).

Precisely where those monks and nuns were located is a mystery. Was the appeal simply a convenient fiction designed to confer religious legitimacy on the movement? Was it a call to the very small number of *saṅgha* members still in robes in Cambodia itself or to those who had fled the fighting and were living in neighboring countries? Or was it directed toward the vast numbers of disrobed individuals still alive under the Pol Pot regime? It is difficult to be certain about this, but on 2 December 1978 the National Front for the Salvation of Kampuchea was formed by a congress of around two hundred "workers, peasants, petty bourgeois, intellectuals, Buddhist monks and nuns, young people, women, ethnic minorities, [and] patriotic insurgents" (Slocomb 2006, 386).

With Vietnamese backing, the Khmer Rouge were overthrown, and the People's Republic of Kampuchea (PRK) was established in January 1979. Heng Samrin became president of the Front's fourteen-person Central Committee, which included Ven. Long Sim, described as "a revolutionary monk for over 50 years"— he had apparently been a close associate of Sao Phim, the former head of the Khmer Rouge Eastern Zone (Marston 2008, 7)—acting as representative for the *saṅgha* (Vickery 1986, 161). The original committee membership was subsequently increased by the addition of thirteen or fourteen "dignitaries, intellectuals, monks and representatives of ethnic minorities" (Slocomb 2003, 162).

Long Sim had been the *cau adhikār* of Wat Pi Ampil, Romduol district, and the *anugaṇ* of the same district before Democratic Kampuchea. It is claimed that he was the first monk to be ordained by the Front, quite possibly in Kampuchea Krom, where he had previously fled. In the early years of the PRK he was regarded to be the most senior monk in Cambodia, and in that role he participated in official delegations to the Soviet Union and Mongolia. However, given the murky history of early PRK Buddhism, there is some suspicion that Long Sim was never properly reordained. He was never allocated a monastery but lived at Party headquarters (Marston 2008, 7), and he seems to have had a wife and a child—he had married after disrobing during Democratic Kampuchea. He had thought that they were dead, but when he discovered that they were still alive, he disrobed and fell out of public view. More than likely he also fell out of favor with the authorities.[12]

Ven. Long Sim. (Documentation Center of Cambodia)

## Restoration of the *Saṅgha*

Even though few people had any immediate concerns beyond the need for survival, a partial restoration of Buddhism was one of the Front's first acts on coming to power, and gradually some of the more extreme antireligious policies of the previous regime were rolled back. The fourth element of the Front's eleven-point program addressed "the right to freedom of opinion, association, and belief." However, this was intended to apply, in a highly restricted sense, only to Buddhism and Islam. Christianity was not accorded such freedoms. Indeed, in 1982 Chea Sim, chair of the National Assembly, is reported to have said that "the Christian religion [by virtue of its foreignness] has no place in the People's Republic of Kampuchea."[13]

It seems that, in the earliest phase of the PRK, religion was manipulated largely for cosmetic and propaganda reasons. There is, of course, nothing new about this, and it is common to hear Cambodian monks compared to the banana leaf on which food is served—once the meal is over, it is simply thrown away. In Löschmann's words (2005, 46), PRK Buddhism was reestablished in its "instrumental form." For all intents and purposes the new state continued the previous regime's suppression of Buddhism, since such suppression was in line with the socialist emphasis on rationality, science, and the dignity of work.[14] As if to emphasize the changed circumstances and to generate useful propaganda, a delegation of the communist-sponsored Asian Buddhist Conference for Peace (ABCP) made an official visit to Cambodia in April 1979 to "investigate the crimes of the Democratic Kampuchea period."[15] A small group led by Ven. Tep Vong, representing the Buddhist Association for the National Salvation of Kampuchea, also attended the fifth congress of the ABCP in Ulan Bator in June of the same year. In a speech replete with revolutionary jargon and entirely devoid of any significant reference to Buddhist practice or doctrine, the Cambodian delegation made the point that "Chinese big nation hegemonic expansionism [had] imposed on Kampuchea an extremely brutal regime which brought to our nation a genocide never before seen in history."[16]

Under the auspices of the Front's Central Committee and the Ministry of Cults and Religions, an "Asiatic Week" (5–12 April 1980) was launched at Wat Langka, Phnom Penh. Sao Phan, an official representing the ministry, stressed that the week was an expression of the framework adopted at the Ulan Bator meeting. As such, it celebrated opposition to American

Monks attending the trial of Pol Pot and Ieng Sary, Phnom Penh, 1979. (Documentation Center of Cambodia)

imperialists and Chinese reactionaries, who both threatened peace in the Asian region (*Sārbătarmān Kambujā,* 9 April 1980).

The initial feelings of euphoria that naturally followed the overthrow of a despised regime soon petered out, and popular opinion concerning the PRK quickly soured. This was perhaps unsurprising, given that the PRK had Cambodia's traditional enemy, Vietnam, as its active backer. In these circumstances the Front was obliged to look around for something to bolster its waning legitimacy. The two strongest institutions in the country had always been the *sangha* and the monarchy, but the regime could hardly play the royal card, for Sihanouk was at this time actively engaged in forming a new alliance with the Khmer Rouge and Son Sann's Khmer People's National Liberation Front (KPNLF) to oppose the PRK.[17] The members of the *sangha,* on the other hand, were not landowners, so it was unlikely that they would be a source of opposition to the government (Löschmann 2005, 46–47). Buddhism's restoration during the early PRK needs to be read in this light.[18]

Monastic ordination in the immediate aftermath of Democratic Kampuchea was difficult for a number of reasons. The most obvious practical problem was that it was impossible to assemble the necessary quorum of fully ordained monks to perform the ritual in a manner that matched ritual requirements. Thus many ex-monks took to shaving their heads and wearing white without the necessary formalities prescribed by *vinaya.* Others unofficially reestablished themselves in monasteries, and such individuals began to form a core of organized Buddhism. Their services were sought, in particular, for the performance of ceremonies to commemorate the dead, for Marxism has nothing to say to personal tragedy and bereavement.

## Unofficial Ordinations

Ven. Nel Mony (b. 1922) was a key figure in the process of unofficial ordinations. A native of Kampong Cham province, he was first ordained in 1943. He became the *cau adhikār* of Wat Angkor Niream, Tbong Khmum district, in 1957. Subsequently appointed *anugaṇ* of the same district, he remained in Kampong Cham until 1974 when, given the intensity of the fighting, he moved to Phnom Penh and took up residence at Wat Unnalom. He was forcibly disrobed in 1976.[19]

After the collapse of the Pol Pot regime, Nel Mony quickly decided to return to the monastic life. On 7 April 1979 he was ordained with four others at Wat Sansam Kosala, Phnom Penh, one of the few city monasteries not being used as barracks by Vietnamese troops at the time.[20] Around a thousand people attended the ceremony, although no formal preceptor was present, and the five candidates merely took their vows in the presence of the Buddha and a selection of sacred writings containing the Buddha's teachings (*dhamma*).

Ven. Nel Mony.

Some Party officials appear to have supported the event, the robes being furnished by Phnom Penh Party secretary Vann Sen and Minister of Commerce Tang Sarim (Hayashi 2002, 213; Marston 2008, 11). Several months later around twenty monks from Wat Sansam Kosala and nearby Wat Stung Meanchey reportedly joined a large gathering of cadres and workers outside the Phnom Penh railway station to express their support for the presence of Vietnamese troops in Cambodia (*Sārbătarmān Kambujā,* 22 July 1979).

Nel Mony subsequently went on to ordain at least five hundred additional monks—including Vens. Noun Nget and Las Lay, both of whom would rise to a high rank in the national ecclesiastic hierarchy—at Wat Sansam Kosala as well as in some provincial locations.[21] His status as persona grata is further supported by his provision of written statements to the August 1979 trial of Pol Pot and Ieng Sary, although he did not attend in person, arguing that it was not right for a monk to be involved in procedures that could result in a death sentence.[22] Trial records indicate that some thirty-nine monks signed a report, dated 13 June 1975, that was used as evidence, and this document makes it clear that sixty-eight monks, including many of the signatories, were already residing at Wat Sansam Kosala.[23]

Ven. Thim Pok was another monk to reemerge early in the PRK, this time in the Battambang area. He had initially refused to disrobe when the Khmer Rouge commanded him to do so, and even after he was forced to enter the lay life, he continued to wear a monk's belt under his black clothes, an apparently rather common practice during Democratic Kampuchea, as we have seen. He was reordained as a novice in 1979 by an *achar* at Wat Pothi Vong in Battambang and rapidly began admitting new monks to the order.[24] However, in 1981 he was called to Phnom Penh, where he underwent an additional, official ordination procedure. His preceptor on that occasion was Ven. Tep Vong.[25] On returning to Battambang, he lived at Wat Piphittearam and became the province's *megaṇ.* He worked hard to reestablish Buddhism in difficult circumstances and died of old age in 1987.[26]

A similar pattern was repeated across the country,[27] and we have good evidence of monks returning to their pagodas, especially monks who were quite old and had no surviving or easily located relatives.[28] In Dang Tong district, Kampot province, very few young monks returned to the *saṅgha* after 1979, for most of the monks from that district either had been forced into marriage or had died after they were disrobed and sent as soldiers to the front. But some older ex-monks did return, in part because their families had perished during Democratic Kampuchea and they had no one to support them.[29] Meanwhile, in Stung Treng province, a few old monks trickled back to Wat Kandal Spean Thmor,[30] and Ven. Suon, an elderly man who had disrobed in 1960, was reordained at his old pagoda in Prek Pok village, Kampot province.[31] Similarly, at Wat Nokor Bachey Ba-Ar, a famous monastery still housing an old Angkorian-period *prāsād*, the first group to arrive back wore white robes. Some of these, including the subsequent *cau adhikār*, Ta Man, sought reordination as 1979 unfolded.[32]

Ven. Em Phoeung, the current *megaṇ* of Kampot province, has claimed that he was ordained by Ven. Chan Sang in Takeo in 1980 but was obliged to undergo reordination by Tep Vong at Wat Unnalom, Phnom Penh, in 1981. More than fifty other monks from most of Cambodia's provinces were also reordained at this event.[33] It is clear that Tep Vong was kept quite busy after his elevation to head of the monastic order.[34]

## Official Ordinations

The PRK authorities kept a tight rein on extragovernmental activities, and for this reason, on 19 September 1979, seven "carefully chosen" former monks, all with between twenty and sixty years' former service, were given permission to ordain.[35] Reinforcing the significance of the event is that the ceremony's president was Chea Sim. Marston (2008, 2) refers to it as a ritual "charter of the new state."

The ceremony took place at Wat Unnalom and was supervised by Theravāda monks from Vietnam, headed by Thich Bou Chon, adviser to the Central Commission of Vietnamese Theravāda Buddhism and supported by Ven. Gioi Nghiem. The rest of the ordination committee consisted of a mixture of Khmer who had fled to Vietnam during the Democratic Kampuchea period and some ethnic Khmer from Kampuchea Krom (Keyes 1994, 60n36).[36] The seven who were reordained were Kaet Vay from Kampong Thom province; Din Sarun from Kampong Cham; It Sum, Noun Nget,[37] and Prak Dith, all from Takeo; Ken Vong from Prey Veng; and Tep Vong from Siem Reap. Some—Kaet Vay, for example—had disrobed from their nonofficial monastic status a little earlier.[38] The seven were clearly held in high regard by the new Party apparatus, and most went on to assume high-profile roles.

## Ven. Kaet Vay

Kaet Vay (1895–1991) was the exception among the seven reordained monks, in that he exercised any widespread influence for only a short period.[39] He was the oldest monk in the group and consequently became the country's chief monk and national preceptor (*upacchāy(n)*), ordaining many new monks very quickly after he assumed this position.[40] However, the authorities do not appear to have been entirely happy with Kaet Vay's labors; he may, for example, have been ordaining too many young men who, it was assumed, should have been working to reconstruct the country. Whatever the reasons—some say that he was uncomfortable with his official role, others that he was simply just too old and set in his ways—Kaet Vay could not adjust to life in Phnom Penh, and after a few months he returned to his native province of Kampong Thom. On arriving there, he ordained ten young monks, and despite their being younger than the government-regulated age of ordination, they stayed nearby and looked after him.[41]

Kaet Vay was a member of the Kuoy tribal minority. He had entered the Mahanikay at Wat Choam, Prasat Sambour district, and subsequently became the *cau adhikār* of Wat Lpeas in Stung Saen district.[42] The Khmer Rouge had arrived in that area in 1970, but not much changed until the pagoda was completely destroyed during a battle, probably in 1973.[43] The monks moved on to various pagodas, where they resisted forced disrobing for almost a full year. An ultimatum finally came on 27 January 1976, but Kaet Vay refused. It seems that some local cadres had once been his students, so out of either respect for such an eminent monk or fear of his powers—he was a well-known practitioner of traditional healing—he was able to continue practicing Buddhist rites.

Like Paen Sen, Kaet Vay moved to a small cottage built by local people and furnished with a number of small Buddha images. This was located at Sambour village, the chief of which allowed an old woman to bring him food on a regular basis.[44] During this period, Kaet Vay pretended to be blind and kept a dog that barked if any suspicious person came near. He wore white robes outside his cottage, especially during the day, and the traditional orange monk's robes at night when he was inside. He was occasionally approached to conduct prayers for the dead, and he sometimes received visits from the chief of the collective and from other senior cadres who were happy about this arrangement as long as news of it did not filter out to higher-ups. Apparently the local officials had reported that all monks in the area had been disrobed and that Kaet Vay was requested to stay in his cottage, where he was assigned the light work of collecting and preparing medicinal herbs.[45]

After his brief period as national preceptor, Kaet Vay dwelt temporarily at Wat Intry Samvirak in Kampong Thom town, where his replacement as Cambodia's chief monk, Ven. Tep Vong, often came to pay his respects. But he soon moved back to Wat Lpeas, which he helped rebuild. He lived on a state salary of 700 riels, but "bad people always cheated him." He died there in 1991 at age ninety-six.[46]

As far as I am aware, Kaet Vay is the only monk to have been singled out in official recognition of his having remained in robes throughout the Pol Pot period. As we have already seen, however, there were others. Nevertheless, in a radio broadcast Chea Sim acknowledged that Kaet Vay was the only monk who successfully struggled against the Khmer Rouge, and Tep Vong has also confirmed that Kaet Vay practiced the ten monastic precepts and lived as a "man of virtue" (*anak sīl*) during Democratic Kampuchea.[47]

## Ven. Tep Vong

Tep Vong was born on 12 January 1932 at Trapeang Chork village, Chreav commune, Siem Reap district. He was ordained at age fifteen by Ven. Hing Mao (d. 1966), the *cau adhikār* of Wat Bo in the provincial capital, where he stayed until 1975, apart from a brief spell when he disrobed temporarily to help his parents. When the Khmer Rouge arrived, the residents of Wat Bo, both monastic and lay, were quickly ordered to write their biographies. These documents were used to separate out various groups of evacuees, and Tep Vong was forced to join a party that moved off in a northerly direction, eventually ending up in Preah Vihear province. Fifteen of the sixty monks who left Wat Bo with him ended up there. They were all expected to work and could not rely on alms. The base monks of the region fared a little better than the outsiders because they were able to get food from family members. But even though some old villagers secretly gave rice to the new monks, their life was very difficult.

During this time, Tep Vong was accused of secretly worshipping the Buddha. He also refused to disrobe and get married, a decision that incurred the wrath of some Khmer Rouge. He was arrested, but when the village chief died, he was released from prison.[48] In October 1975 the head of the commune committee announced that there were no more monks in Cambodia, and a few days later an armed group arrived. The remaining monks—three from Wat Bo plus twelve base monks—all agreed to disrobe. None of them were killed, and Tep Vong returned to his home village, where he worked as a carpenter.[49]

Tep Vong was the youngest member of the September 1979 ordination party. He had also given tearful evidence at the trial of Pol Pot the previous month, to the effect that the Khmer Rouge had executed fifty-seven monks, including three of his own nephews. Interestingly, he had attended court in monastic robes, even though he was not a monk at this time, at least as far as the Front was concerned. Immediately after the official ordination event, Tep Vong was given the title *braḥ vinay dhamm saṅgh,* indicating that he would have responsibility for monastic discipline. But he became the president (*pradhān*) of the *saṅgha* after the "retirement" of Ven. Kaet Vay. He was, after all, a loyal supporter of the Front and a good friend of the governor of Siem Reap.

Yet there was considerable opposition to Tep Vong's appointment by those would had "unofficially" entered the *saṅgha* before 19 September. Nel Mony was present at this event and has said that it marked a turning point

Ven. Tep Vong in 2001.

in his own status. As we have seen, his own 7 April ordination was initially supported by the authorities, but later it was deemed illegal.[50] Furthermore, Vann Sen, his original sponsor, had been expelled from the Party around this time, although whether his association with the ordination ceremony was a factor is unknown. Thus Nel Mony was detained for three months in 1980 at Wat Unnalom, where he remained in robes, was supplied with a servant, and seems to have been well treated. Nevertheless, with some reluctance, he voluntarily defrocked in July 1982.

Nel Mony was not the only monk somewhat hostile to the new position of Tep Vong. To many of those who had been ordained several months earlier, the issue was one of seniority, for in the traditional Theravāda *saṅgha* the period of time a monk has been in robes is the decisive factor in determining his rank. If we leave aside that some monks had lived throughout the whole of Democratic Kampuchea without disrobing, the case of Tep Vong is especially complicated, for another prominent monk of the immediate post–Democratic Kampuchea period, Ven. Uk Rorn, was the original preceptor of one of the Vietnam-based monks who had served as a member of Tep Vong's own reordination committee. Yet Tep Vong subsequently reordained Uk Rorn.[51]

Tep Vong attending the trial of Pol Pot and Ieng Sary, Phnom Penh, 1979. (Documentation Center of Cambodia)

It is easy to see that anomalies of this kind would do much to disrupt the fragile solidarity that existed between members of the fledgling PRK *saṅgha.* Moreover, it has been difficult for surviving members of the September 1979 seven to break free from the implications of their "official" status, leaving some of their enemies to accuse them of being "Vietnamese monks in Khmer robes."[52]

## Official Circulars

A PRK circular of 19 August 1979 stated that monks had the same rights and duties as all other persons. They were, for example, expected to hold identity cards and to respect government regulations. As full citizens they also had the right to vote, a right that—Laos excepted—was at variance with electoral procedures in the rest of Theravāda Southeast Asia (Löschmann 2005, 51).[53] This policy was adopted to promote rationality and political insight among the monkhood and to liberate the *saṅgha* from outmoded forms of thinking.

For associated reasons monks were not permitted to engage in mendicancy, and as "state employees" they were expected to cultivate vegetables on monastery grounds for their own consumption, even though this was clearly in contravention of the norms of monastic discipline (*vinaya*). However, as things began to relax, monks were allowed out of their monasteries for one hour every morning, and older members of the laity were permitted to visit the local pagoda in the evenings after the day's work had been completed. Alms giving, however, continued to be discouraged, even though for the laity it has always been one of the principal ways to accrue religious merit (*puṇy*). The government clearly expected laypeople to focus their limited resources on more explicitly social benefits (Löschmann 1991, 18–19, 21).

Management committees, composed of a majority of lay members representing the secular authorities, were set up for individual monasteries. In this way the government was able to outmaneuver uncooperative senior monks (W. Collins 1998, 52). These lay representatives also ensured that a proportion of the donations received by the monastery were redirected to the building of hospitals, roads, and schools. The few foreign observers to visit during the period reported that portraits of Marx and Ho Chi Minh were prominently displayed alongside Buddha images in the few functioning *wat*s (Luciolli 1988, 187).

Provincial ordination commissions were also established, and prospective monks were now obliged to write a full biography that was to be properly studied at village, commune, district, province, and national levels.[54] This would ensure that anyone tainted by crimes associated with Pol Pot, Ieng Sary, and Khieu Samphan could be excluded. But it left the door open for former Khmer Rouge who were not part of this particular faction, and it seems that many ex-cadres did reenter the *saṅgha*. The *cau adhikār* of Wat Ang Serei, Kampong Tralach district, for example, appears to have been the former director of a prison in Krang Skea commune.[55]

A reduction of the quorum from ten to five monks for a higher ordination was also introduced. This was perfectly valid from the *vinaya* perspective. However, the requirement that no male under the age of fifty could be ordained[56]—a measure ostensibly designed to maximize the forces of production, enhance the defense of the country, and ensure "the sound functioning of family relationships given the overall scarcity of men"—was not. In addition to the age requirement, candidates had to be unmarried, obey the rules of the pagoda, and stay put in one place (*Kampuchea* 1982). These restrictions were not lifted until 1988.[57]

Temporary ordinations were also forbidden, although the authorities appear to have actively encouraged the ordination of handicapped men, a message contrary to the rules of monastic discipline, on the grounds that they were not economically active and could best be cared for in a monastic setting. As time went on, ordination became somewhat easier, although local authorities still retained the right of veto.

In mid-1979 Ros Samay was appointed special minister of state, with a fairly wide brief that included international economic cooperation, jurisdiction, and courts, as well as Buddhism and other religions (Slocomb 2003, 64).[58] On 5 December 1980 a circular entitled *Concerning the Implementation of the Policy on Religion* (no. 453/80KB) announced the formation of a Department of Religion within the Front's Central Committee (ibid., 181).[59] Many of these documents were signed by Chea Sim, who as well as being sponsor of the "official" monk ordinations of September 1979, had been a monk himself before the civil war (Löschmann 1991, 21n11, 24).

The political leadership of the PRK tried to tackle the problem of "outmoded" thinking in the religious realm, through a three-stage process called "preserve-overcome-update" (Löschmann 2005, 52). The 5 December 1980 circular made four important points related to the freedom to practice religion in the PRK: all religious issues were to be resolved in a democratic fashion and any decisions reached had to be approved by the revolutionary state authority; the law on religious freedom of belief had to be implemented according to the law of the state; the masses had to be mobilized in such a way that the enemy, who might use religion to endanger the state, would be frustrated; and the clergy and religious organizations that did worthwhile work for the nation and the people were to be protected.[60] A good example of such a monk was Ven. Aom Em, age sixty-one, from Wat Khnong Veang, Oudong district, who was reported as participating in "rebuilding all sectors" of society (*Kampuchea* 1981a).

Between 29 May and 1 June 1982, Heng Samrin, the general secretary of the Kampuchean People's Revolutionary Party (KPRP), addressed the First National Buddhist Monks' Congress, at which he extolled Cambodian Buddhism as a religion in harmony with democratic principles. These views were repeated in circular dated 1 October 1982 (no. 02-82). Buddhism would "last forever," it stated, not least because the Buddha had urged his followers not to split into parties or factions (*Kampuchea* 1982). This document also praised the positive historical contribution of Buddhists to society, particularly those with a nationalist outlook like Achar Mean (Son Ngoc Minh), Tou Samouth, and Hem Chieu.[61]

Official policy also spelled out the ways in which Buddhism was compatible with Marxism. Monks were expected to maintain the unity of nation, push the people to work for development, and encourage the masses to be angry with Pol Pot. But those who preached that the deaths of "three million Cambodians" under Pol Pot was the result of karma were to be condemned, for such views served the plans of the enemy.

Monks were also required to promote the notion that Vietnam, Russia, and Laos were the friends of the Cambodian people and that the United States, China, and Pol Pot were most definitely not. The fostering of good relations with Buddhists in Vietnam and Laos was a further aim. To this end, Tep Vong made visits to the Soviet Union and to Mongolia, so that he could discover more about the appropriate model of church-state relations in a socialist setting (Try 1991, 359).[62] Ven. Oum Sum[63] attended the sixth conference of the foreign ministers of Cambodia, Vietnam, and Laos in Ho Chi Minh City on 6–7 July 1982 as a representative of Phnom Penh monks. In his speech he stated that, with the establishment of the PRK, Cambodians were now free to believe in Buddhism once more. He endorsed the Front's opposition to Chinese support for GRUNK (the Royal Government of National Union of Kampuchea) and applauded a recent but cosmetic withdrawal of

Ven. Oum Som. (Documentation Center of Cambodia)

some Vietnamese soldiers from Cambodian territory. A fellow Cambodian monk, Ven. Am Uon, condemned Sihanouk as a reactionary and warmly applauded the recent role of Cambodia's Vietnamese friends (*Phnom Penh News* 1982).

On 14–18 July 1984 the Vietnam Buddhist Saṅgha (VBS) sent a delegation carrying quantities of Buddhist literature to Phnom Penh, and periodic contacts continued until the Vietnamese withdrawal from Cambodia in 1989 (Vietnam Buddhist Saṅgha 1990, 124, 136–137).[64] We can say that Cambodian Buddhism was slowly beginning to reengage with a wider Buddhist world, even though this contact was restricted to the communist bloc. Nevertheless, the authorities were especially suspicious about the activities of foreign monks staying in Cambodian monasteries. The concern was further developed in a circular dated 10 September 1986 (no. 05-86), also signed by Chea Sim. The document declared that too many illegal and foreign monks, particularly from Vietnam, were present in the country's *wats*.[65] Such individuals were not working to reconstruct the country, many were entering the *saṅgha* through bribery, and none possessed the necessary identity card (*chāyā*), according to the circular. Particular concern was expressed about the activity of monks coming from Kampuchea Krom, but the circular urged the authorities to deal with the problem by using "cold" methods (i.e., administrative procedures, as opposed to "hot," or coercive, ones).

In due course an official document, entitled *Buddhism and the Fatherland,* defined the correct relationship between religion and state (Löschmann 1991,

25n20). At the Second National Buddhist Monks' Congress, in 1984, Heng Samrin reminded his audience that they must be prepared to fight to protect the state against its enemies—characterized as the hordes of Māra, a god believed by Buddhists to be the embodiment of evil—for the existence of the state was the necessary condition for the flourishing of Buddhism itself.[66] Heng Samrin urged monks to be vigilant with regard to their fellows who might be using the ordained state for acts of subversion. He also advised them that they should "completely discard unhealthy beliefs" (Keyes 1990, 62) and hold true to the example of the Buddha, who had "abolished classes in his lifetime." The latter statement is not an entirely accurate characterization of the Buddha's position on the Indian caste system, but it served to remind listeners that the Buddha's message was one of equality, democracy, and collective existence.

Around this time the government laid down eight conditions for the proper regulation of the *saṅgha:*

1. to learn the significance of the political line
2. to educate the laity with regard to party ideas
3. to model themselves on the Buddha and fight the enemy
4. to preserve and cultivate the patriotic and revolutionary spirit exemplified by monks like Ven. Hem Chieu[67] and Achar Mean
5. to preserve the cultural heritage
6. to promote and improve production among the people so that their living standards may be enhanced
7. to assist in building social service establishments
8. to carry out all of the above to achieve victory (Yang Sam 1987, 85)

As Löschmann (2005, 46) observes, the new government viewed "the potentially progressive doctrinal teachings and traditions of Buddhism" as a contribution "towards converting the material interests of the people *into the non-material*" (my italics). An anonymous document titled *Address Given by the Religion Commission to the International Seminar on the Aftermaths of the Genocidal Regime and the Prevention of Its Recurrence,* which, on the basis of internal evidence, must have been written after Min Khin produced his July 1983 report, was also very sympathetic to Buddhism. It recognized that monasteries had traditionally been places of asylum and psychological relief, shelters for waifs and the unfortunate, places of physical healing, meeting places for all strata of society, storehouses of knowledge, and locations for creativity in literature, arts and crafts, arithmetic, and so on. The document also noted that the almost total liquidation of Buddhism during Democratic Kampuchea had caused "psychological trauma and a loss of spiritual balance" to people across the country and that this had consequences both materially and spiritually. The people had become pessimistic about the future, for they were in "boundless despair," while the youth had been transformed into uncivilized and ignorant fanatics. It concluded by asserting that the spiritual consequences of the destruction of Buddhism in Cambodia were much more severe than any material impact, by a factor of ten to twenty.

## Disrobing Unofficial Monks

Although the government was committed to strong levels of regulation, the weakness of its bureaucratic systems meant that many of the proposals settled at congresses and in official documents were ineffectively implemented. Restrictions on monastic ordination and caps on monastic numbers could easily be circumvented by the establishment of unofficial *wat*s. In rural areas young monks seem to have circulated in significant numbers, even though their ordinations had not been registered. Wat Long in Chhlong district, for example, had only two official monks, but it also had another ten who had ordained clandestinely,[68] and one of my informants reported that although he was only in his late teens in 1980, he was ordained and avoided official disapproval simply by keeping a low profile.[69] I have also interviewed a number of older monks who claim to have been secretly teaching Pāli long before the study of Buddhist literature was officially tolerated toward the end of the 1980s.[70]

There were many isolated incidents of monk disrobing in the early PRK period, but the policy seems to have accelerated in both regularity and quantity as the 1980s progressed. The need for manpower to service the increasingly disastrous K5 plan, which aimed to physically seal off the border with Thailand through the construction of a physical barrier between the two states, was an important driving factor (Slocomb 2003, 229–230).[71] But not all attempts to return monks to the lay life were successful. At some point between 1984 and 1985 Tep Vong held a mass meeting at Wat Pa'av, Batheay district, at which he tried to encourage over six hundred young monks to disrobe. But Ven. Krouch Saret, the district's *anugaṇ,* successfully argued that they would disrobe of their own accord once they had served long enough to become good marriage partners.[72] This, however, was not the end of the story. Krouch Saret came under official pressure, and he eventually left the district, moving first to Phnom Penh and then to America.[73]

In early 1979 monks from Kampuchea Krom began to trickle back across the border. It seems that they were reluctant to wear their robes in public, and they generally kept themselves hidden from the authorities. Two Khmer Krom monks stayed two to three years at Wat Me Sa Thngak, for instance. But the Front made difficulties for them, claiming that they did not possess the right documents, even though it was very easy for ordinary Vietnamese to live in the area at that time.[74] The story of Ven. Nhem Kim Teng is instructive in this context. He had spent most of Democratic Kampuchea in exile in southern Vietnam and was reordained in Preah Trapeang province (Trà Vinh) before returning to Cambodia. But because his ordination had not been done under the auspices of the Front, he did not have a proper identity card and was regarded as an unlawful monk. As such, he could not take up an official office in his monastery, such as *grū sūtr* or *cau adhikār.* Neither could he eat in the *sālā chān'* or teach about the *dhamma* or monastic discipline (*dhammavinaya*). Eventually he was worn down by low-level bureaucratic opposition, and he underwent an official ordination ceremony in 1987.[75]

The situation was far worse for monks with roots in Vietnam, for as we have seen, the receipt of Buddhist teachings from other countries was not permitted (Vickery 1986, 161). The reason for the large-scale migration is connected to the socialist reconstruction of southern Vietnam following the communists' victory of 30 April 1975. With Buddhist practice now under suspicion, quite large numbers of monks decided to cross the border into Cambodia. But this rarely improved their lot. Ven. Yeoung Seak is a case in point. Originally from Khleang province (Sóc Trăng), he arrived in Kirivong district, Takeo province, in 1979. At that time around sixty monks were living nearby, 70 percent of whom came from the other side of the border. In Vietnam itself Yeoung Seak had worked for the Ministry of Nationalities, but because he was regarded as a staunch Theravāda monk, the authorities wanted to defrock him. He was subsequently imprisoned from 1975 to 1979, and it was his release from captivity that prompted the move to Cambodia. Unfortunately he was almost immediately caught up in the PRK authorities' suspicion of foreign agents within the *saṅgha.* He was defrocked and imprisoned in Cambodia from 1984 to 1987. Only on release was he officially reordained, the ceremony taking place at Wat Unnalom with Ven. Oum Soum as his preceptor.[76]

## Buddhist Infrastructure: Phnom Penh and Beyond

In a report prepared for the August 1979 trial of Pol Pot, Nel Mony asserted that during Democratic Kampuchea "several principal temples of our 26 pagodas in Phnom Penh were sacked."[77] With this in mind, repair of the country's pagodas had been incorporated into the Front's program. Yet work proceeded slowly. The reestablishment of pagodas was closely supervised, and new foundations could not be started willy-nilly. However, by 1981 some rebuilding was taking place, and a number of *kathin* ceremonies had occurred. A good example was Wat Sre Ampil, close to National Route 1 to the south of the capital. There, by 1983, the chief monk and a local lay-woman had refurbished its damaged buildings and created a number of new *kuṭī*s (Ouch Sophany 2004, 31).

Although the state did not allocate funds for such undertakings—they were largely financed by local communities—a sympathetic official might sometimes donate materials (Vickery 1986, 162–163). And if that sympathetic official happened to be a senior member of the government, things could move very quickly. Chea Sim, for example, helped rebuild the *wat* in his wife's village of Kamchay Meas within a few years of his taking power.[78]

A man who became an *achar* at Wat Unnalom, Phnom Penh, immediately after the fall of Democratic Kampuchea claims that when he arrived at the pagoda on 19 September 1979, the buildings were in surprisingly good condition. The compound, on the other hand, was full of around four years' worth of garbage, and some superficial damage had been caused by people lighting fires to cook food. The thing that upset him the most, however, was that the library of Ven. Chuon Nath, a highly significant repository of Khmer and Buddhist culture, had entirely vanished. It was also reported that unidentified persons had thrown a highly venerated photograph of Chuon Nath into the river that flowed nearby.[79]

This report tallies well with other accounts of the state of Phnom Penh *wat*s. Wat Mohamontrei was in fairly good condition, although its pre-1975 murals had been erased.[80] A good number of pagodas were also intact in Battambang and Siem Reap, for the infrastructure of these towns had generally not been badly damaged by war (Sher 2004, 116), and the same applied to many rural areas, especially those away from the eastern provinces where US bombing had obliterated vast tracts of habitation in the early civil war period. In the historically significant Srey Santhor district of Kampong

Cham, for instance, most *wat*s had survived Democratic Kampuchea intact, and only one, Wat Lvea Te, had been destroyed.[81]

There is some evidence to suggest that this situation deteriorated after the establishment of the PRK and that many pagodas that had survived the previous nine years of fighting succumbed once the situation stabilized. Peace is, of course, a relative concept, and hostilities continued in many parts of the country. But as Cambodia gradually opened up to the outside world once more, the seductive power of the international art market made its presence felt, and Noun Nget's claim that there was a lot more looting of monasteries after 1979 than before has a ring of truth to it.[82]

Furthermore, Vietnamese forces were now heavily garrisoned in strategically significant locations, and pagodas, as they had in the past, offered the most convenient sites for establishing barracks.[83] In Battambang, for example, Wats Sangke, Kandal, Po Veal, and Bo Knong remained as Vietnamese army bases until 1992, and the undercroft of Wat Kandal was used as a prison throughout most of this period.[84] The *brah vihāra* of Wat Sangke had been used as an ammunition store during Democratic Kampuchea and was still well stocked with ordnance when Vietnamese troops arrived. It was totally destroyed by explosions—whether by accident or by design is difficult to say—during one week in the early PRK period.[85] Other pagodas were also devastated by explosions well after Democratic Kampuchea had ended.[86]

I take these to be isolated incidents rather than an indication that the Vietnamese were themselves engaged in an anti-Buddhist campaign. Indeed, it is difficult to identify many examples of willful sacrilege. More often than not troops used buildings for military purposes without any explicit intention to destroy. Indeed, on some occasions they may have made efforts to rehabilitate Buddhist structures so that they could be employed for their original purpose. A case in point is a *wat* in Kandal province that had apparently been damaged in the conflict and was later repaired by the Vietnamese in 1982 so that monks could be invited back.[87]

Another revealing incident relates to Wat Mathar, a pagoda in Kampong Thom province. After Democratic Kampuchea its previous *cau adhikār,* Chan Chhet, returned. But at eighty years of age, he was too old to resume that position, and in any case he now had a wife. Because he could not be reordained, he decided to install himself as an *achar.* The first task he undertook was to clean off the black paint that the monks had smeared over the murals of the *brah vihāra* before 1975 to protect them once the monks realized the antireligious nature of Khmer Rouge ideology. Sometime later, in 1984, an old monk called Ta Kay was installed as the *cau adhikār*, but the Vietnamese had by this time decided to use the pagoda as the military base. There was considerable local disquiet about this turn of events, however, and the troops moved out when they became aware of the level of opposition (An Rasmey 2004).

## *Saṅgha* Growth, Unification, and (Re)politicization

Given the number of "unofficial" monks, it is difficult to be certain about the *saṅgha*'s rate of growth in the early PRK period. In an interview with the *Globe and Mail* (Toronto) in September 1981, Tep Vong claimed 3,000 ordained monks and 700 pagodas under construction nationwide. But a more scholarly estimate in the same year concluded that only 500 monks had been fully reordained, with a further 1,500 entering the *saṅgha* as novices (Keyes 1990, 61). A year later Cambodian officials were computing a total of 2,311 monks in 1,821 monasteries, an overall decrease of around 60,000 monks since the Khmer Rouge seized power (Yang Sam 1987, 81).[88] This averages out at less than two monks per monastery, a figure well below the limit of four imposed by the government in an attempt to prevent the monasteries from expanding and becoming potential foci of unrest. There were some exceptions to this, particularly in Phnom Penh, where 170 monks were officially in residence during 1981.

The monastic order in Cambodia had been divided into two fraternities since 1855, when King Ang Duong imported the newly formed Thommayut from Siam. King Norodom subsequently established Wat Botum Vaddei as the order's headquarters, adjacent to the Royal Palace in Phnom Penh. But unlike in nineteenth-century Thailand, where the new order was introduced without significant opposition, in Cambodia tensions between monks of the two fraternities have been a recurring phenomenon (Bizot 1976, 9).[89] These tensions were exacerbated by the French, who regarded the Thommayut monks to be politically suspect because of a supposed allegiance to the Siamese court (Forest 1980, 143). The order's aristocratic orientation and Thai connections put it into a doubly difficult relationship with the Khmer Rouge, who regarded even the most innocent of contacts with foreign states as treasonable acts.[90] As has already been noted, the Khmer Rouge also favored rural monks over those based in the cities. For these reasons we might suppose that Thommayut monks suffered greater persecution during Democratic Kampuchea than did their Mahanikay fellows, but the evidence is inconclusive. Certainly, official resistance to the Thommayut was a feature of the early PRK period. Indeed, many prominent figures at that time argued that *sangha* unification would help eliminate the elitist, unpatriotic, and monarchical influences of the Thommayut.

In June 1981 the fourth congress of the Party resolved that "the National Front for the Salvation of Kampuchea must be constantly enlarged and developed and must have a political line acceptable to each social layer, in particular the monks, intellectuals, [and] the ethnic minorities" (quoted in Try 1991, 39). In September of the same year, Tep Vong was "elected" the head of a unified monastic order. To underscore the changed circumstances, he did not adopt the traditional title of *samtec sangharāja* (His Excellency, king of the *sangha*), for such a title would have been inappropriate in a socialist setting. Instead he was referred to as "president" (*pradhān*).[91]

The unification was unprecedented, although something of the sort had been suggested as early as July 1937, when the newspaper *Nagara Vatta* condemned Buddhist factionalism and recommended the end of differences between the parties on the grounds that the Khmer race should be united in "one Buddhism" (Edwards 2004, 79). The new unified order, or "Front order" (*brah sangh ranasirsa*), was the only form of Buddhism now to be tolerated. As a "solidarity Buddhism without sects" it effectively dissolved the boundaries between the pre-1970s Thommayut and Mahanikay fraternities (*nikāya*). This change seems to have been modeled on parallel developments in Vietnam, where Theravāda and Mahāyāna Buddhism had been unified in the early 1960s, and in Laos.[92] A senior Cambodian monastic source stated that after unification "our monks are neither Mahanikay nor Thommayut but Nationalist monks" (quoted in Yang Sam 1987, 86). Yet as some commentators have noted, the practice of the unified order was oriented around Mahanikay interpretations of monastic discipline (*vinaya*).[93]

This meant that old Thommayut pagodas in Phnom Penh, like Wat Botum Vaddei and Nuon Moniram, lost their original affiliation. Wat Keo Preah Phloeung, by contrast, was leveled in 1979 and the land redeveloped for housing officials (DC-Cam 1996b, 41).[94] Many local *sangha*s, however, largely went their own way while appearing to do as they were officially bidden—a typical deployment of James Scott's "weapons of the weak." Thus, Wat Koki Thom in Svay Rieng province had been Thommayut, but the monks who recongregated there in the early PRK period simply "pretended to be Mahanikay."[95] And as already noted, in Kampong Cham province Ven. Paen Sen also chose to ignore the official line on the unified *sangha*.

The politicization of the monastic order was now as explicit as it had ever been under any previous Cambodian regime. In 1980 Pen Sovann, secretary-general of the KPRP, said: "As far as monks are concerned, our Front has a well-defined political line: to respect the traditions, mores and customs of our people. All monks who have direct relations with the people are members of the Front" (quoted by Kiernan 1982, 181). Three monks served on the Party's Central Committee (Thion 1983, 317), and Ven. Tep Vong, now chairman of the *brah saṅgh raṇasirsa,* also occupied the post of vice president of the Khmer National Assembly. Indeed, by late December 1981 he had also became one of the four vice presidents of the National Council of the Front (Slocomb 2003, 166).[96] This paradoxical position informed his public utterances. As an example, he had argued that some types of political violence might be condoned from the Buddhist perspective, specifically citing the activities of the Buddhist-inspired Issaraks of the 1950s (Löschmann 1991, 24).

When the PRK Constitution had first been debated, some thought was given to whether or not monks might run for government office. An official document from the Central Propaganda and Education Commission, the unsigned and undated *Study Document for the Election to Choose People's Revolutionary Committees for the Commune and Sangkat,*[97] however, urged monks, who were "citizens with rights and obligations like other citizens," to clarify the following points when they were preaching to the people in the run-up to the elections of February and March 1981: they should not listen to enemy propaganda, and they should be sure to cast their own vote, but only for "good" candidates (Slocomb 2003, 78).

## Buddhism in the Late PRK Period

In the mid-1980s the Soviet authorities had already decided to scale back their commitments around the world. Mikhail Gorbachev's October 1985 suggestion to Afghan president Babrak Karmal that he would soon have to "figure out how to defend [his] . . . own cause" did not augur well for the Vietnamese, who were highly reliant on cheap Russian fuel. It was only a matter of time, then, before Vietnam would have to withdraw from Cambodia.

As a result of a rapidly changing internal and international political situation, restrictions on the ordination of monks were lifted in mid-1988, and Radio Phnom Penh began each day with a broadcast of Buddhist liturgies from various city monasteries. A fresh wind of religious toleration and openness was beginning to blow. The constitution of the new State of Cambodia (SOC) in April 1989 restored Buddhism as the state religion, Prime Minister Hun Sen apologized for earlier government "mistakes" toward religion in a series of talks around the country, and senior leaders engaged in acts of conspicuous Buddhist piety.[98] In this new atmosphere monk numbers grew rapidly;[99] pagoda reconstruction received a massive boost, particularly since funds for large-scale merit-making activities were now flowing into the country from an extensive Cambodian diaspora; taxes on pagodas were abolished; and Buddhist education, including Pāli schools, began to reemerge.[100]

With the Vietnamese finally withdrawing in September 1989, Cambodia prepared for the restoration of the monarchy. In Theravāda Buddhism there is a long-standing impetus toward purification and reform following times of crisis or dynastic transition. After the Burmese sack of Ayudhya in the 1760s, the Siamese *sangha* was in a dismal condition for many decades, and it was this situation that led Rama IV to introduce major monastic reforms. Similarly, when Ang Duong began his reign as king of Cambodia in 1848, he made it a priority to replace Buddhist texts destroyed during wars with Siam and Vietnam. There is a clear parallel here with the situation after Democratic Kampuchea, and developments following the end of the communist period should be read in this light.

Norodom Sihanouk returned from exile in November 1991 and resumed the traditional function of supreme patron of the *sangha.* In December the *brah sangh ranasirsa* was dissolved, and Sihanouk appointed chief monks (*sangharāja*) for each of the two pre-1975 monastic fraternities. Tep Vong became the Mahanikay patriarch, and Ven. Bour Kry, a prominent figure from the Cambodian community in Paris, took charge of the Thommayut. Pagoda councils, comprising the *cau adhikār,* the *grū sūtr stām,* and the *grū sūtr chven,* were reinstituted in 1991. This institution had been unknown in the 1980s, partly because individual *wat*s often did not have even three resident monks (Löschmann 2005, 56).

Full restoration of both ecclesiastical hierarchies followed in February 1992. The Ministry of Cults and Religions was also reestablished at this time. Its initial goals were to reform the ecclesiastical structures that existed before 1970, to develop monk education, and to reestablish the Buddhist Institute, a center of research and higher learning that was originally founded by the French.

The development of Cambodian Buddhism throughout the 1980s has been a journey from virtual extinction to a simulacrum of normality in which most of the institutions created during the colonial period were reestablished. At the time of writing, furthermore, the numbers of monks in robes equates well to that at the end of the 1960s. In this very restricted sense, then, one can say that Buddhism has been reborn in Cambodia, and even if it is still far from maturity, it is moving incrementally toward that goal. But this is window dressing. The problems afflicting the *saṅgha* today, in terms of both leadership and future direction, are deep and seemingly intractable, for the Khmer Rouge effectively eliminated Buddhism's intellectual and spiritual elites, and the PRK, although not entirely cynical in its policy on religion, was never interested in reviving traditional learning. Only now are there some encouraging signs of new growth, but well-motivated and well-educated young monks are thin on the ground. Buddhist hierarchical structures certainly changed with the establishment of the Kingdom of Cambodia in the early 1990s, but the senior personnel remain largely the same. As a result, corruption, cronyism, and stagnation are rife, with many middle-ranking figures jostling for the top positions soon to be vacated by members of the current ecclesiastical gerontocracy.[101] The Cambodian monastic order is, in fact, the mirror of a wider society. Those desiring spiritual and intellectual reform are vulnerable, and they must take care not to press their demands too assiduously.

# Conclusion

Since 1979 the Cambodian political landscape has shifted from a uniquely extreme and nationalistic communism to one marked by a strange amalgam of postconflict democratization, dominant party authoritarianism, and unregulated market liberalism.[1] As Buddhism has begun the process of recovery following its almost total liquidation, it has had no option but to accommodate itself to these bewildering and unpredictable currents of change.

In the PRK the monastic order had little freedom to reestablish itself along pre-1975 lines, since it was required to act as a partner in a project of national reconstruction determined by the governing regime. It suffered from heavy-handed ideological manipulation, its institutional growth was significantly curtailed, and it was forced to develop along narrowly patriotic lines that few surviving independent-minded and traditionally educated monks had the influence to moderate.

The pagoda is not always the place of sanctuary imagined by those seeking escape from the vicissitudes of the political, yet the monkhood did slowly manage to carve out a niche that was protected from the worst excesses of government interference, and with the general easing of restrictions following the withdrawal of Vietnam from the country around 1989, it regained some of its prerevolutionary forms and functions. But despite these changed circumstances a small group of old monks who had been selected to steer the *sangha* through the early days of its reestablishment rose to commanding heights within the ecclesiastical hierarchy, where they promoted a xenophobic worldview and sought to cement their own position through the construction of a carefully choreographed form of state Buddhism. Critics of the arrangement had little choice but to keep their heads down and eke out a marginalized existence. For this reason the more traditional currents of Buddhist practice and belief took a little longer to reemerge. But monks whose charisma derived from a purported ability to manipulate the sacred through magic began to gain a wide following in the immediate post-1993 era of liberal economic reform, some significantly benefiting from the patronage of wealthy ex-communists and members of the mushrooming business sector. In the process they were incorporated into the religio-political establishment (Harris 2006).

Potentially influential members of the *sangha* who were further removed from the paraphernalia of the state, by contrast, suffered from levels of suspicion that have sporadically flared into outright persecution from the ruling party and its ecclesiastical placemen. This has especially been the case for an emerging Phnom Penh–based Buddhist intelligentsia largely composed of younger monks. But it has also been a factor in the difficulties experienced by certain more senior figures who survived Democratic Kampuchea and PRK outside the country and returned in the early 1990s to initiate projects of renovation or reform, often funded by foreign individuals or organizations.

The run-up to the first post–Democratic Kampuchea elections in May 1993 marked a turning point in Buddhist engagement with the international community. Before this time the government had ensured that the only connections deemed appropriate for Cambodian Buddhists were those with Buddhists in other socialist settings. But the massive influx of foreign aid workers during the UNTAC period ensured that the floodgates would now be definitively breached, with Cambodia rapidly becoming one of the most heavily colonized countries in the world in terms of nongovernmental organizations (NGOs) and their related activities (Trannin 2005). Soon tens of million of US dollars were flowing annually through these organizations into the economy, affecting all levels of Cambodian life, including the practice of medicine, human rights, rural development, banking, art, culture, the rewriting of laws, urban planning, environmental matters, women's issues, education, disarmament, demining, and so on. Religion was also significantly affected, not least because many NGOs felt the need to channel their activities through reliable partners with a wide geographical footprint and moral influence throughout the country. As was previously noted in connection with the PRK's need to establish legitimacy, the *sangha* has always been well situated to perform such a role. But this can come at a cost.

Underlying this process one may dimly detect an outlook that has remained a constant from the French era, through the short period between national independence and the civil war of the early 1970s, the initial stages of Democratic Kampuchea, and into the People's Republic of Kampuchea.

For over a century all regimes, be they colonialist, communist, socialist, or republican, have sought to disengage Cambodian Buddhism from its traditional roots through the introduction of a modernist emphasis on the value of the monk's engagement in socially progressive activity. This was just as much to the fore in the attitudes of many international donors post-1993. Yet, given its almost total destruction only a little over a decade previously, the *sangha* was just beginning to emerge from its chrysalis and thus was especially vulnerable to external manipulation, particularly given that most monks now had only the barest grasp of basic Buddhist principles (Marston 2009, 227–236). As a result the contemplative life, which is arguably the central element to which all aspects of Buddhist doctrine and practice must ultimately tend, remains—with a few signal exceptions—as fragile now as at almost any point in the last half century.

From the Theravāda Buddhist perspective, many of the crimes committed during the period covered in this book were of the utmost seriousness, and all guilty of such offenses must suffer for their actions both in this life and in future existences, for they are subject to the ancient law of karma. The basic constitution of the universe (*dhamma*) entails that this must be so, and there can be no escape from the consequences of one's improper acts: "Not up in the air, nor in the middle of the sea, nor going into a cleft in the mountains; Nowhere on earth is a spot to be found where you could stay and escape your evil deed" (*Dhammapada* 127). In this sense the idea of a formal tribunal to determine guilt or innocence, or to confer sanctions on the guilty, might appear to be redundant. But from its inception Buddhism has also recognized the need for formal public rites designed in various ways to achieve two goals: to assist in bringing the disturbed minds of both perpetrators and their victims back to a state of moral and spiritual calm and to positively reconfigure the moral order. As far as Cambodia is concerned, while the medieval Khmer law codes tended to emphasize sanction and retribution, this outlook would in time shift away from a concern over the determination of guilt or innocence toward the primary value of reconciliation of the parties to a dispute (Engel 1978, 107–108), reflecting the Theravāda ethical values that rose to prominence after the fall of Angkor.

This book is intended to stand as a memorial, however imperfect, to those whose lives were overwhelmed by the desperate events that beset Cambodia in the 1970s. I also hope that it may be of value to those with responsibility to determine the outcome of the current Extraordinary Chambers in the Courts of Cambodia for the Prosecution of Crimes Committed during the

Period of Democratic Kampuchea. The Cambodian state, stretching from the colonial period to the present, has never been entirely integrated into Cambodian society, yet organized Buddhism can contribute to the resolution of this rupture through active promotion of a worldview that enshrines ethical values and acceptable behaviors reflecting the deeper structures of reality. The overcoming of resentment and anger related to past atrocities may never be entirely possible, but if the notion that a perpetrator's injurious actions may reveal something important about wider flaws at every level of society is contemplated, perhaps the outrage felt in some quarters about the continuing culture of impunity will in time dissolve into a kind of moral sadness. This may, in turn, lead to the emergence of a more just and compassionate Cambodia.

# NOTES

## Introduction

1. ICH/12.
2. For a study of the Buddha's predictions of decline in the Cambodian context, see de Bernon 1994.
3. Not all scholars agree that Langdarma was an anti-Buddhist. For an opposing perspective, see Yamaguchi 1996.
4. For a discussion of early Chinese communist views on the significance of Buddhism to Chinese history, see Ch'en 1965.
5. The insistence on monks engaging in productive labor did not hold the same negative resonances in China—for it was largely in line with historical tradition—as it would in Theravāda Southeast Asia, where such activity is specifically forbidden by the rules of monastic discipline (*vinaya*). For various reasons that have not been sufficiently investigated, the practice of monastic landholding was very poorly developed in Cambodia before Democratic Kampuchea. For this reason, the Khmer Rouge never needed to worry about expropriating monastic property.
6. From "On the New Democracy," in Mao 1967, 155.
7. The interview transcripts (in Khmer with some partial English translation) and audiotapes associated with this project are held at the Documentation Center of Cambodia (DC-Cam) and are designated with "BAC" in the center's cataloguing system. Additional interviews conducted by the author are designated by "ICH" in this work. Details of all relevant BAC and ICH materials are provided in the bibliography.
8. Conducted in refugee camps on the Thai-Cambodian border and in Phnom Penh, this work resulted in Chantou Boua's 1991 article, "Genocide of a Religious Group: Pol Pot and Cambodia's Buddhist Monks," which represents the first systematic attempt to deal with the Khmer Rouge's treatment of Buddhism in Cambodia based on oral sources. These interview transcripts are designated by "D" in the DC-Cam cataloguing system. All of those that are relevant to this study are further described in the first section of the bibliography.
9. Ciorciari and Chhang (2005, 224–234) give a good account of the documentary sources housed at DC-Cam. Also see Heder and Tittemore 2004, 6–7.
10. For a discussion of the difficulties involved in using confessions under torture as historical evidence, see Heder and Tittemore 2004, 28ff.
11. These intelligence reports are designated by "L" in the DC-Cam cataloguing scheme.
12. The DC-Cam holds 19,763 individual biographies of cadres and soldiers.
13. *Yuvajan Niṅ Yuvanārī Padivatt(n)* (Revolutionary youth), *Daṅ' Paṭivatt(n)* (Revolutionary flag), and *Daṅ' Raṇasirsa* (Flag of the front) were distributed to officials on a monthly basis throughout 1975–1978.

14. DC-Cam claims to have 1,166,307 of these handwritten documents on file.
15. This number is an exaggeration, for in the entire history of Cambodia there had never been this many *saṅgha* members. Ministry of Religion statistics suggest that there were around 65,000 monks in robes in the early 1970s, but this number must have been massively reduced by the time the Khmer Rouge took Phnom Penh.
16. The tribunal considered the following stories:

    When Kan Man, a former student of archaeology, left Phnom Penh and arrived in his home village in Prey Veng province, he and other villagers were forced to participate in the destruction of the local pagoda, Wat Por Loas, in Prey Kdouch hamlet. His Buddhist sympathies made it difficult for him to wield the sledgehammer, and he hid some of the precious objects he was expected to smash. It appears that on 27 January 1976 he was denounced, imprisoned in a toilet, and tortured savagely until he lost consciousness and died.

    A certain Sang, age sixty, was forced to disrobe and marry at Memot commune, Memot district, Kampong Cham. His wife subsequently died of exhaustion, and that night he recited prayers and put candles, incense, and flowers on her grave. He was discovered and arrested. But on his release he visited the grave again. He was taken away and never seen again.

    A married couple, Mi, age sixty-five, and his wife, Tuch, age sixty-three, were caught performing Buddhist rites in their cottage in Sras Pring hamlet, Cheung Prey, Kampong Cham. They were arrested along with thirty-four other family members, including some children, and all were massacred.
17. For a good account, see Fawthrop and Jarvis 2004, 40–41.

## CHAPTER ONE: Unraveling of the Buddhist State

1. Concerns about the status, character, and external control of Buddhism influenced the overall motivation of many participants in what became known as the Umbrella War (Harris 2005a, 137–144; Locard 2006–2007).
2. Chandler (1996, 199) characterizes Sihanouk's Buddhist socialism as a "ramshackle ideology."
3. A long-standing opponent of Sihanouk and a leader of the Khmer Serei (Free Khmer) movement, Son Ngoc Thanh served as prime minister of Cambodia in August–October 1945 and again in March–October 1972.
4. Ministry of Religious Affairs statistics, quoted in Try 1991, 148. The numbers do not differentiate between novices and fully ordained monks.
5. See the following reports in *Réalités Cambodgiennes:* "Samdech preside à la pose des *seima* d'un nouveau temple," 14 February 1969, 5; "En Kandal, Samdech inaugure le nouveau temple de Monastère Chumpou Prœk," 14 March 1969, 6; "Un nouveau monastère en Kompong Chhnang," 28 March 1969, 6.
6. Under torture, Preap In confessed to membership in the Khmer Serei and to having received US Central Intelligence Agency backing to overthrow Sihanouk. Sihanouk claimed to have "no inhibitions in signing the death warrant" and ordered that a newsreel of the execution be played in the country's cinemas for

a month after the event (Corfield 1994, 34). The effect of this was to appall a significant proportion of the population, and the issue still recurs from time to time in more recent Cambodian political discourse. The country's current prime minister, Hun Sen, for example, has threatened to show the newsreel again as part of his campaign to discredit the ex-king (*Cambodge Soir,* 5 April 2005).

7. Norodom Sihanouk 1964, 98. Kiernan (1985, 231, 252) reports the arrest of a monk from Prey Veng province as an alleged communist sympathizer the previous year.

8. Lon Nol's younger brother Lon Non was another key player in the Khmer Republic. He believed himself to be a reincarnation of Akinet, an ascetic magician with supernatural eyes of fire who is mentioned in the Khmer version of the *Rāmāyaṇa,* the *Rāmakīrti* (Corfield 1994, 113). For a contemporary source on Lon Nol's "otherworldly" approach to politics, see Henry Kamm, "Lon Nol Reads No Newspapers and Never Uses a Telephone," *New York Times Magazine* 13, December 1970.

9. To this end Lon Nol established a pseudoscholarly journal and the grandly named Khmer-Mon Institute. Indeed, one of the first delegations to be sent abroad by the new government was headed by the institute's director, the prominent antiroyalist Keng Vannsak (Khing Hoc Dy 1990, 2:72).

10. The term derives from the ethnonym "Tamil," a word that seems to have entered Khmer as a result of contact with Sri Lanka, probably via Thailand. As such, it reflects the racial antipathies of some Sri Lankan missionary monks. On the role of Buddhist nationalism in the conflict between Sinhalese and Tamils in Sri Lanka, see Tambiah 1992, 123ff.

11. Predictions of the Buddha (*Buddha daṃnāy*) had circulated in Cambodia for at least a century. For a study and translation of some of the relevant sources, see de Bernon 1998a.

12. Lon Nol, *Le neo-khmerisme* (Phnom Penh; Imprimerie Decho-Dandin, 1972), quoted in Martin 1994, 130, and Slocomb 2006, 383.

13. Two predominantly Vietnamese Catholic churches in Phnom Penh were attacked by mobs on 13 March 1970. One month later about eight hundred Vietnamese men were rounded up and shot dead at Chrui Changvar (Corfield 1994, 68, 96). Arson and rape were widespread, and the government actively contributed to the mayhem by ordering the closure of all private schools, most of which were Catholic and serving pupils of Vietnamese origin.

14. Adopted at a congress in Peking on 3 May 1970.

15. BAC/02.

16. For example, Phath Chhavny (D16013) reported Lon Nol spies in his pagoda, Wat Srah Reangsey, in the period 1972–1973.

17. Lon Nol government intelligence report L01700, dated December 1972. The two other intelligence reports were made by Ven. Serei Tos, from Sangke district (L01698, undated; but L07377, a copy of this document, is dated 21.12.72), and Ven. But Ngoy, also from Sangke district (L01699, undated).

18. BAC/04; BAC/05.

19. The Cambodian Buddhist *saṅgha* has, since the late 1860s, been divided into two monastic fraternities, the smaller, urban and more elitist Thommayut and the larger, predominantly rural Mahanikay. There is no disagreement between the two on matters of doctrine but they differ in their attitude toward certain aspects of monastic ritual.

20. Huot Tat (1891–1975) was born at Psar Oudong, Kampong Speu province, and entered the religious life when he was seven years of age. He succeeded Chuon Nath as Mahanikay chief monk on 25 September 1969 and was executed by the Khmer Rouge soon after they took Phnom Penh on 17 April 1975. See "Biographie de son éminence Samdech Preah Pothiveang Huot Tat," *Le Sangkum* 13 (August 1966), 25–30.

21. Tep Loeung (1883–1975) came from Kirivong district, Takeo province. He was ordained in 1904 and eventually settled at Wat Botum Vaddei, Phnom Penh. He undertook higher Buddhist studies in Thailand and was appointed *cau adhikār* (chief monk) of Wat Nuon Moniram, Phnom Penh, in 1928. On 28 April 1966 he succeeded Ven. Phul Tes as temporary Thommayut patriarch and ascended to the rank of *samtec saṅgharāja* (His Excellency, king of the *saṅgha*) in 1970. He died of natural causes on 15 April 1975, two days before the Khmer Rouge takeover. See "Samdech Preah Sudhamma Thipati Preah Saṅghanayok de l'ordre Dhammayutti Gandharo Tep-Luong," *Le Sangkum* 19 (February 1967), 23–30.

22. Dated 20 May 1970, the statement appeared in *Cambodge Nouveau* 1970b.

23. In my view the notion of "excommunication" makes no real sense and holds no precise meaning in the Theravāda Buddhist tradition. Sihanouk seems to agree that "excommunication" is incompatible with Buddhist traditions, yet he did, nevertheless, call on Huot Tat to "excommunicate" Lon Nol and his followers (Norodom Sihanouk 1970, 16).

24. This may have been an example of political naïveté, for several months later Huot Tat was striving for impartiality in a letter he wrote to all parties, urging reconciliation (Corfield 1994, 169). In 1973, in a feeble attempt to assuage monastic criticism, the government abolished the title of *samtec* for civilians. Henceforth it would be a purely monastic title (Martin 1994, 141).

25. The relevant Lon Nol government intelligence reports from this period are L03581, dated 10.6.71; L03582, dated 23.6.71; and L03583, dated 25.6.71, which contains details of Ven. Nget Tuon's interrogation.

26. At the end of his interrogation, Nget Tuon was disrobed and forced to join the Lon Nol army. It seems that Bunchhan Mul, Huot Tat, and other named individuals were involved in the decision to make Nget Tuon do this.

27. Chandler (1999, 99) feels that the monks may have been soldiers in disguise. This seems odd to me. Sihanouk had spent two short periods in robes and, as the constitutional protector of Buddhism, could be expected to be able to identify someone masquerading as a monk.

28. Khieu Chum wrote an autobiography, a relatively rare Cambodian genre at the time it was composed. See Khieu Chum (Khīev Juṃ), *Jīv pravatti nai dhammapālo bhikkhu khīev juṃ* (Autobiography of Dhammapalo Bhikkhu Khieu

Chum), the appendix to *Buddhavidyā rīoeṅ puṇy-pāp* (Buddha's knowledge of merit and demerit) (Phnom Penh: Trai rat(n), 1967). For further information on Khieu Chum's career, see Harris 2008.

29. *Manifesto of the Committee of Intellectuals for the Support of the Salvation Government,* 18 March 1970, quoted in Edwards 1999, 387.

30. Commenting on the rapid turnover in government ranks, Son Ngoc Thanh said, "These changes may be a little hard for Westerners to understand. The Khmer revolution is not like Western politics, it is not strictly logical, it is more like a complex piece of Angkor sculpture that unfolds slowly to the viewer" (quoted in Slocomb 2006, 383). Khieu Chum brokered the resignation of Son Ngoc Thanh as prime minister following demonstrations and a bombing some months later. The latter stood down from office to make way for Long Boret the morning after a long conversation with Khieu Chum at Wat Langka.

31. His significant post-1970 works are *Buddhasāsanā prajādhipateyy sādhāraṇaraṭṭh* (Buddhism, democracy, and republic; 1971) *Prajādhipateyy cās' duṃ* (Ancient democracy; 1972); and *Sakal cintā gaṃnit srāv jrāv* (Universal mind: Thoughts for research; 1972).

32. Sometime after Hem Chieu's death in prison, around mid-March 1945, his co-accused—Nuon Duong, Pach Chhoeun, and Bunchhan Mul—were released from Poulo Condore. When they crossed into Cambodia, they were met by a delegation of friends that included Pang Khat (Bunchhan Mul 1971).

33. Also see *Cambodge Nouveau* 1970c, 23.

34. Heng Mengly, a Phnom Penh–based monk, claimed that some monks held demonstrations (no date provided) against Lon Nol and that Huot Tat was obliged to organize a meeting to deal with their grievances (D16140).

35. The article also contained a table indicating monks killed, injured, and arrested by VC/NV from 18 March 1970 to 30 June 1972 on a province-by-province basis (Dik Keam 1972, 26).

36. See *Khmer Republic* 1971b; Ministère de l'Information 1971, 53; and Thach Saret 1971, 17–18.

37. *Cambodge Nouveau* 1972. Also see Sak Sutsakhan 1980, 112.

38. See *Koḥ Santibhāb* 1972a, 1972c. Also see *Nokor Thom* 1972.

39. BAC/21.

40. BAC/03; BAC/04.

41. BAC/34. In the south of the country, pagodas in the vicinity of Kampong Trach were used by both sides (DC-Cam 2004 [K07478]). A late 1973 Lon Nol government intelligence report (L04365) also describes an enemy plan to attack the National Army base at Wat Svay Meas, Kandal province.

42. A monk who had been studying at Wat Unnalom in the early 1970s reported that many of his colleagues talked about the policies of the revolutionaries and some argued that they should be given the support of the *saṅgha* (BAC/08).

43. His letter also pointed out that the only teachers still active in rural areas were monks, some of whom were very experienced, for everyone else had run away to the city (*Rāstracakr* 1972b).

44. One of these, a monk named Om Mam Prum Mani, claimed to be an incarnation of Jayavarman VII (Chandler 1991, 205). By 1972 Lon Nol is said to have been spending around US$20,000 a month on astrological consultations (Corfield 1994, 41). However, not everyone benefited from these indulgences. Fifty-five of the hundred-odd people held under arrest in Queen Kossamak's house in March 1973 were astrologers who had rather unwisely predicted the overthrow of Lon Nol before the end of April 1972 (Lee 1976, 455).

## CHAPTER TWO: Buddhism and the Origins of Cambodian Communism

1. Like so many Khmer words, "Issarak" derives from a Pāli term, in this case *issara* (lord, master, or chief). A Khmer Issarak (Independence) movement had been founded with Thai government support in Bangkok in 1940. A very loose alliance of different groups, the Issaraks eventually split into two camps. One was leftist in orientation and in due course morphed into the United Issarak Front and finally into the Communist Party of Kampuchea. The second, the Khmer Serei (Free Khmer), was antimonarchist and republican and was associated with Son Ngoc Thanh.

2. Sihanouk, for example, mentions that Son Ngoc Minh was the leader of a mixed group of communist auxiliaries recruited in Cochinchina but admits to being unsure of who he is. Son Ngoc Minh may have been involved in an incident on 12 April 1954 when a mixed Vietminh/Khmer-Vietminh detachment massacred around one hundred passengers on a train from Phnom Penh to Battambang, including some thirty monks (Norodom Sihanouk 1958, 194, 199).

3. BAC/38.

4. Son Ngoc Minh and Tou Samouth had been the only two Khmer on an ICP body called the All Cambodia Special Ad Hoc Committee. Son Ngoc Minh had previously chaired the National Liberation Committee, while Tou Samouth was responsible for the Issarak Association (Heder 2004, 25).

5. One of my informants, Chea Sot, had joined Tou Samouth as his secretary in 1948. At this point the latter had already disrobed. Chea Sot first met Son Ngoc Minh in 1951, becoming his secretary soon after (BAC/38). Also see Heder 1983.

6. A photograph of the monks attending the meeting may be found in Christian 1952.

7. Also known as the Khmer People's Revolutionary Party.

8. VWP Telegram of June 1952 (quoted in Heder 1979b, 2). It also seems that the Vietnamese, drawing on Lenin's *Left-Wing Communism: An Infantile Disorder,* classed the Cambodian revolution as infantile. See Nuon Chea 1987.

9. The Vietnamese had maintained monastic contacts in Cambodia in the hope that those contacts would come up with concrete support for the struggle, but by the time of the split, the Vietnamese had become disillusioned. As a Viet Minh Committee for Phnom Penh document intercepted by the French and dated 11 September 1951 peevishly notes, "Contrary to what they promised us, the monks have not yet presented any Cambodian candidates [for the movement]" (quoted in Kiernan 1981, 167).

10. Prom Samith and Nuon Chea, who eventually became deputy secretary of the Communist Party of Kampuchea, were among the select group of the "best and brightest" Khmer revolutionaries to relocate to northern Vietnam following the Geneva Agreements of 1954 (Engelbert and Goscha 1995, 47). Nuon Chea returned to Cambodia soon afterward. Chea Sim, who claimed to have joined the revolution in 1948, had also been a monk, firstly in Svay Rieng and subsequently at Wat Unnalom (1952–1954). He seems to have met Tou Samouth and Chea Soth around this time (Kiernan 2007, 63).

11. The crucial role of the Khmer Krom Buddhists in the Vietnamese liberation movement is illustrated by the example of Huynh Cuong. He was the secretary of the Cochinchina Khmer Buddhist Association from 1943 and graduated from the Buddhist Institute in 1945. Later he worked as an inspector of Pāli schools in the western Mekong Delta before gaining election to the National Liberation Front Central Committee in 1962 (Kiernan 1985, 24).

12. The quotations are from Kiernan 1985, 93.

13. On the cordial relations between monks and the Issarak movement, see Pok and Moorthy 1998, in which a senior monk from Wat Mohamontrei, Phnom Penh, is quoted as claiming, "If anyone was going to be killed for being a French spy, and if the monks knew about that, the monks would successfully request the pardon from the Issarak to release that person."

14. Kong Sophal's brother, Kong Sophear, subsequently compiled a popular biography of Hem Chieu, titled *Achar Hem Chiev* (Phnom Penh: Bannalay Niseut, 1972).

15. See Kiernan 1975.

16. Y144, DC-Cam.

17. Nuon Chea (also known as Long Bunruot and Runglert Laodi) may have spent some time as a Buddhist monk. He certainly resided at Wat Benjamabopit when he first arrived in Bangkok, in 1942, to study (Murashima 2009).

18. Saloth Sar's "Buddhist upbringing and calm, unruffled manner" may have won Tou Samouth's confidence (Short 2004, 100).

19. Pol Pot has sometimes been accused of murdering Tou Samouth, but this seems unlikely. The latter was probably executed by Sihanouk's secret police. In an interview with Nate Thayer (1997a), Pol Pot vehemently denied that he had any involvement in Tou Samouth's death.

20. Nuon Chea and Sao Phim were important exceptions (David Chandler, pers. comm., 2006).

21. In 1971, for example, Nuon Chea issued an order calling for the execution of anyone connected with Son Ngoc Minh. See DC-Cam 1996b.

22. DC-Cam 1996b. Saloth Sar's home village of Prek Sbauv, Kampong Thom province, did not have a monastery, although there was one upriver. Surprisingly, given the generally poor rural coverage of the order, it belonged to the Thommayut.

23. Norodom Sihanouk's (1980, 155) claim that "the most fanatic Khmer Rouge soldiers were from the mountain and forest regions" combines the primordial fear of wilderness with terror of the Khmer Rouge, whose executions tended to happen

at night, a time traditionally connected with danger, disorder, lack of civilization, and violence. Keyes (2006, 17) also notes that Thai communist insurgents of the 1960s called themselves "forest fighters" (*tahan pa*) for the same reasons. He argues that both Thai and Cambodian communist revolutionaries, unlike at least some in the Communist Party of Vietnam, failed to understand the moral and mythological universe of the rural people they claimed to represent.

24. In a 1991 interview, Chea Sim told Ben Kiernan that "Pol Pot was a kindly person, simple, with a mass view" and that "people would praise him as the kindliest person of all" (quoted in Kiernan 2007, 76).

25. See Stuart-Fox (1996, 80) on the use of ceremonial fans in Laos.

26. For further relevant details of Son Sen's biography, see BAC/28; BAC/29; and Heder 2004, 46. On King Monivong's establishment of the Tripiṭaka Commission in 1929, see Harris 2005a, 120.

27. Ta Mok was also known as Chhit Chhoeun, Eang Eng, and Nguon Kang.

28. Nget Kheng, a fellow monk from the same village, remembered that at that time Ta Mok was very gentle; he would never even slaughter a fish or a chicken. See Sann 2000.

29. For further biographical details, see DC-Cam n.d. (PAT [Promoting Team Accountability] Reports TKI09714 and TKI0079).

30. Thayer 1997b. I have arrived at the date of 1942 by extrapolating from information volunteered in this interview.

31. He seems to have commanded groups in both Kong Pisei district of Kampong Speu and his home district of Tram Kak.

32. See Heder 1999.

33. Chandler (2000, 89) notes that autobiographical writing was rare and had a low literary status before Democratic Kampuchea, when the self-critical life story (*pravattirup*) became a key element in the work of S-21.

34. Chandler et al. 1988, 234. Also see Chandler 2000, 64–65.

35. For information on a number of other senior leftists with early links to the *saṅgha*—such as Koy Thuon (1933–1977), northern zone secretary from 1965 to 1975, and Meah Mut, a monk from Wat Langka who eventually rose to become the effective commander of the Khmer Rouge navy—see Harris 2007, 88–91.

36. Wats Unnalom, Langka, Prochumvong, Kamsam, and Stung Slot are mentioned in the relevant documentation. See J.913, a manuscript with a rogue class mark in the DC-Cam cataloguing system.

37. L0749, a Lon Nol government intelligence report dating from the civil war period.

38. J.913. This group needs to be distinguished from an earlier movement with the same name that was active in the Mekong Delta region in the early 1960s. The earlier group was named after the printed magical devices worn by its members for protection and associated with a monk called Samouk Seng, who had connections with various wizards and healers in the Seven Mountains (Thất Sơn) area to the south of Châu Đốc. In 1961 the White Scarves changed their name to the Struggle Front of the Khmer of Kampuchea Krom. See Harris 2009, 110–111.

39. L0140, a Lon Nol government intelligence report.
40. The Khmaer Sa appear to have been active in Chhlong district and the area immediately to the south of Kratie town but were also operating in Kampong Svay district, Kampong Thom province, and they may have had their origins in Stoung district, around San Chikor. My Samedy (2000, 200) reports that the White Khmer had fifty armed personnel who planned to attack a Khmer Rouge office at Kampong Trabek district in early January 1978. Khmer Rouge subsequently came from Takeo to kill anyone they suspected of supporting Chan Chakrei (BAC/12; BAC/16), and the White Khmer "soon died out" (An Rasmey 2004, 27).
41. Supposed associates of Chakrei were quickly hunted down. Achar Kang, whom the Khmer Rouge suspected of being chief of the Khmer Serei in the Southwestern Zone, was personally arrested by Ta Mok and sent to S-21 on 2 October 1976, and Meah Mut, chief of Military Division 164, was subsequently ordered by Son Sen to track down Achar Kang's wife (Ea 2005, 125–126). It seems that Meah Mut, Achar Kang, and the otherwise unknown Achar Rot, among others, had all been part of a communist monks' cell active at Wat Langka and Wat Koh. They entered the Party in March 1968.
42. Before becoming editor of *Pracheachon* (*Prajājan*) in the mid-1950s, Chou Chet (ca. 1926–1978) had been a Buddhist monk, first in his home village of Banteay Thmei, Kampong Cham, then at Wat Rokakong, Kandal, and finally at Wat Keo Preah Phloeung, Phnom Penh (Kane 2007, 92). He fled Wat Keo Preah Phloeung with a number of like-minded monks, including Tou Samouth, soon after the US bombing of Phnom Penh on 7 February 1945. Immediately before the fall of Phnom Penh in April 1975 he was responsible for the communists' Religious Affairs, a role described by Short (2004, 305) as a "ghost portfolio." Subsequently becoming secretary of the Western Zone, Chou Chet was arrested in March 1978 and executed several months later.

## CHAPTER THREE: Buddhism and Khmer Communism

1. Duch was also known as Kang Kek Ieu, Ta Pin, and Hong Pen. After being baptized an evangelical Christian in the Sangke River, Battambang, on 6 January 1996 by Cambodian-born pastor Christopher LaPel, Duch admitted to his involvement at Tuol Sleng. Pastor LaPel claims that he first met Duch in 1995 when the latter attended a two-week Christian leadership seminar in Chamkar Samrong village. Duch went on to establish a church in his village of Ruluoh, Svay Check district, and worked for at least two nongovernmental organizations, the American Refugee Committee and the Christian-based World Vision, both of which were impressed by his commitment and efficiency (Dunlop 1999). For biographies of Duch, see Chandler 2000, 20ff.; and Dunlop 2005. Duch was found guilty of crimes against humanity, torture, and murder and sentenced to thirty-five years' imprisonment on 26 July 2010. The sentence was subsequently adjusted to take account of his eleven years in pretrial detention. A controversial

five-year deduction was also made because the detention period exceeded the maximum allowed under Cambodian law.

2. While a high proportion of males traditionally entered the *saṅgha* at some point in their lives, only a small minority of the population ever entered the CPK. There are clearly other differences; Buddhism, for example, is more tolerant of those who do not embrace its ideals.

3. Comprising trousers, shirt, cap, scarf (*kramā*), sandals, and bag.

4. AOM, Indo/RSC/675, dated 22 June 1943, quoted in Locard 2005, 32.

5. For a contemporary, yet critical, response to the accusation that "monks are leeches," see Thach Saret 1971.

6. Saloth Sar 1952, 357–361. Khieu Samphan, a fellow Paris-based student and important member of the CPK, was still calling Cambodia a "Buddhist country" in 1959 (ibid., 103).

7. With regard to the more general issue of French intellectual influence on the Khmer Rouge, Khieu Samphan is reported to have said, "Prime Minister Pol Pot and I were profoundly influenced by the spirit of French thought—by the Age of Enlightenment, of Rousseau and Montesquieu" (*Le Monde,* 31 December 1998).

8. For a contemporary survey of the territory, see Benz 1965. In 1956, *New Age,* the journal of the Communist Party of India, published a series of articles by Rahul Sankrityayan and others, seeking to explain the compatibility between Buddhism and communism (Gard 1962, 63).

9. Such contentious visions of Buddhism were bound to come under challenge. In the 1950s the Yahan Byo Ahpwe (Young Monks' Association) was a focus for opposition to communism, and one of its prominent members, U Kethaya—also known as "the American *pongyi* [monk]"—wrote a number of pamphlets on the topic, funded by the Ford Foundation (D. E. Smith 1965, 301–302). See, for example, his *Proclamation on the Subject of Dangers to the Buddhist Religion by the Headquarters of the All Burma Young Monks Association* [in Burmese] (Mandalay: Pitaka Electric Press, 1959).

10. See, for example, *Panya* (Intellect) (Phranakhon: Samnakphim Ruamsan, 1954) and *Witthaya sat mai lœ Phra Sìan* (The new science and Mettaya Buddha) (Phranakhon: Phræphittaya, 1970).

11. Its Thai title is *Kwampen 'anitchang khong sangkhom.* For a discussion of the work, see Morell and Morell 1972.

12. The five principles were mutual respect for one another's territorial integrity and sovereignty, mutual nonaggression, mutual noninterference in domestic affairs, equality and mutual benefit, and peaceful coexistence. Also mentioned in Norodom Sihanouk 1958, 202.

13. While on a visit to China, Pol Pot said that "Comrade Mao Tse-tung's works and the experience of the Chinese (cultural) revolution played an important role at that time" (*FBIS [Foreign Broadcast Information Service] Daily Report—People's Republic of China,* vol. 1, 3 October 1977, A20–A21). Some internal sources referred to the Cambodian revolution as a "Super Great Leap Forward."

14. The policy was implemented in Democratic Kampuchea. Money was reintroduced by the PRK on 25 March 1980 (Kiernan 1982, 173). For a detailed treatment of the social, economic, and political consequences of the early stages of Vietnamese occupation, see Heder 1980.

15. Significant differences also existed between a largely nonbureaucratic, Indian-derived, Khmer attitude toward governance and the Vietnamese orientation toward managerialism deriving from Confucian sources (Newman 1978, 20–22).

16. Nuon Chea was in this region at the time.

17. In Harris 2010, I attempt to argue that the "emptying" of Phnom Penh had a religious and ritual significance.

18. Mak Phœun (2003, 53–54) also provides two 1972 Khmer Rouge statements that appear to give some support to Buddhist monks. The first indicates that nothing should be done against the liberty of the cult, while the other argues that monks cannot be regarded as traitors because the latter kill and pillage, acts that are entirely contrary to the discipline of the Buddha.

19. Vorn Vet, also known as Sok Thouk, became the minister in charge of industry, fisheries, and railways in October 1975. Eventually he rose to the rank of deputy prime minister before being executed in 1978.

20. "Confession of Bam Oeun," an S-21 confession held at DC-Cam with the classmark D00215, quoted by Ea 2005, 5n35.

21. Lon Nol government intelligence report L07175.

22. D16129 (Chhun Chim).

23. Quoted in Norodom Sihanouk 1980, 49.

24. L00682, dated 28 November 1974, detailing the interrogation of Ven. Vong Sarin, the former *cau adhikār* of Wat Traeuy Sla, Sa-ang district.

25. L02439.

26. L02457, dated 6 July 1974.

27. D16131. For additional assertions that "the Buddha was a foreigner," see Mak Phœun 2003, 61. Ponchaud (1990, 234) maintains that the Khmer Rouge (like the French before them) were especially hostile to Cambodian Buddhist links with Thailand.

28. L07193. There was some basis in the belief that the United States was manipulating Southeast Asian Buddhists as part of its anticommunist crusade. See Operations Coordinating Board 1957.

29. L04260; L04274.

30. Also see Mak Phœun 2003, 51.

31. *FBIS Daily Report—Asia and Pacific,* 6 January 1976, H1–H9. The 1954 Chinese Constitution similarly states that "every citizen of the People's Republic of China (PRC) shall have freedom of religious belief," but the starting point here is that the majority should be free not to believe. Freedom of belief, then, is a minority right, and minorities are not expected to interfere in the rights of the majority. In the PRC, the term "religion" is interpreted in the strict sense of ritual, doctrine, and belief. As such, the prophetic role of religion is most definitely ruled out (Yu 1987, 373) and comes under the legal heading of counterreligious activity.

32. From the late 1960s on, both Pol Pot and Ieng Sary employed tribal bodyguards

from the Jarai and Tampuon peoples. They were regarded as particularly faithful to the revolution (Kiernan 1996, 302).

33. Also see Hinton 2005, 84. The song may have been composed sometime before 1975. The blood motif was preserved in the national anthem of PRK, which included the words "the blood-red flag with the towers [of Angkor Wat] is raised and will lead the nation to happiness and prosperity" (Ministère de l'Information de la Presse 1979, 9–10).

34. This is my interpretation of the previously quoted term "good."

35. The most explicit hints come from Hinton (2002, 71), who suggests, "The actions and ideology of the Democratic Kampuchea regime seem to draw heavily on pre-existing forms of cultural knowledge. . . . The Khmer Rouge leaders were also inspired by traditional conceptions of purity, particularly the idea of the universal monarch who, because of his moral superiority and enlightenment, is able to purify society by bringing order and coherence." More recently Hinton (2005, 126) has described the Khmer Rouge's "high-modernist authoritarianism" as having been colored by local categories.

36. Minutes of CPK Standing Committee meeting, 1 June 1976, quoted in Short 2004, 324.

37. Kiernan is quoting Simon Leys' (1986, 165–166) characterization of the Chinese Cultural Revolution leadership.

38. Keng Vannsak, for example, had "embraced an obscure quasi-Buddhist doctrine called ascetology, founded by a paralysed French academic, Dr Gorelle, in the belief that it would help him control his sexual desires at a time when the struggle for independence was paramount" (Short 2004, 59).

39. As in the slogan "Everyone must rely only on oneself" (*khluon dī bịn khluon*) (Locard 1996, 56). On parallels with the North Korean concept of self-reliance/ self-determination (*chuch'e*), see Kiernan 2006, 199. By the mid-1950s, *chuch'e* was seen as a creative and specifically North Korean modification of Marxism-Leninism. It underpinned the regime's insistence on Spartan austerity, sacrifice, discipline, and so forth and was regarded as an almost spiritual foundation of Kim Il Sung's rule to the extent that, by the 1970s, *chuch'e* was called Kim Il Sungism.

40. This is an explicit reference to the very popular *Vessantara Jātaka,* an account of the future Buddha's penultimate life in which he gives away his royal elephant, his kingdom, and his wife and children in an effort to perfect the important virtue of generosity. For an extended discussion of the mythicopolitical significance of this text, see S. Collins 1998, 497–554.

41. Radio Phnom Penh, 24 January 1976, in BBC Summary of World Broadcasts FE5117/B/1–2.

42. The practice of burying an offender in earth up to his or her neck for a period of time is also attested in Thai and Burmese traditional law texts. See Manu (1874), 11, as quoted in Huxley 1991, 344n13. On the concept of "disproportionate revenge," see Hinton 1997, 233.

43. Communist Party of Kampuchea Central Committee 1976 (Sos and Jackson 1989 translation, 287). Other examples of Khmer Rouge terminology revealing

appropriation of traditional Buddhist terms include *mārgā nayopāy,* "policy line" (original meaning of *mārgā:* "path"); *mitt,* "comrade" (original meaning: "friend"); and *vaṇṇa,* "social class" (original meaning: "caste"). For more detailed discussion, see Carney 1977, 65–77; Marston 1997, 163; and Hinton 2005, 145.

44. Communist Party of Kampuchea Central Committee 1978 (Sos and Jackson 1989 translation, 294). In Thailand at approximately the same time, Phraya Anuman Rajadhon was using the symbol of the stupa as an analogy for the hierarchical structure of traditional Thai society, with the king in the dewdrop at its highest point (Suwanna Satha-Anand 2006, 174–175, 180).

45. Parallel experiments had been made by Mao. It also seems unlikely that notions of class war and anticapitalism had any great appeal in Vietnam (Bayly 2000, 612–613).

46. This strategy was also employed by the Mongolian Communist Party in the late 1920s. See Sarkisyanz 1958, 626. The precepts, both negative and positive, are listed in Yang Sam 1987, 70. The set does not appear to be fixed. Huy Vannak (2003, 17) gives a list of the twelve moral precepts (*sīladhamm dāṁn dap' bīr pakārah*). Ith Sarin, an inspector of primary education who spent time in the maquis as a candidate Party member throughout most of 1972, however, gives fifteen:
    1. Be modest and simple to the people.
    2. Don't take bribes.
    3. Beg pardon of the people for any wrongs.
    4. Behave in a refined unobtrusive manner following the traditions of the people.
    5. Don't go beyond bounds of propriety with women.
    6. Don't drink.
    7. Don't gamble.
    8. Don't touch money, property of the people, or of Angkar.
    9. Have a burning rage towards the enemy.
    10. Engage in manual work.
    11. Work well with colleagues.
    12. Constructively conduct criticism and self-criticism sessions.
    13. Don't depend on others, foreigners in particular, to make the revolution.
    14. Maintain the image of mastery of the task at hand.
    15. Realize that though the task may be difficult, the struggle will be victorious.
    (Carney 1977, 50–51, quoting from Ith Sarin 1973)

47. *FBIS Daily Report—Asia Pacific,* 6 January 1975, H1–H9. Khieu Samphan appears to have been a particularly ascetic figure. For a general, though fundamentally Eurocentric, discussion of revolutionary asceticism, see Mazlish 1976.

48. D02123, an S-21 confession held at DC-Cam.

49. BAC/08.

50. Hinton 2002, 70, quoting Marston 1994, 110.

51. *Cpāp'* were mainly composed by monks and are part of the basic curriculum of monastic education. On the contrast between the "practical" or "ritual" canon and the "formal canon" in Sri Lanka, see Blackburn 1999.

52. It is worth noting that the meaning of the term *cakrabatra* has migrated a good deal in modern Khmer. Traditionally it referred to a righteous Buddhist king (Pāli *cakkavatti*). Since the Democratic Kampuchea period, it has connoted "imperialist."

53. It is, perhaps, no coincidence that the revolutionary saying "We strive to become our own masters step by step" (quoted in Chandler et al. 1988, 96) is surprisingly similar to the message taught by the famous Cambodian monk-activist Mahaghosananda in the 1990s.

54. Marston 1997, 168–169, quoting from Picq. That the leaders of the regime remained unidentified for far longer than security considerations required may also be connected to the idea of self-abnegation.

55. The pseudonym "Ho Chi Minh" meant "he who enlightens" (Duiker 2000, 248). Part of this name was borrowed by the founder of the Cambodian communist movement, Son Ngoc Minh. For a discussion of the etymology of Angkar, see Hinton 2005, 127–128. For "enlightenment" in the Khmer Rouge context, see ibid., 132.

56. Communist Party of Kampuchea Central Committee 1977a (Heder translation, 19).

57. Communist Party of Kampuchea Central Committee 1977b (Heder translation, 18).

58. *FBIS Daily Report—Asia Pacific,* 6 January 1975, 1–9. Martin (1981, 17) supplies illuminating diagrams of Cambodian rice-field boundaries before and after the arrival of the Khmer Rouge. Chea Sim claims that Angkar's "offensive to raise earthworks," in which vast areas of land were turned into a checkerboard of precisely measured rice fields, was initiated on 1 January 1976 (Kiernan 2007, 75).

59. An obvious objection here is that this vision is a feature of Mahayanist texts, like the *Sukhāvativyuha Sūtra,* and entirely inappropriate in the Cambodian Theravāda context. In response one might point to the work of Bizot, who has convincingly argued for the presence of "Mahayanist" elements in certain of the unreformed Buddhist practices that flourished before the Democratic Kampuchea period.

60. Ritual suicide and probable human sacrifice were linked to goddess cults practiced in the Indian Pallava kingdom of the seventh through the ninth centuries. It is possible that such rites were exported to Cambodia. The last human sacrifice there took place at Ba Phnom in April or May 1877, when two prisoners of war were beheaded during a royally sponsored ceremony of "raising up the ancestors" (*loeṅ anak tā*), a festival still held in a highly modified form at the beginning of each growing season. It is significant that the rite occurred in *bisākh.* That month is sacred to Kālī, the Brahmanical deity most particularly associated with *anak tā* Me Sa, the "white mother" of Ba Phnom (Chandler 1974). The human sacrifice of a criminal seems to have occurred annually at a site on the northeastern slope of the mountain. Evidence also suggests that Buddhist monks based at nearby Wat Vihear Thom were involved in a number of unspecified prayer rituals, including prayers for the dead, during the first few days of the rite. However, they withdrew some time before the coup de grâce on the final day, a Saturday. The direction that blood spurted from the severed neck was used to predict the nature of the coming rains. Ritual decapitation is also attested in two other nineteenth-century

Cambodian locations, Thboung Khmum and Kampong Svay, where appanage chiefs (*stec trāñ*) established their initial authority through the performance of a human sacrifice (Leclère 1894, 194; Porée-Maspero 1962–1969, 1:246–248).

61. The charge of nihilism has been leveled at Buddhism by Western philosophers and theologians since the time of Schopenhauer.

62. In Democratic Kampuchea the term *kasāng,* usually translated as "to build," was often employed in the context of "building up socialism." But Marston (1994, 113–114) has shown that *kasāng* had a dual meaning. It signified both "to build up" and "to tear down."

## CHAPTER FOUR: Dealing with Monks

1. BAC/45.
2. BAC/14.
3. BAC/59.
4. BAC/24.
5. BAC/07.
6. BAC/50.
7. BAC/64.
8. BAC/53.
9. Wat Prey Koki, Chan Trea district, was liberated in 1972, and the monks had no further contact with the country's ecclesiastic hierarchy in Phnom Penh after that time. Nevertheless, in contrast to the experience of monks at most other *wat*s, they "lived normally until final victory" in April 1975 (D16139). Also see BAC/46, BAC/56, and BAC/62.
10. Lon Nol government intelligence report L0612.
11. BAC/02.
12. D16014.
13. BAC/03.
14. An interviewee from Wat Athikaram (Wat Thmei), Kuk Cho subdistrict, Siem Reap, also recalled being invited to a festival at Angkor Wat four days after the Khmer Rouge took over. He was transported there by truck with thirty-six others. They were all shot. He was hit five times but survived (DC-Cam 1995).
15. D16116.
16. D16122.
17. Kratie and Stung Treng provinces are regarded as the safest places to have lived during the Democratic Kampuchea period, and this circumstance affected the general treatment of Buddhism there. To give two illustrations: Wat Roka Kandal, near Kratie town, was allowed to select a new *cau adhikār,* Kru Khan, when its old chief monk, Ven. Srei Ou, died in 1973 (BAC/16). And Ven. Keo Savann, the last *cau adhikār* of Wat Chey Mongkul, Sesan district, Stung Treng, was appointed as late as 1976 (BAC/63).
18. L04700.
19. L04710.

20. L03583. Kiernan (1985, 346) claims that Ta Mok made a first call for monks to disrobe and join his army at a meeting of more than three thousand monks in Kampong Chhnang.
21. L03207.
22. L05448. *Wat*-based meetings were clearly very common. One Khmer Republic intelligence report relates that in November 1973 around three hundred people attended a learning strategy meeting at Wat Trapeang Po, Kampot province. The teacher was thirty-year-old Pov, a "Khmer from Hanoi." Two weeks later a similar session was held at Wat Pang Kruos in Kampong Chhnang province (L04103).
23. Another abbot appears to have confirmed these sentiments when he referred to the "yoke of the demon Lon Nol" (Thion 1993, 14). In early 1973 a man confessed to having attended a revolutionary meeting of the army, laypeople, and monks. The attendance, mainly consisting of people from Phnom Penh, was very large; the intelligence report mentions the remarkable figure of forty thousand, including six hundred monks (L02638).
24. According to Yang Sam (1987, 60), three basic kinds of committees were formed by the monk association chapters:
    1. social affairs: to ensure monks engaged in mutual criticism sessions
    2. economic affairs: to ensure monks produced their own food and donated surpluses to troops on the front line
    3. cultural affairs: to ensure monks received communist propaganda
25. L07290.
26. D16132.
27. L07267.
28. I am grateful to Steve Heder for alerting me to this document, held at DC-Cam with a classmark of O106.941Th.
29. Sao Sophal's activities as a propagandist of monks are also mentioned in a Lon Nol–period intelligence report of 24 October 1974 (L02888).
30. L00682. That this was not an isolated event is confirmed by L01918, a Lon Nol intelligence report dated 17 July 1974, about the situation in Kampong Cham.
31. It seems that many of the revolutionary monks active in this area came from Romeas Hek in Prey Veng province. A flavor of the hostility and fear evoked by monks working for the Khmer Rouge is given in the account of Ven. Om Tit. When he arrived in the country he recognized some monks who had previously been given responsible roles by the communists, but they refused to acknowledge him (D16121).
32. BAC/37.
33. BAC/02.
34. BAC/03; BAC/04. It seems that Try ordered a certain Dong to kill a man named Chheuy (BAC/03).
35. Ven. Uk Mut became the *megan* of Battambang province after the PRK period. After 1979 he was the *cau adhikār* of Wat Kdol before moving to Wats Slaket and Bo Knong. At the time of writing, he was based at Wat Po Veal. When I

asked Uk Mut about Try, he was reluctant to say much beyond that Try sometimes "re-educated monks who misbehaved" (BAC/06).

36. E.g., L00676.
37. BAC/54.
38. BAC/56.
39. D16016. A Lon Nol government intelligence report (L00229) from the same period suggests that unidentified senior front monks at both the district and provincial levels carried pistols or had bodyguards with AK-47s. Also see L02479, L00676, and L00601.
40. BAC/19.
41. L00546.
42. L00586.
43. D16130. This document also mentions a visit of Hon, Heng, and Dem Khon to Wat Sokan, Bakan district, where they ordered monks to evacuate.
44. BAC/08.
45. Also see D16130.
46. BAC/01.
47. BAC/03. According to a document on the history of Wat Norea during Democratic Kampuchea (one of the few such documents I have found), the pagoda became a base for Lon Nol soldiers early in the civil war period. Although there was fighting nearby between 1970 and 1974, the *wat* remained safe. Indeed, the *cau adhikār,* Ven. Tes Thang, and a number of lay devotees were making plans to build a new *brah vihāra.* But in 1975 the fighting intensified. All of the area's monks, who had by now congregated at Wat Samraong Knong, fled the fighting and went to Wat Pothi Knong. Three days after 17 April 1975 the entire population was ordered out of Battambang town. The *cau adhikār* of Wat Samraong Knong and a party of other monks—including Thon Rom, Thun Sovan, Chhit Ruom, and Ven. Ngin Phlek, deputy chief monk of Sangke district—were sent back to Wat Samraong Knong and forced into laboring at cultivation and dam building. They were placed under the control of a *ganah sangh* with a gun. At a later point they were forced to disrobe, and by April 1976 there were no monks left at the *wat* (Huot Robiep 2004, 2).
48. D16117.
49. BAC/04.
50. D16141.
51. BAC/02.
52. L07675.
53. L07210.
54. L00715.
55. L00614.
56. BAC/56.
57. L01918.
58. BAC/03.

59. D16133
60. BAC/10.
61. D16016.
62. BAC/03.
63. BAC/01.
64. L05049.
65. DC-Cam 2004 (K07478).
66. D16141.
67. D16143.
68. D16122; D16144.
69. For a history of Khmer Buddhism in the Mekong Delta, see Harris 2009.
70. BAC/42.
71. Ponchaud (1990, 236) has argued that, unlike Chinese and Vietnamese communists, the Khmer Rouge did not really engage with the concept of "reeducation." They preferred self-criticism (*svăy didīen*), and if this did not work, there was always straightforward torture, forced confession, and extermination. Ponchaud links this difference to dissimilarities in prior religious outlook. For the Chinese and the Vietnamese, Confucianism, with its insistence on moral reformation, provides a logic for reeducation. Buddhism, on the other hand, emphasizes the doctrine of karma and the possibility of future suffering in hell. Such ideas contributed to a Khmer tendency toward violent and exemplary punishment, in the hope that this might mitigate future torments. After hearing many reports from refugees, Ponchaud concluded that "one cannot help observing a certain complicity between the executioner and his victims, each of them accepting the tragic rules of the game by which they were governed" (ibid.).
72. BAC/41.
73. BAC/46.
74. BAC/37.
75. It appears that Thach Kong was subsequently killed by the Vietnamese authorities (BAC/65).
76. The *cau adhikār* of Wat Sokha Phi, Kaoh Sampeng district, Stung Treng province, did flee to Laos, but he was a married man at that time (author's interview, 30 June 2005; regretfully, his name was not recorded). He asserted that around fifty thousand other Khmers from the province did the same, though few of them were monks.
77. BAC/59.
78. BAC/60.
79. BAC/63.
80. There are parallels between the ways in which both Lao and Thai communists approached Buddhism. The Communist Party of Thailand, for example, was not especially negative about Buddhism, although it did criticize monks alleged to have a rightist outlook (de Beer 1978, 155). Also see Yuangrat (Pattanapongse) Wedel 1981; and Morell and Morell 1972.
81. BAC/08.

82. BAC/02; BAC/08. Thai intelligence sources suggest that Sek Sam Iet became a key figure in the Khmer-controlled black market on his arrival in the country.
83. By the early 1990s some fourteen *wats* in the various border camps were housing more than four hundred monks (Peter Gyallay-Pap, pers. comm., 2002). Khao I Dang camp had a large Mahanikay pagoda, Wat Pothirot, with between forty and eighty monks and novices (Guthrie 1992, 54–55). These camps were controlled by assorted Cambodian political factions, a factor that influenced monastic affiliation. Site B contained pro-Sihanouk monks, those at Site 8 were pro–Khmer Rouge, and Site 2, which was temporarily the second-largest Khmer "city" in the world and the fourth-largest concentration of people in Thailand, contained supporters of Son Sann, one of Sihanouk's former prime ministers but by now a leader of anticommunist resistance forces.
84. DC-Cam 2004 (K07478).
85. BAC/06.
86. BAC/59.
87. BAC/63.
88. BAC/29.
89. BAC/46. For further information on Uk Rorn, also see D16139.
90. BAC/06.
91. BAC/08.
92. BAC/48. Also see Chantou Boua 1991, 234.
93. D16019.
94. BAC/01.
95. D16129.
96. D16134. Also see Chantou Boua 1991, 235.
97. D16123.
98. D16117.
99. BAC/60.
100. Sometimes monks were given the clothes of people who had recently died. See, for example, BAC/45.
101. Also see my interview with Ven. Noun Nget (ICH/07).
102. BAC/02.
103. D16124. Since Wat Mang Sala was a Thommayut pagoda, there seems no good reason to suppose that the revolutionaries treated members of this order any more harshly than their Mahanikay coreligionists. The Mahanikay is the second of Cambodia's two traditional Buddhist fraternities (*nikāya*). It is larger, more rural, and less socially elitist than the Thommayut, so one might have assumed that its members would have fared slightly better during Democratic Kampuchea.
104. BAC/63. The last *cau adhikār* of this pagoda, Ven. Keo Savann, was not appointed to his post until 1976. Informants have claimed that there was always enough food at the pagoda and that none of its monks were ever killed. Chantou Boua (1991, 235) also interviewed one monk who said he had remained in robes until January 1977.
105. BAC/03. Also see L04257.

106. D16142. When Ven. Hin Yang was evacuated from Wat Langka in Phnom Penh, he believed that it would be for only three days and that the Khmer Rouge would not disrobe him (BAC/39).
107. BAC/11.
108. D16121.
109. D16146.
110. BAC/12.
111. D16120.
112. D16130.
113. BAC/46.
114. D16126.
115. BAC/49; BAC/50.
116. BAC/42. For another account of a prison for monks, see DC-Cam 1996c, which mentions a facility at Phnom Phlov Trey, Kandal. Between 1975 and 1977 one hundred monks were held there, and only two survived, Mao Chhayavuth and his brother.
117. Some old monks were simply left alone when they refused to disrobe. They were not especially harassed, but neither was it possible for them to receive alms from villagers. A very few managed to survive until 1979, but others were not so fortunate. Because they were weak and of advanced age, their living circumstances took a toll. One of Tep Vong's old teachers, Ven. That Bin, had not been punished when he refused to leave the order. But he starved to death around February 1976. He was seventy years old (D16116). The old *cau adhikār* of Wat Norea, Ven. Prum Norm, died under similar circumstances in September 1977 at the age of seventy-six (BAC/03). He had been appointed the pagoda's chief monk in 1939.
118. D16139.
119. BAC/21. Chong Hieng was reordained in 1979 by Ven. Oum Sum and died at the age of ninety-one.
120. BAC/04.
121. This seems also to be the basis of the policy to compel Muslims to eat pork. Single members of the Cham community were also told that they should be prepared to marry non-Muslims (Ysa 2006, 109–110).
122. BAC/11.
123. D16016.
124. BAC/12.
125. BAC/52.
126. D16132.
127. ICH/10.
128. This probably happened in Svay Rieng province (D16145).
129. On the contentious issue of "Buddhist warfare," see Jerryson and Juergensmeyer 2010.
130. L00545.
131. L00639.
132. BAC/16.

133. L02457.
134. L01903. The report names them as Wat Tasas, Wat Prey Rorng, and Wat Samraong.
135. L00576. Ven. Suu, the *cau adhikār* of Wat Antung Veoun, Kratie province, also became a military commander (BAC/16).
136. BAC/49; BAC/51. These reports are confirmed by Hun Khor (DC-Cam 2004 [K07478]), who described a monks' unit formed to fight the Vietnamese. It was based at Slep Leur, Kantuot Cheung commune, Kampong Trach district.
137. L00578.

## CHAPTER FIVE: Buddhist Practice and Material Culture under the Khmer Rouge

1. A variety of Khmer Republic intelligence reports written between 1974 and 1975 confirm this fact. See Lon Nol government intelligence reports L07569, L02480, and L05970.
2. BAC/63.
3. BAC/37.
4. L06780.
5. L05549.
6. L00614; L00676; L05970.
7. L00610.
8. L06780.
9. L00709.
10. BAC/12; L00225.
11. L00685. An undated intelligence report mentions monks still active in Zone 203. They were allowed to officiate at *bhjuṃ piṇḍ,* the New Year celebration, and funerals. However, if the laity prepared food for five monks, they were expected to feed around fifteen soldiers or to donate 200 to 300 riels (L00599). A similar document mentions that half of all the donations to the *saṅgha* had to be given over to Angkar. Monks were additionally required to pay a tax of 1 riel per month (L02617).
12. L00575.
13. L00593.
14. BAC/10.
15. L00119.
16. BAC/33.
17. Also see Simon-Barouh and Yi Tan Kim Pho 1990, 100–102, 110–111.
18. Short (2004, 347) observes that Nuon Chea allowed his pious mother to maintain a Buddhist monk, "almost certainly the only practicing bonze in the country," to perform ceremonies on her behalf. I believe that there were rather more monks around than this, although their activities were less visible. There is a strange parallel here: Stalin refrained from persecuting the Georgian Orthodox Church because he was frightened of his mother, who had wanted him to become a priest!
19. BAC/33.

20. Ven. Las Lay (b. 1914) is currently a senior member of the Mahanikay hierarchy, holding the position of *brah dhammalikhit*. He was ordained at Wat Sbeng, Khum Thieu, Kandal province, at the age of twelve and moved to Phnom Penh the following year, where he subsequently came under the influence of Ven. Chuon Nath (ICH/10). Ven. Uk Mut remembered receiving nighttime invitations from relatives of the dead, asking him to perform funerary rites. He also administered traditional healings by blowing and spitting (BAC/06).

21. Also see D16143.

22. BAC/17.

23. BAC/04.

24. BAC/06.

25. BAC/08. For further examples of Buddhist practice during Democratic Kampuchea, see the secret meditations of Ven. Chhun Chim (D16129) and Ven. Pin Suen (BAC/11). Also see Locard and Mœung Sonn (1993, 192); and Simon-Barouh and Yi Tan Kim Pho 1990, 183. Boun Sokha (1979, 165) mentions an old defrocked monk in Svay Chrum district, Kampong Chhnang, who always recited his prayers in a low voice before going to bed, and Pin Yathay (1980, 38, 273), a nonpracticing Buddhist, describes his performance of a rite of protection for his son. Sihanouk likewise performed private devotions (Mak Phœun 2003, 60n47).

26. BAC/08. This informant was insistent that So Chit was never invited to conduct funerals.

27. D16142.

28. BAC/12.

29. D16116. For further examples, see BAC/61 and ICH/04.

30. BAC/23.

31. BAC/64.

32. BAC/17.

33. D16117.

34. I regret that this study almost completely neglects the fate of Buddhist nuns (*ṭūn jī*) under Pol Pot. However, we know that many flourished in the pre-1975 period. Wat Kdei Romduol, Battambang district, housed around 170 of them in 1970 (BAC/04). Wat Roka Kandal, near Kratie, was also a big center, even accommodating *ṭūn jī* from Vietnam (BAC/16). When the Khmer Rouge arrived at Wat Slaket, Battambang district, they forced the pagoda's old nuns to return to their families, but it seems that these women were not forced to marry (BAC/05). On the general subject of nuns in Cambodia, see Löschmann 2000.

35. BAC/21.

36. For a detailed discussion of the cult of the *anak tā*, see Forest 1992 and Ang Chouléan 1986. Judy Ledgerwood (pers. comm., 2003) points out that such reports need to be considered alongside other stories in which the Khmer Rouge unsuccessfully tried to take action against the *anak tā*—explosives used to blow up their houses did not work, the cadres got sick, and so forth.

37. For evidence that a prior Buddhist education may have modified the behavior of even quite ardent cadres, see Pin Yathay 1980, 148–149; and Locard and Mœung Sonn 1993, 42.

38. ICH/09.
39. Dith Pran was punished for secretly gathering rice in autumn 1975. Beaten and then tied to a tree for two days, he anticipated execution. After being unexpectedly released, he shaved his head in a traditional expression of Buddhist piety, telling the Khmer Rouge that this was a cure for migraine. He also later described secret devotions he had performed, including lighting candles for the dead, throughout the period (Maha Ghosananda 1992, x–xi). Shapiro-Phim (2002, 188) mentions a similar case of ritual head shaving.
40. BAC/01. Chu Kroeng died before the end of Democratic Kampuchea.
41. Locals today believe that Hoy Keum tried to use magic against the communists, who were, initially, very polite to him.
42. BAC/10; BAC/11.
43. BAC/54.
44. BAC/53.
45. BAC/55.
46. BAC/56.
47. BAC/06.
48. BAC/03.
49. L03256.
50. L04386.
51. L04374.
52. L05593.
53. BAC/24.
54. BAC/01. The same procedure was adopted at nearby Wat Samraong Knong (Huot Robiep 2004).
55. Thion was allowed to visit selected CPK zones, and all of his interviews were thoroughly vetted by the Party (David Chandler, pers. comm., 2006).
56. Wat Salaneti, Chhlong district (BAC/10), and the Chunleung village pagoda in Khsach Kandal district (BAC/36) are further examples of Buddhist monasteries damaged by aerial bombardment.
57. BAC/42.
58. BAC/43.
59. BAC/23.
60. BAC/31.
61. BAC/34.
62. Ismael's account is given in BAC/27 and is broadly confirmed in BAC/33 and BAC/36. Another member of the demolition team, Lun Long, had been a prisoner at Prek Ta Moak, charged with a moral offense in 1977. He later stated that, in all, eighty men were incarcerated there and that none had previously been monks. He met Ismael at Koh Oknha Tei and believed that the work group was composed of seven families, some of whom he named when he was interviewed (BAC/33).
63. So Ny stated that when the team was trying to break up a Buddha statue, "there was an accident because of the magic of the god" (BAC/48).
64. BAC/33.

65. The dismantled *wats* included Wat Tep Montrei near Prek Preah Prosop; Wat Me Ban, Wat Prek Bang Kang, and Wat Chor Cheng, all in Khsach Kandal district; and Wat Leur at Koh Oknha Tei. It took two months to destroy Wat Leur (BAC/33). Another informant who was a member of Ismael's team for only two months remembered working on the following pagodas: Ta Moeum (which had already been damaged by bombing), Ang Cheng, Koh, Prek Bang Kang, and Me Ban. However, he believed that the work was done between late 1976 and early 1977 (BAC/36).
66. BAC/27.
67. It appears that the district security chief was called Dum and that So Ny was Dum's deputy, with a responsibility for security (BAC/33). So Ny was replaced when soldiers arrived in the area from the Southwestern Zone (BAC/27). In the PRK period he was imprisoned for eight years before being released without charge (BAC/48).
68. Miwa (2000, 468), however, claims that the city contained a total of seventy-six pre-1975 *wats*. Also see de Nike et al. 2000, 145, document 2.1.2.01. This is an issue that deserves more detailed research.
69. DC-Cam 2003a (TKI012).
70. DC-Cam 2003b (KTI0365). The interviewee, Hau Li (alias Soar), remembered seeing Khieu Samphan drive by the site after the cathedral's destruction.
71. D16117.
72. Both vehicles and spare parts were exported from the Wat Mangalavan factory to China (Guthrie 2002, 63).
73. DC-Cam 2002b (KHI0040).
74. Also see D16116.
75. David Hawk was the project coordinator.
76. D16012. Also see D16014.
77. D16017.
78. D16140.
79. D16020.
80. BAC/55; BAC/56.
81. D16012.
82. BAC/16.
83. The cadres destroyed the Buddha images, and the workers collected the usable stones. See DC-Cam 2002c (KDI0126).
84. BAC/48.
85. D16012. For more on the religious, and specifically esoteric, significance of Phnom Sampeou before the outbreak of civil war, see Bizot 1980.
86. BAC/48.
87. BAC/15.
88. Although by no means exhaustive, a table of 103 provincial prisons during Democratic Kampuchea given by Kane (2007, 306)—itself derived from DC-Cam's Mapping the Killing Fields of Cambodia project (1995–2000)—also indicates that many were located in former pagodas.

89. The bodies were subsequently disinterred and placed in a *cetiy* (funerary monument) (Locard 2004, 52–53).
90. D16012; D16014. The official responsible for this prison was called Kech Pen.
91. D16140.
92. D16116.
93. D16131.
94. BAC/01. Intriguingly, the Khmer Rouge do not seem to have taken gold from the teeth of the dead, although informants have told me that graves were robbed after 1979 for this specific purpose (e.g., BAC/15).
95. D16130.
96. *Complaints of the People from Kandal Province,* dated 25 September 1983 and quoted in Ea 2005, 50. Also see DC-Cam 1983 (D00821).
97. I am grateful to Youk Chhang (pers. comm., 2005) for this information.
98. BAC/60.
99. D16013.
100. D16120.
101. DC-Cam 2002a (KDI0134).
102. BAC/64.
103. BAC/53.
104. BAC/12.
105. D16016. For a discussion of the ritual and religious significance of these canoes, see Harris 2005a, 65.
106. BAC/14.
107. For a study of Buddhist painting in Cambodia, see Roveda and Sothon Yem 2009.
108. BAC/56.
109. BAC/54.
110. Also see Short 2004, 283.
111. D16124.
112. BAC/12.
113. D16120.
114. I am grateful to Olivier de Bernon (pers. comm., 2004) for pointing this obvious fact out to me. We do know, however, that in pre–Pol Pot times fragments of ancient texts were sometimes used as medicines that were administered by smoking.
115. For a discussion of the mystical significance of traditional writings, see Harris 2005a, 82–83.
116. D16016.
117. D16017.
118. D16130.
119. For a probable variant on this story, see *Phnom Penh Post* 1994.
120. It now forms the largest collection in the country—the National Library only has 800 manuscripts—and is held in a library that bears his name in his old monastery. Since July 1991 the École Française d'Extrême-Orient has sponsored research into the identification and conservation of surviving Buddhist manuscripts under the

auspices of the Fonds pour l'Édition des Manuscrits du Cambodge (FEMC). Its first publication provided an inventory of Buddhist texts found in Phnom Penh and Kandal province. See de Bernon, Kun, and Leng 2004.

## CHAPTER SIX: Monk Mortality and the Destruction of Institutional Buddhism

1. One survivor of the Democratic Kampuchea period has commented on the similarity between Khmer Rouge class analysis and the traditional modes of ordering society: "People got divided into three classes: the workers, the farmers and the upper class. It was just like at the pagoda [with its novices, monks, and abbot]" (Luco 2002, 66).

2. Vairon (2004, 55) has suggested that the category of *anak ceḥ diṅ*—a term that implies someone who possesses the knowledge to do various things (i.e., technical mastery)—can be divided into four subcategories: Sihanoukists, Khmer Rouge leaders, other elements of the Left, and patriotic high functionaries opposed to US policy in the region. But none of the subcategories is explicitly related to the *saṅgha,* although many monks would have been Sihanoukists in the sense that they recognized the old Theravāda notion that the protection of a righteous ruler is absolutely indispensable to the proper functioning of institutional Buddhism.

3. The widening of the net meant that "members of the second tier Islamic elite: *hakim, haji* and *tuon*" (Heder 2005, 399) were also targeted.

4. Heng Samrin, who was in the audience, remembered Pol Pot saying that "no monks were to be allowed, no festivals were to be allowed any more, meaning 'wipe out religion' [*lup sāsanā*]" (quoted in Kiernan 2007, 72).

5. ICH/19. Only two of the ten survived Democratic Kampuchea, but the deaths of the others were mainly due to old age, overwork, or illness. For discussion of the role of the *pāragū,* see de Bernon 1997; and Harris 2005a, 51, 114.

6. For documentary evidence on the persecution of Islam, see Front d'Union pour l'Édification et la Défense de la Patrie Kampuchéenne 1983a and 1983b. The latter work includes a list of non-Cham Muslims (i.e., Pakistanis, Indians, Arabs) killed at Tuol Sleng on pages 20–21. The first Khmer Rouge attacks on the Cham Muslim minority occurred around 1972 in the Southwestern Zone by order of Ta Mok. Women were forced to cut their hair short in the Khmer style, the traditional sarong was banned, and restrictions were placed on religious activities. Nevertheless, policy toward the Cham was not always hostile; rather it depended on local conditions and the attitude of regional cadres. However, by mid-1978 the massacre of Cham, even those who obediently followed all the restrictions placed on them by the authorities, arguably constituted a campaign of racial extermination. In a pioneering study of the issue, Kiernan (1988, 17, 30) concluded, "It seems inescapable that over one-third of the Chams, about 90,000 people, perished at the hands of the Pol Pot regime." Also see Ysa 2002, 2006.

7. L00685, a Lon Nol government intelligence report dating from the civil war period. Ven. Chhut was killed on 28 April 1974.

8. This pagoda was the backdrop for the arrest of François Bizot in October 1971 (Bizot 2000, 53).
9. BAC/23.
10. BAC/14.
11. D16019.
12. D16013.
13. BAC/25.
14. BAC/24.
15. BAC/10; BAC/15; BAC/16. I have been told that a few years ago one of the executioners took some people to the site, where they found strips of robe, a belt, and the remains of Hong Peng.
16. BAC/16.
17. L02423.
18. See L01700, for example.
19. BAC/02; BAC/05. Also see D16013.
20. D16013.
21. BAC/17.
22. BAC/12.
23. BAC/53.
24. BAC/19.
25. For an eyewitness report of the execution of Ven. Pin, the *cau adhikār* of Wat Pothi Voan Hanchey Krom, following his refusal to disrobe, see BAC/11 and BAC/12. Eyewitness accounts of mass executions of monastics are rare. The only examples I have been able to identify are those that were presented at the 1979 trial of Pol Pot and Ieng Sary.
26. D16142.
27. D16017.
28. L06777. This intelligence report also mentions the death of Ta Morm, the chief monk of Wat Trapang Ondaek, Takeo province. This pagoda was turned into a Zone 13 message office.
29. BAC/30; BAC/34.
30. BAC/42. Also see D16139.
31. BAC/21.
32. BAC/51. This informant knew of another monk who met the same fate, Ven. Tean Nak of Wat Ou, Kampong Trach. Two Kampong Thom monks, Ven. Chim of Wat Chan Serei and Ven. Chhem of Wat Chaom Leu, who had refused to work because it was against Buddhist discipline, also had their robes removed, forcibly in the case of the latter, before they were killed in 1973 (BAC/34).
33. BAC/61; BAC/63. See BAC/59 for information about three other senior monks killed in various districts of Stung Treng: Ven. Kham My, the *cau adhikār* of Wat Hang Khor Ban; Pao Hing, the *cau adhikār* of Wat Kangchor; and Siv Thorn, a *bālăt* (senior monk of the second rank) of Wat Kandal. This informant stated that these three, along with Ven. Nou Sin, were all taken away in a boat at night after refusing to disrobe.

34. Wat Prang is home to a now badly damaged stupa dating from the reign of King Ang Duong (r. 1845–1860). It originally contained a Buddha relic brought from Sri Lanka by *saṅgharāja* Tieng. A history of Wat Prang was written by Huot Tat and edited by Chuon Nath. Also see BAC/20.

35. BAC/29.

36. BAC/52. For a breakdown of ecclesiastical titles, see Harris 2005a, 236. So Hay was number two in the monastic hierarchy, holding the title of *brah bodhivăns*. Kem To was a member of the Tripiṭaka Commission and the chief of national examinations on *patimokkha* (rules of monastic discipline). He held the monastic title of *brah dhammalikkhit* (Khin Sok 1999, 36n3). Sek Neang, who held the title of *brah dhammaghosācāry,* was the monk in charge of Buddhist national primary education. He may have been killed in Preah Sdech district, Prey Veng (D16146). For further information on Sek Neang, see D16145.

37. D16145.

38. D16029. One monk, Ven. Som Sereivath, was a passenger in the car and survived Democratic Kampuchea. I have not been successful in tracking him down.

39. Of the twelve, only Ven. Oum Sum and Ven. Heng Leang Hor (also known as Ta End) survived Democratic Kampuchea.

40. ICH/16. So Hay was the *cau adhikār* of Wat Nirot Reangsey, across the river from Phnom Penh on National Highway 1. Before that, he had been *grū sūtr stăṃ* (right-hand assistant to the abbot) at Wat Kork Kak, Kat Phluk commune, Baset district, Kampong Speu.

41. Pon Sompheach held the monastic title of *brah vaṇarat(n)*.

42. Pang Khat, So Hay, and Khieu Chum had all been part of the circle of the nationalist monk Hem Chieu before he was arrested in 1942. Pang Khat was imprisoned, first in Phnom Penh and subsequently at the Central Prison in Saigon, for his involvement in that year's "Umbrella War" demonstration.

43. Also see Yang Sam 1987, 58–59.

44. The report also lists Wat Prey Lvea, Kandal province, as a National Army base.

45. D16116.

46. We also know that there were about sixty-five thousand monks in Cambodia at this time, for an average *wat* population of around nineteen monks.

47. The monk representative at this meeting, chaired by Ven. Men Chhorn, was Oum Sum, one of the two surviving members of the Tripiṭaka Commission. In his speech he called on the United Nations to expel GRUNK (the Royal Government of National Union of Kampuchea), so that the PRK could take up its seat as the legitimate government of Cambodia.

48. Pagoda statistics are also offered on a provincial basis—e.g., Battambang, 312; Stung Treng, 12; Kampong Speu, 182; Phnom Penh, 47; Kandal, 298; Takeo, not given; etc. The document also mentions that 108 mosques were destroyed.

49. By 1990 this figure had risen to 2,667.

50. The PRK trial (in absentia) of Pol Pot and Ieng Sary in August 1979 also appears to have generated some troublesome statistics related to the Buddhist order. One of its documents, for example, incorrectly states that there were more than 100,000

monks in robes in 1975, a massive overestimate (Groupe de Juristes Cambodgiens 1990, 217).

51. D16116.
52. Ibid.

## CHAPTER SEVEN: Aftermath

1. Yeum came from Kang Ta Neung commune, Kang Meas district, Kampong Cham. Another of these "monks," Daik, also had a gun (BAC/19).
2. The boy was Lim En, now the *cau adhikār* at a Thommayut pagoda, Wat Tuol Sophea Khuon, near Pochentong airport (BAC/18). We know that the communists monitored people who listened to the radio. Before 17 April 1975 they were concerned about the *Voice of the Khmer Republic* on the radio, especially its interviews with prominent monks (Lon Nol government intelligence report, L00579).
3. It appears that Ta Hoy had once been a Thommayut monk in Takeo province (BAC/19).
4. Also known as Rom (BAC/19).
5. On one occasion Ta Ros ordered Paen Sen's biographer, Hong Dy, to walk on a painting of the Buddha that was being used for drying tobacco. Despite terror of reprisals, Dy was more frightened of the consequences of disrespecting the Buddha, and he refused by just sitting quietly. To his surprise and great relief he was not punished. However, Ta Ros certainly felt antipathy toward Paen Sen. On another occasion he asked Dy to fetch him a fishing net to be used to bind and kill the monk. Once again, Dy remained inactive, nothing subsequently happened, and no punishment ensued (BAC/19).
6. Ven. Lim Eng, for example, was ordained into the Thommayut by Paen Sen on 20 February 1979 (BAC/18). Marston (2008, 8–9) gives details of other early PRK ordinations. Dating from February 1979, they were performed by a Cambodian monk named Ta Nep, who had fled to Vietnam as a refugee in the Memot district of eastern Kampong Cham province, close to the Vietnamese border.
7. Hong Dy's (1989) manuscript is a biography written for Paen Sen's cremation.
8. BAC/32.
9. The story of Nut presented here is an amalgam of information contained in BAC/25, BAC/26, BAC/30, and BAC/31.
10. Ironically, the *wat* committee at Wat Prek A Chi, no doubt under strong pressure from the ruling Cambodian People's Party, voted to join the Mahanikay in the early 2000s.
11. D02129.
12. BAC/22; BAC/37; BAC/40; BAC/67. Tep Vong told me that Long Sim retired simply because he was old and weak.
13. Quoted in "Religion in Kampuchea" 1988, 170. Only in *Circular Concerning Becoming a Buddhist Novice* (National Council of the United Front for the Construction and Defense of the Motherland Kampuchea 1989), signed by Chea

Sim and dated 24 April 1989, was full freedom to practice religion, at least for Buddhists, granted. It was issued one week before the PRK was dissolved into the new State of Cambodia (SOC). Slocomb (2003, 182) notes that the circular "was merely recognizing what was already a *fait accompli.*"

14. As Ponchaud (1989, 172–173) has pointed out, Buddhist modernism was built on the assertion that the Buddha's teachings were based on scientific and rational grounds. If one accepts this premise, obstacles to the accommodation of the doctrinal and practical resources of Buddhism to the socialist world picture would be substantially reduced.

15. The visit is mentioned in a letter responding to some criticisms of the prominent scholar of Cambodian history Michael Vickery by a Sri Lankan monk, Ven. Wipulasara Thera, who had been a delegation member and the general secretary of the World Buddhist Sangha Council. The letter was published in the *Phnom Penh Post* (Wipulasara 1994). On the ABCP, see Vietnam Buddhist Sangha 1990, 19–20, 60–61, 115–116.

16. De Nike et al. 2000, 146–147, document 2.1.2.02. For a flavor of ABCP proceedings, see the document produced by the follow-up conference, *Peace through Harmony* (1982).

17. Son Sann (1911–2000) was the president of the National Assembly in 1952, the first governor of Cambodia's National Bank (1955–1968), and prime minister (1967–1968). In June 1970 he moved to Paris, where he unsuccessfully sought to bring about a resolution of the civil war. As a devout lay Buddhist he became convinced that the troubles of the Khmer people were the result of their non-Buddhist conduct. He also conceived the possibility of a "third force" in Cambodian politics and seems to have gained the support of the Mahanikay *saṅgharāja,* Ven. Huot Tat. Sihanouk, on the other hand, accused Son Sann of being "a dreamer, not a man of action" (quoted in Corfield 1994, 136). Sihanouk also "shied away from the older man's Buddhist moralizing, and his austere personal style" (Chandler 1990, 58).

18. Try (1991, 39) describes the PRK's attitude toward Buddhism as a "mariage idéologique bouddhico-marxiste."

19. See BAC/67; and Hayashi 2002, 209ff. Marston (2008, 10) claims that Nel Mony never formally disrobed. According to Marston, when Nel Money was asked to do so, he refused, even though villagers warned him that he would be killed. But the authorities allowed him to live as a monk so long as he dressed as they did. He was not required to do heavy labor and was therefore able to live "as if" he were a monk. He also kept his monastic robes about his person.

20. The four other monks were Chhem, Phonn, Mom, and Seth (BAC/67).

21. Ven. Chhun Chim was ordained in May 1979 at Wat Sansam Kosala by Nel Mony and reordained by Tep Vong a little later at Wat Unnalom (D16129). Ven. Pok Som Ann was also ordained with a group of eighty others by Nel Mony at Wat Sansam Kosala in August 1979 (D16146).

22. However, he did assign ten of his fellow monks to attend!

23. The report was reviewed by a committee of Phnom Penh monks and authenticated by Ven. Nel Mony, the Buddhist clergy representative (de Nike et al. 2000, 145, document 2.1.2.01).
24. See BAC/01, BAC/03, and BAC/06.
25. One of my informants (BAC/03) thought that Long Sim was the preceptor, but this seems unlikely to me.
26. BAC/05.
27. Marston (2008, 19) suggests five categories of individuals reentering the monastic order at this time: (1) those who simply put on robes without any attempt at ceremony; (2) those who assumed the monkhood in a ceremony in front of a Buddha image; (3) those ordained by men who claimed to have never left the monkhood during the Pol Pot period; (4) those ordained by monks who spent the Pol Pot period outside of Cambodia; and (5) those who crossed national borders to be ordained at *wat*s in neighboring countries.
28. For a brief description of the restoration of Buddhism in Bakham, Cheung Prey district, Kampong Cham, see Ly Heng and Demeure 1992, 212.
29. BAC/51.
30. BAC/61.
31. BAC/50.
32. BAC/53.
33. BAC/52.
34. Tep Vong performed a Phnom Penh–based ordination of around twenty-five individuals in late September 1979, quickly followed by a ceremony for six others at Wat Damnak, Siem Reap (ICH/16). An old monk from Stung Treng, Ven. Nou Thang Nak, also told me that he was reordained in 1980 at Wat Unnalom by Tep Vong—along with Ta Nou of Wat Khatteyaram and Ta Ma of Wat Srekrasaing, both in Kratie province, and Ta Deng of Wat Veun Seng, Ratanakiri (BAC/59).
35. For a contemporary report on the ceremony, see Summary of World Broadcasts 1979. For a Vietnamese-language account, see Lê Hưũ Dan 1995. The ordination ceremony (*pabbajjā upasampadā*) was held in the traditional manner (Bizot 1988, 121).
36. Nel Mony (BAC/67) claimed that not all of the monks who attended the September 1979 ordination were Khmer from Kampuchea Krom. Some—including the *grū sūtr*, whom he had known at Wat Mohamontrei before Democratic Kampuchea—were Vietnamese wearing Khmer monks' robes. He maintained that eight monks came from Vietnam, but the most senior of them died almost as soon as he arrived in Phnom Penh. All of the others, who were quite young, mysteriously died within two years of arriving back in Vietnam.
37. Noun Nget had been a base monk at Wat Prey Chnor, Takeo, and claimed to have retained his vows (this expression is usually a veiled reference to forced marriage) throughout Democratic Kampuchea, despite being forced to defrock at the end of *vassā* 1975. By 1986 he was the senior figure in a *saṅgha* of only three monks living at Wat Langka, Phnom Penh (BAC/28).

38. De Nike et al. 2000, 149, document 2.1.2.03. Also see *FBIS Daily Report—Asia and Pacific,* 21 August 1979, quoted in Yang Sam (1987, 69). Marston (2008, 30) suggests that this group of monks, except Tep Vong and Kaet Vay, had been ordained previously with Nel Mony.
39. One source (Ros Chantrabot 2000, 20) suggests that Kaet Vay was an original member of the Salvation Front. This seems most unlikely.
40. Kaet Vay ordained several groups—of ten and then of twenty monks—in Phnom Penh before the end of the year (BAC/35). Also see BAC/29, BAC/30, and D16133, the last of which describes Ven. So Chhem's reordination by Kaet Vay at Wat Unnalom on 17 December 1979.
41. BAC/34.
42. Also known as Wat Samraong Meanchey.
43. I have been unable to establish the date of the battle.
44. Others also brought him occasional food, including the interviewee of BAC/34.
45. According to one informant (BAC/30), Kaet Vay lived in this manner until he escaped to Vietnam in late 1978 or early 1979, possibly with some ex–Khmer Rouge who rose to prominence in the early PRK. It is difficult to verify the Vietnam connection, but Kaet Vay's subsequent career suggests that he was not involved in the formation of the Front that invaded Cambodia in December 1978.
46. The story represents a synthesis of elements gleaned from BAC/30, BAC/34, BAC/35, BAC/40, and BAC/66.
47. BAC/40.
48. Tep Vong claimed that in the early PRK period he was imprisoned and sentenced to four years of forced labor (Danois 1980, 73).
49. D16116. For details of Tep Vong's life after the Democratic Kampuchea period, see Moung Ra and Chheung Bun Chhea 2001.
50. BAC/66.
51. BAC/37. Also see D16139.
52. Or "Khmer bodies with Vietnamese minds" (*khluon khmaer khuor kpāl yuon*); see Hinton 2002, 90. The matter is clearly sensitive. When Michael Vickery (1986, 196n9) questioned Mme. Peou Lida, the vice president of the PRK Salvation Front who was also responsible for religious affairs, she denied any explicit Vietnamese involvement in the reordinations. Nevertheless, Tep Vong's opponents refer to him as a "false monk" and "a Communist . . . [who] has always been devoted to the Vietminh" (Martin 1994, 237).
53. Vickery 1986, 161. With regard to the rights and duties of monks, one source claims that monks were expected to pay higher taxes than most other workers ("Religion in Kampuchea" 1988, 169). It also seems that a number of monks were among the 148 candidates who contested the PRK elections of 1 May 1981 (Heder 1998). Sometimes it is incorrectly asserted that monastic voting was first introduced in Cambodia in the run-up to the 1993 election sponsored by the United National Transitional Authority in Cambodia (UNTAC).
54. Some scholars have suggested that biographical writing in Khmer started in Democratic Kampuchea, but Löschmann (2005, 49) argues that it was a fairly

long-standing practice—citing a circular of 12 October 1920 mentioned by Imbert 1961, 134n1.

55. DC-Cam 1996a.

56. Similar policies occur in Vietnamese history. During the nineteenth century, for example, the government controlled ordination into the Buddhist order through a system of certification. Certificates could be obtained only by those over the age of fifty, with good morality and a knowledge of scripture (Nguyên Thê Anh 1993, 110). Rama IV, king of Siam, also tried to ban all men between the ages of twenty-four and seventy from entering the *saṅgha* (Ishii 1986a, 73).

57. The measure had been introduced by Circular no. 3 of 1980, which makes it all the more peculiar that, in an official newspaper article after that date, a photograph appears of a young monk, Nget Ngen—the *cau adhikār* of Wat Sre Nor Nong, Ang Ta Soam commune—along with a statement that monks like him had been working hard in the fields or constructing schools and hospitals, in an effort to participate in rebuilding the country (*Kampuchea* 1981b).

58. Ros Samay was the cousin of Pen Sovann, who, on 1 December 1981, was removed from office as prime minister. He and Ros Samay were arrested the following day. In late January 1980, Ros Samay and Tep Vong attended the Muslim community of Chraing Chamres' celebrations for Mohammed's birthday (*Sārbătarmān Kambujā*, 1 February 1980).

59. Many of these early primary source materials are particularly valuable, but few have survived. Provincial offices of the Front Department of Religion were ordered to burn them all after the Vietnamese withdrawal from Cambodia and the establishment of the State of Cambodia in 1989. Fortunately most are reproduced in Löschmann 1989. Ly Sovir (1999) also contains a good selection.

60. But clergy or religious organizations operating illegally or conducting activities contrary to the welfare of the people and nation were not to be tolerated. The overall intent, then, was to ensure that the monastic order did not become a threat to the fledgling state. This is also the theme of *Concerning the System of Entering the Buddhist Monkhood* (no. 24—82SR), dated 5 June 1982, which focused its attention on the restoration and containment of the monastic order, not on its development (cited in Slocomb 2003, 180–182).

61. *FBIS Daily Report—Asia and Pacific,* 2 June 1982. It is interesting that Hem Chieu was generally referred to by the title *achar* in the PRK period. An *achar* is technically a senior lay Buddhist rather than a monk. Yet Hem Chieu did rise to public prominence after he had been defrocked and sent to jail, so the lay designation does make some sense. Recasting monastic heroes in this way would certainly have been more attractive to the communist authorities. Frings (1997, 813) makes the point that early heroes of the anticolonial struggle—for example, Achar Sva (led rebellion 1864–1866)—were given their honorary title well after the actions for which they became famous, and often by communists who, one would have thought, would have been keen to avoid the unwelcome associations the title evokes. Forest (1992, 88) confirms the association of *achar*s and "mouvements de contestation" (protest movements). It is important to note that Hem Chieu has

been regarded as a Khmer hero by all Cambodian regimes since independence. Both Lon Nol and his first minister, Son Ngoc Thanh, attended the ten days of ceremonies following the return of Hem Chieu's ashes to Phnom Penh on 4 June 1972 (*Khmer Republic* 1972, 27).

62. A limited number of young monks were sent for further training to Nepal, India, and Sri Lanka in the early 1980s.

63. At the time of the 1982 conference of foreign ministers, Ven. Oum Sum held the title of *braḥ sāsanāmuni*. Oum Sum was born in Thboung Khmum district in 1918 and became a novice in 1934 at Wat Neaty Reangsei in his home village. He moved to different monasteries a number of times, eventually arriving at Wat Saravan, Phnom Penh, in 1942, where he became a student at the Pāli High School (D16117). Before Democratic Kampuchea, he was the *cau adhikār* of Wat Keo Preah Phloeung, Phnom Penh, a pagoda that survived the hostilities intact but was razed at some point in 1979 (DC-Cam 1996b, 21). As has already been noted, Oum Sum was one of the two Tripiṭaka Commission members to survive Democratic Kampuchea (BAC/29).

64. On 25–30 January 1987 a Cambodian Buddhist delegation, headed by Ven. Oum Sum, paid another friendly visit to the VBS in Ho Chi Minh City. Conversely, representatives of the VBS attended a conference of monks at Wat Nirot Reangsey, Phnom Penh, on 4–5 September 1989.

65. The circular also contains useful information on recent publications of Buddhist literature by the authorities.

66. Vickery (1994, 110) has observed that adherence to a pure Marxist ideology may have been pretty minimal even at the beginning of PRK. He notes that as the years progressed, Heng Samrin's " 'Marxism-Leninism' was hardly more than the strong state ideology that animates several Southeast Asian capitalist regimes."

67. It seems that the PRK authorities blamed Sihanouk for the arrest and forcible defrocking of Hem Chieu (Frings 1997, 818).

68. D16016.

69. The informant was Ven. Hay Sahim, from Pralay village, Tang Krasaing commune, Prasat Sambour district, Kampong Thom. He was ordained in 1979, when he was about eighteen years old, by Ven. Kaet Vay (BAC/30).

70. E.g., Ven. Las Lay (ICH/10).

71. K5 caused great hardship and internal dissension within the country. See Luco (2002, 78ff.) for a discussion of the impact that drafting young men into the K5 plan had on village life and economy.

72. There is a traditional view in Southeast Asia that a period of time spent as a monk "cooks" a young man and renders him a more satisfactory husband.

73. ICH/18.

74. BAC/45.

75. BAC/37.

76. BAC/65.

77. De Nike et al. 2000, 145, document 2.1.2.01. The report had been reviewed by a committee of Phnom Penh monks and authenticated by Ven. Nel Mony, the Buddhist clergy representative.

78. D16116.
79. BAC/66.
80. D16121.
81. D16143.
82. ICH/11.
83. There appear to have been about 224,000 Vietnamese soldiers in Cambodia in 1979. This figure fell to about 100,000 by 1988 (Quinn-Judge 2006, 219).
84. BAC/08.
85. D16019.
86. Wat Khmuonh in Kampong Cham province had a large ammunition bunker that also went up in an enormous explosion when it was attacked by Vietnamese troops (D16140).
87. D16125.
88. DeVoss' (1980, 62) claim that "of 80,000 Cambodian monks, 50,000 were murdered—often beaten to death—during the three years of Pol Pot's savage rule" must be treated with considerable caution.
89. A largely urban fraternity, the Thommayut has always been much smaller than the Mahanikay in terms of membership and geographical spread. A 1959 inventory assigned 1,725 of the country's monasteries to the Mahanikay and 106 to the Thommayut (Chuon Nath and Samdech Preah Mahāsumedhādhipatī 1976, 41). In the mid-1990s around 3 percent of the monastic population belonged to the Thommayut, according to the Centre for Advanced Studies and the Ministry of Cults and Religious Affairs (1996, 23). It was only in December 1991 that the two orders were re-created, after Sihanouk appointed Ven. Tep Vong and Ven. Bour Kry patriarchs of the Mahanikay and Thommayut, respectively. But even after this date there has been a willful confusion of ecclesiastical titles and ongoing disputes over the control of some pagodas (Löschmann 2005, 56–57; Harris 2005a, 214–215).
90. Chantou Boua (1991, 229). Also see Ponchaud (1990, 234) on the Khmer Rouge's assertion that Buddhism is a foreign religion.
91. Administrative posts were also created at the provincial and village levels, with village presidents effectively acting as pre-1975 *achar*s. See Vickery 1986, 162; and Gyallay-Pap and Tranet 1990, 367.
92. In Laos the new head of the Unified Saṅgha Organization was also called president (*pathan*), not the more customary term *phra sangkarat*. However, Evans (1990) has shown that the vast majority of Lao peasants, who were entirely acculturated to habits of deference, paid little or no attention to these language reforms. Since such persons constituted a linguistic majority, it was only a question of time before the official terminology had been eroded and old patterns of usage were reestablished. The same general principle holds true for Cambodia. Unsuccessful attempts to unify the two monastic fraternities also took place in early 1940s Thailand, where some government ministers interpreted (wrongly it turned out) the *1941 Saṅgha Act* as having precisely that effect (P. Jackson 1989, 74).
93. As Keyes (1994, 64) has noted, "It appears that the modernist approach to Buddhism first championed by the Thommakay faction of the Mahanikay order may be the most favoured in the PRK."

94. For a legendary history of the pagoda, see Svay Muoy 1972. One also hears frequent rumors that sacred writings and precious Buddha images from Wat Unnalom were transported to Ho Chi Minh City following the defeat of the Khmer Rouge. Such rumors may, of course, be motivated by little more than anti-Vietnamese sentiment.
95. D16016.
96. Tep Vong, even though he was a monk, stood as a candidate in elections and was voted into the National Assembly (Slocomb 2003, 82).
97. A *sangkat* is an administrative district within a city or large town.
98. One such act was the construction of an ossuary shrine to those who died in Democratic Kampuchea, replete with explicit Buddhist cosmological motifs, at the killing field of Choeung Ek, on the outskirts of Phnom Penh.
99. It is estimated that the number of monks in the period 1985–1989 was about 7,250, but by 1990 the figure had risen to around 16,400, of whom 6,500 were novices (Keyes 1994, 63).
100. By 1990 twenty-six Pāli schools, based on the 1950s–1970s model, had opened (Löschmann 1991, 22).
101. For discussion of the ecclesiastical gerontocracy in neighboring Thailand, see Taylor 1999, 178, and the more forthright McCargo 2004, 158.

## Conclusion

1. For a recent collection of essays on Cambodia's political reconstruction since 1979, see Öjendal and Lilja 2009.

# ABBREVIATIONS AND GLOSSARY

| | |
|---|---|
| ABCP | Asian Buddhists' Conference for Peace. |
| achar (*ācāry*) | A lay Buddhist ritual specialist. *Achar*s are also often involved in the administrative, educational, and moral life of a Buddhist *wat*. |
| *ahiṃsā* | Noninjury or nonviolence. |
| anak sīl | A man of virtue. |
| anak tā | An ancestral or tutelary spirit, often the focus of a popular cult. Sometimes rendered as *neak tā*. |
| Angkar (*aṅgkār*) | The revolutionary organization that controlled the Communist Party during the Democratic Kampuchea period. |
| *anugaṇ* | Deputy chief monk—e.g., of a province. |
| *bālăt* | A senior monk of the second rank. |
| *baray* | An artificial lake constructed for ritual and irrigation purposes, usually dating from the Angkorian period. |
| *bhikkhu* | A Buddhist monk (literally, "beggar") who has undergone the higher ordination ceremony (*upasampadā*). |
| *bhjuṃ piṇḍ* | A solemn annual ceremony of merit-making for dead ancestors. Often rendered as *phcum ben*. |
| *bodhi* tree | The place of the Buddha's enlightenment. |
| *braḥ grū* | An honorific title for a teacher. |
| *braḥ saṅgh raṇasirsa* | The unified "Front" monastic organization of the PRK period. |
| *braḥ vihāra* | The principal sanctuary of a Buddhist *wat*. |
| *brahmavihāra* | Four meditations—on loving-kindness, compassion, sympathetic joy, and equanimity—collectively known as the divine abidings. |
| *Buddha daṃnāy* | Predictions of the Buddha. |
| *cakkavatti* | A righteous Buddhist monarch. Literally, a "wheel turner," for such an individual is believed to turn the wheel of *dhamma*. |
| *calăt* | A Khmer Rouge–period mobile work unit—*calăt yuvajan* for males and *calăt yuvanārī* for females. |
| *cāp' phtoem bī sūny* | Starting from zero. |
| *cau adhikār* | The chief monk or abbot of a Buddhist *wat*. |
| *cetiy* | A funerary monument, often in the form of a stupa. |
| Cham | Cambodia's largest minority group, almost exclusively Muslim. |
| *chāyā* | A monastic ordination certificate that also serves as an identity card. |

| | |
|---|---|
| *Cpāp'* | Medieval didactic poems in Khmer that have moral and behavioral themes. |
| CPK | Communist Party of Kampuchea. |
| *damiḷ* | An atheist, a communist, or a devil. |
| *dhamma* | An important and multivalent Pāli term. Primarily it refers to the teachings of a buddha, but it may also denote the basic constitution of reality. |
| *dhammavinaya* | The Buddha's teachings (*dhamma*) and discipline (*vinaya*). |
| EFEO | École Française d'Extrême-Orient. |
| FBIS | Foreign Broadcast Information Service |
| FEMC | Fonds pour l'Édition des Manuscrits du Cambodge. |
| FUNK | Front Uni Nationale du Kampuchéa (National United Front of Kampuchea), an umbrella organization for anti–Lon Nol forces formed by Sihanouk after he was deposed in 1970. |
| *gaṇaḥ saṅgh* | A special cadre appointed to maintain revolutionary discipline in the *saṅgha* at the level of the *wat*. |
| *grū* | A teacher or person possessing a high level of traditional skills. |
| *grū sūtr* | A monk assistant to a *cau adhikār*. Usually there are two of these in a *wat* (*grū sūtr stāṃ* and *grū sūtr chveṅ*), each with his respective sphere of responsibility. |
| GRUNK | Gouvernement Royal d'Union Nationale du Kampuchéa (Royal Government of National Union of Kampuchea), a Beijing-based government in exile during the Khmer Republic period, consisting of a coalition between Sihanouk and the Khmer Rouge. |
| *haji* | A title given to a Muslim who has made the pilgrimage to Mecca. |
| hakim | An Islamic dignitary. |
| ICP | Indochinese Communist Party. |
| Kampuchea Krom | A region of southern Vietnam with a significant Khmer population. Also known as Lower Cambodia. |
| *kathin* | A ceremony (*puṇy*) marking the end of *vassā* in which laypeople offer new robes to monks as a means of making merit. |
| Khmer Serei (*khmaer serī*) | Free Khmer. |
| KPNLF | Khmer People's National Liberation Front. |
| KPRP | Kampuchean People's Revolutionary Party. |
| *kramā* | A traditional Cambodian scarf. |
| *kuṭī* | A hut or dwelling house for monks. |
| KWP | Khmer Workers' Party. |
| Mahanikay | A name applied to the largest of Cambodia's two monastic fraternities (*nikāya*). Literally, "great group." |
| Māra | An evil god. The Buddhist embodiment of ignorance. |

| | |
|---|---|
| *megaṇ* | A chief monk, usually of a province. |
| *nāg* | A serpent spirit. |
| *nikāya* | A fraternity of Buddhist monks. Sometimes mistakenly referred to as a "sect." |
| *pabbajjā* | The ordination ceremony of a novice monk (*sāmaṇera*). |
| Pāli | The canonical language of Theravāda Buddhism. |
| *pāragū* | A Brahmanical priest employed to conduct rituals in the Royal Palace. Often rendered as *baku*. |
| *pāramī* | A guardian spirit. Sometimes rendered as *boramei*. |
| *paticcasamuppāda* | Dependent origination. A fundamental teaching of the Buddha that stresses the interdependence of all conditioned things. |
| *patimokkha* | The rules of monastic discipline. |
| *prāsād* | A Brahmanical or Mahayana Buddhist temple, usually dating from the pre-Angkorian or Angkorian period. |
| *pradhān* | A president. |
| PRK | People's Republic of Kampuchea. |
| *puṇy* (Pāli *puñña*) | A meritorious act, especially a religious ceremony or festival. |
| *Rāmakīrti* | The Khmer version of the Indian epic poem *Rāmāyaṇa*. |
| *sālā chān'* | A building within the monastic compound used for eating and teaching and for accommodating guests. |
| *sāmaṇera* | A novice monk who has undergone the Buddhist lower ordination ceremony (*pabbajjā*). |
| *samtec* | A highly honorific title. |
| *saṅgam niyam braḥ buddhasāsanā* | A Buddhist-oriented community. |
| *saṅgam rāstra niyam* | People's Socialist Community. |
| *saṅgh mūlaṭṭhān* | A term employed by the Khmer Rouge to denote a "base," or rural, monk. |
| *saṅgh ṭap' prāṃ bīr mesa* | April 17 monks—i.e., those who came under Khmer Rouge control only after the taking of Phnom Penh on that date. |
| *saṅgh thmī* | A term employed by the Khmer Rouge to denote a monk from the areas of Cambodia liberated after 17 April 1975. Literally, "new monk." |
| *saṅgha* | The order of Buddhist monks and nuns. |
| *saṅgharāja* | "King of the *saṅgha*," the chief monk of a fraternity (*nikāya*) of monks. |
| *sangkat* | A district of a city or large town. |
| Sangkum | The shortened and customary form of *saṅgam rāstra niyam*. |
| *sāsanā pratikiriyā* | A reactionary religion. |
| *sati* | Mindfulness. |
| *sīmā* | The ritual boundary of a Buddhist monastery. |
| *srok* | A district or subdivision of a province. |

| | |
|---|---|
| stupa | A funerary monument, especially associated with relics of the Buddha, Buddhist saints, and kings. |
| Thommayut (Pāli *dhammayuttika*) | A reformist and socially elitist monastic fraternity (*nikāya*) introduced into Cambodia in the nineteenth century from Thailand. |
| *Tripiṭaka* | The Theravāda Buddhist canon, written in Pāli and consisting of "three baskets" (three collections): *vinaya, sutta* (the discourses of the Buddha), and *abhidhamma* (the higher teaching). |
| *ṭūn jī* | A Buddhist nun. |
| UIF | Unified Issarak Front. |
| UNTAC | United National Transitional Authority in Cambodia. |
| *upacchāy(n)* | A monastic preceptor. |
| *upasampadā* | A higher ordination ceremony. |
| *vaṇṇaḥ* | Social class. |
| *vassā* | The annual three-month rainy-season retreat for monks, usually lasting from July to October. |
| VBS | Vietnam Buddhist Saṅgha. |
| Ven. | An abbreviation for "Venerable," a Western-derived title of respect. Used for monks. |
| *vinay aṅgkār* | The rules of personal and social conduct imposed during the Khmer Rouge period. |
| *vinaya* | The rules of monastic discipline constituting the first section of the threefold canon (*tripiṭaka*) of Theravāda Buddhist sacred writings. |
| VWP | Vietnam Workers' Party. |
| *wat* (*vatt*) | A Buddhist monastery, or *vihāra.* Often referred to as a pagoda in Cambodia. |
| *yuon* | A derogatory Khmer term, of uncertain origin, for the Vietnamese. |

# BIBLIOGRAPHY

## Unpublished Materials

DC-Cam Buddhism and Communism (BAC) Interviews—conducted by the author, usually with the assistance of Prum Phalla of the Documentation Center of Cambodia (DC-Cam). Tapes and transcripts in Khmer and English are held at DC-Cam. The name of the interviewee appears immediately after the reference number. Locations are indicated in the following manner: place (usually a Buddhist temple), village, commune, district, and province.

BAC/01. Sim Koeun at Wat K'dol, O Tum Nup, K'dol, Battambang, Battambang, 2.9.03.

BAC/02. Chhuon Vang at Wat Samraong Knong, Samraong O Trea, Samraong Knong, Ek Phnom, Batambang, 2.9.03.

BAC/03. Tun Tim at Wat Norea, Ta Kok, Samraong Knong, Ek Phnom, Battambang, 2.9.03.

BAC/04. Sor Phak at Wat Kdei Romdoul, Romdoul, Chamkar Samraong, Battambang, Battambang, 3.9.03.

BAC/05. Set Seun at Wat Slaket, Slaket, Slaket, Battambang, Battambang, 3.9.03.

BAC/06. Uk Mut at Wat Po Veal, Ratanak, Ratanak, Battambang, Battambang, 3.9.03.

BAC/07. Tan Vong at Wat So Phy, So Phy 1, Ratanak, Battambang, Battambang, 4.9.03.

BAC/08. Hat Saray at Wat Sangke, Romchek 4, Ratanak, Battambang, Battambang, 4.9.03.

BAC/10. Seng Thieng at Wat Pothi Voan Hanchey Leu, Hanchey 2, Hanchey, Chhlong, Kratie, 21.1.04.

BAC/11. Vong Sreng at Wat Pothi Voan Hanchey Krom, Hanchey, Hanchey, Chhlong, Kratie, 21.1.04.

BAC/12. Heng Pum at Wat Pothi Reangsey, Phum Thmei, Khsach Andet, Chhlong, Kratie, 21.1.04.

BAC/14. Meas Suon at Wat Pothi Preuk, Kanchor, Cheu Teal Phluh, Chhlong, Kratie, 21.1.04.

BAC/15. Van Voan at Wat Kratie, Kratie, Kratie, Kratie, Kratie, 23.1.04.

BAC/16. Seum Khan at Wat Rok Kandal, Roka Kandal, Roka Kandal, Kratie, Kratie, 23.1.04.

BAC/17. Peng Somrat at Preah Thmey, Preah Thmey, Kean Svay, Kandal, 29.1.04.

BAC/18. Lim Eng at Wat Tuol Sophea Khuon, Prek Trea, Trapeang Krasang, Dangkao, Phnom Penh, 6.5.04.

BAC/19. Hong Dy at Wat Sovann Kiri, Cheung Chhnok, Tang Krang, Batheay, Kampong Cham, 7.5.04.

BAC/20. Oum Son at Wat Preah Prang, Knong Veang, Veang Chas, Oudong, Kampong Speu, 19.5.04.

BAC/21. Son Nieng at Wat Veang Chas, Knong Veang, Veang Chas, Oudong, Kampong Speu, 19.5.04.

BAC/22. Sin Khin at Thnal Banteay, Angk Snuol, Kandal, 19.5.04.

BAC/23. Nou Song at Wat Tep Pranam, Tep Pranam, Vihear Luong, Ponhea Leu, Kandal, 20.5.04.

BAC/24. Srey Khlang at Wat Preah Put Nippean, Preah Nippean, Preah Nippean, Kong Pisey, Kampong Speu, 21.5.04.

BAC/25. Khieu Nem at Wat Kandal, Preak A Chi Ti Muoy, Preak A Chi, Kroch Chhmar, Kampong Cham, 22.5.04.

BAC/26. Hun Sovann at Preak A Chi Ti Bey, Preak A Chi, Kroch Chhmar, Kampong Cham, 22.5.04.

BAC/27. Ismael at Kampong Krabei, Kampong Kor, Kampong Siem, Kampong Cham, 23.5.04.

BAC/28. Prak Prum at Wat Langka, Boeng Keng Kang Muoy, Chamkar Mon, Phnom Penh, 25.5.04.

BAC/29. Heng Lieng Hau at Wat Preah Put, Veal Vong, 7 Makara, Phnom Penh, 26.5.04.

BAC/30. Hay Sahim at Wat Mohamontrei, Oulampik, Chamkar Mon, Phnom Penh, 15.6.04.

BAC/31. Yeng and But at Wat Antong Vien, Antong Vien, Thei, Kratie, 04.7.04.

BAC/32. Kim Lin at Wat P'chha, Trapang Pring, Ou-Russey, Kratie, 05.7.04.

BAC/33. Lun Long at Vihear Suor Chheung, Vihear Suor, Khsach Kandal, Kandal, 21.8.04.

BAC/34. Tim Him and Hing Pheat at Wat Samraong Meanchey, Sambuor, Prey Kuy, Steung Sen, Kampong Thom, 21.8.04.

BAC/35. Tong Ma at Wat Sen Sirei, Kampong Samraong, Sra Yov, Stung Sen, Kampong Thom, 22.8.04.

BAC/36. You Baoy at Chun Leung, Rokar Chun Leung, Khsach Kandal, Kandal, 09.10.04.

BAC/37. Ven. Nhem Kim Teng at Wat Prey Chhlak, Prey Chhlak, Prey Chhlak, Svay Rieng, Svay Rieng, 14.10.04.

BAC/38. Chea Sot at Cambodian People's Party Headquarters, Tonle Bassac, Chamkar Mon, Phnom Penh, 15.10.04.

BAC/39. Hing Yan at Royal Academy, Kakap, Dangkao, Phnom Penh, 19.10.04.

BAC/40. Ven. Tep Vong at Wat Unnalom, Chey Chumneah, Daun Penh, Phnom Penh, 19.10.04.

BAC/41. Noek Chhuon at Wat Po Thmey, Bavet, Bavet, Chan Trea, Svay Rieng, 21.10.04.

BAC/42. Kham Sek and Peou Thoeng at Wat Sang Samei, Tuol Sdei, Tuol Sdei, Chan Trea, Svay Rieng, 21.10.04.

BAC/43. Kao Nheung at Wat Botum Reangsei, Chek, Samraong, Chan Trea, Svay Rieng, 21.10.04.

BAC/44. Sok Toeng at Wat Svay Thloeng, Kaoh Kban Cheung, Samraong, Chan Trea, Svay Rieng, 22.10.04.

BAC/45. Ven. Roat Va at Wat Me Sa Thngak, Por, Me Sa Thngak, Chan Trea, Svay Rieng, 22.10.04.

BAC/46. Lay Neou at Wat Prey Kokir Tauch, Prey Kokir, Prey Kokir, Chan Trea, Svay Rieng, 22.10.04.

BAC/47. Yiey Poun at Trapeang Chhuk, Trapeang Thom Khang Tboung, Tram Kak, Takeo, 23.10.04.

BAC/48. Prum Preung (also known as So Ny) at Kampong Trea, Mesa Prachan, Peareang, Prey Veng, 11.1.05.

BAC/49. Ven. Meas Soeun at Wat Prey Samnang, Prey Samnang, Khcheay Khang Cheung, Dang Tong, Kampot, 13.1.05.

BAC/50. Moa Kann at Preaek Pok, Dang Tong, Dang Tong, Kampot, 13.1.05.

BAC/51. Teng Chien at Wat Twe Sakha Ratanaram, Prey Khmum, Khchey Khang Cheung, Dang Tong, Kampot, 13.1.05.

BAC/52. Ven. Em Phoeung at Wat Chum Kriel, Chum Kriel, Chum Kriel, Kampot, Kampot, 14.1.05.

BAC/53. Long Chuob at Wat Nokor Banchay Ba-Ar, Ampil, Ampil, Kampong Siem, Kampong Cham, 18.1.05.

BAC/54. Ven. Keo Suth and two *achar*s at Wat Pongro, Pongro Kaeut, Pongro, Koh Sotin, Kampong Cham, 19.1.05.

BAC/55. Chhaom Noy at Lve, Lve, Koh Sotin, Kampong Cham, 19.1.05.

BAC/56. Bov Bang at Anlong Doung, Pongro, Koh Sotin, Kampong Cham, 19.1.05.

BAC/57. Ven. Noun Nget at Wat Botum Vaddei, Chatomukh, Daun Penh, Phnom Penh, 25.1.05.

BAC/58. Ven. Soch Sovann at Wat Mohamontrei, Oulamapik, Chamkar Mon, Phnom Penh, 4.2.05.

BAC/59. Nou Thang Nak at Wat Srah Keo Monivong, Thmei, Srah Russey, Stung Treng, Stung Treng, 28.6.05.

BAC/60. Yi Nguon at Wat Pothi Nhean (also known as Wat Preah Ang Thom), Preaek, Stung Treng, Stung Treng, Stung Treng, 28.6.05.

BAC/61. Phieu Kham Suon at Wat Kandal, Spean Thma, Stung Treng, Stung Treng, Stung Treng, 28.6.05.

BAC/62. Ma Sok at Wat Outisaram, Thalabarivat, Thalabarivat, Thalabarivat, Stung Treng, 29.6.05.

BAC/63. Lit Khun at Wat Chey Monkul, Kamphun, Kamphun, Sesan, Stung Treng, 29.6.05.

BAC/64. Ke Kan at Kaoh Sampeay, Kaoh Sampeay, Siem Bok, Stung Treng, 30.6.05.

BAC/65. Yeoung Seak at Wat Samakhi Reangsey, Trea, Stung Meanchey, Meanchey, Phnom Penh, 5.7.05 and 14.7.05.

BAC/66. Prak Ing at Trairot Bookshop, #136, Street 130, Psar Kandal Pi, Daun Penh, Phnom Penh, 15.7.05.

BAC/67. Nel Mony at Wat Saravan, Chey Chumneah, Daun Penh, Phnom Penh, 18.7.05.

1986 Interviews with Monks—conducted under the auspices of the US Social Science Research Council, Indochina Studies Program Project, coordinated by David Hawk. The interviewers were, variously, Chantou Boua, Sharon Brown, and Ben Kiernan. Copies are held at DC-Cam.

D16012. Yuahs Poa at Dongrek Camp Site II, 7.86.
D16013. Phath Chhavny at Nong Chan Site II, 6.86.
D16014. Sam Borin at Wat Nong Samet Site II, 20.3.86.
D16016. Nob Seng at Nong Chan Site II, 5.86.
D16017. Priem Somaly at Dongrek Camp Site II, 3.86.
D16018. Ros Sakun at Khao I Dang Holding Centre, 20.4.86.
D16019. Poeung Sam Oeurn at Ampil Site II, 10.86.
D16020. Chet Khemara at Dangrek Camp, Site II, 3.86.
D16032. Text of BK220904, 21.9.84.
D16115. Ros Rotha at Nong Chan Site II, 6.86.
D16116. Tep Vong at Wat Unnalom, 19.1.86.
D16117. Um Sim at Wat Unnalom, 19.1.86.
D16120. Lum Yun at Nong Chan, Site II, 8.86.
D16121. Om Tit at Wat Mohamontrei, 9.1.86.
D16122. Khieu Oeun at Wat Mohamontrei, 9.1.86.
D16123. Pes Phann at Wat Unnalom, 11.1.86.
D16124. Chhim Chhoun at Wat Unnalom, 11.1.86.
D16125. Chhin Chhom at Wat Moha Reachthann, 12.1.86.
D16126. Ok Khun at Wat Chompou Priksav, 15.1.86.
D16129. Chhun Chim at Wat Svay Att, 17.1.86.
D16130. Keo Sophal at Nong Chan, Site II, 7.86.
D16131. Hom Kim at Wat Unnalom, 6.1.86.
D16132. It Som at Wat Unnalom, 6.1.86.
D16133. So Chhem at Wat Unnalom, 6.1.86.
D16134. Sor Marng at Wat Unnalom, 6.1.86.
D16138. Ken Vong at Wat Unnalom, 6.1.86.
D16139. Uk Ron at Wat Unnalom, 6.1.86.
D16140. Heng Mengly at Dangrek Camp, Site II, 5.86.
D16141. Soeuy at Nong Chan, Site II, 8.86.
D16142. Mao Visothisart at Wat Unnalom, 7.1.86.
D16143. Las Lay at Wat Unnalom, 7.1.86.
D16144. Houl Sovann at Wat Toul Sangke, 8.1.86.
D16145. Itho Tho at Wat Unnalom, 8.1.86.
D16146. Pok Som Ann at Wat Sansam Kosala, 9.1.86.

Ian Harris (ICH) Interviews—conducted solely by the author.

ICH/01. Ven. Bour Kry at Wat Botum Vaddei, Sangkat Chatomukh, Khan Daun Penh, Phnom Penh, 9.12.97.

ICH/02. Hean Sokhom at Center for Advanced Studies, Sangkat Veal Vong, Khan 7 Makara, Phnom Penh, 15.11.99.

ICH/03. Ven. Roth Saroeun at Wat Samraong Andet, Sangkat Phnom Penh Thmey, Khan Russey Keo, Phnom Penh, 16.11.99.

ICH/04. Ven. Dim Phay at Wat Neak Voan, Sangkat Tuk L'ak Muoy, Khan Tuol Kork, Phnom Penh, 16.11.99.

ICH/05. Ven. Bour Kry at Wat Botum Vaddei, Sangkat Chatomukh, Khan Daun Penh, Phnom Penh, 19.11.99.

ICH/06. Ven. Yos Huot at Wat Langka, Sangkat Boeng Keng Kang Muoy, Khan Chamkar Mun, Phnom Penh, 19.11.99.

ICH/07. Ven. Noun Nget at Wat Botum Vaddei, Sangkat Chatomukh, Khan Daun Penh, Phnom Penh, 19.11.99.

ICH/08. Ven. Chin Channa at Wat Unnalom, Sangkat Chey Chumneah, Khan Daun Penh, Phnom Penh, 19.11.99.

ICH/09. Ven. Srey Ith at Wat Kork Kak, Kat Phluk, Basedth, Kampong Speu, 7.2.01.

ICH/10. Ven. Las Lay at Wat Sansam Kosala, Sangkat Boeng Tumpung, Khan Meanchey, Phnom Penh, 14.2.01.

ICH/11. Ven. Noun Nget at Wat Botum Vaddei, Sangkat Chatomukh, Khan Daun Penh, Phnom Penh, 12.7.02.

ICH/12. Ven. Tep Vong at Wat Unnalom, Sangkat Chey Chumneah, Khan Daun Penh, Phnom Penh, 4.8.02.

ICH/13. Ven. Tong Yen at Wat Langka, Sangkat Boeng Keng Kang Muoy, Khan Chamkar Mun, Phnom Penh, 14.1.04.

ICH/14. Ven. Sovanratana at Wat Mongkulvan, Sangkat Monorom, Khan 7 Makara, Phnom Penh, 20.5.04.

ICH/15. Ven. Duang Phang at Wat Maha Ni Tey, Kampong Luong, Ponhea Lueu, Kandal, 20.5.04.

ICH/16. Chhorn Iem at Ministry of Cults and Religions, Sangkat Phsar Kandal 1, Khan Daun Penh, Phnom Penh, 08.10.04.

ICH/17. Ven. Sovanratana at Wat Mongkulvan, Sangkat Monorom, Khan 7 Makara, Phnom Penh, 13.10.04.

ICH/18. Ven. Meas Chhom at Wat Prey Chhlak, Prey Chhlak, Svay Rieng, Svay Rieng, 14.10.04.

ICH/19. Kang Sen at Royal Palace, Sangkat Chey Chumneah, Khan Daun Penh, Phnom Penh, 23.1.06.

ICH/20. Chum Kanal at his office, Sangkat Tuol Svay Prey Muoy, Khan Chamkar Mon, Phnom Penh, 25.1.06.

Unpublished Materials Held at the Documentation Center of Cambodia. Anonymous works are designated "DC-Cam" in citations in the text, as shown in the list below. Items designated with an L- classmark in the DC-Cam cataloguing system are Lon Nol government intelligence reports dating from the civil war period. Where appropriate, details of date and context are supplied when unpublished materials are cited in this book.

Chhang Song. 1996. "Buddhism under Pol Pot."

DC-Cam 1983. "Complaints of People from Kandal Province: Petition of Chin Chil." D00821.

DC-Cam 1995. "Mapping Report—Siem Reap Province," 21–24 October.

DC-Cam 1996a. "A Report: Mapping the Killing Fields of Cambodia." D-4 Kampong Chhnang/a-cb-kh.

DC-Cam 1996b. "A Report: Mapping the Killing Fields of Cambodia." S-19-stoengtreng/a-cb-st. In "Buddhism under Pol Pot" (unpublished MS), ed. Chhang Song.

DC-Cam 1996c. "A Report: Mapping the Killing Fields." H-8-kandal/a-cb-kd.

DC-Cam 2002a. "Interview with Koam Kaet alias Koam Kaek" (biography no. K0475), age 70, in Prek Samraong village, Ta Khmav commune, Ta Khmav district, Kandal province, 26 December (KDI0134—conducted by Phan Sochea).

DC-Cam 2002b. "Interview with Ruoh Aem" (biography K5514), age 43, in Thnal Kaeng village, Kbal Toek commune, Toek Phoh district, Kampung Chhnang province, 13 July (KHI0040).

DC-Cam 2002c. "Interview with Sav Yun," biography K05003, age 61, in Kampung Samnanh village, Kampung Samnanh commune, Ta Khmav district, Kandal province, 27 December (KDI0126—conducted by Phan Sochea).

DC-Cam 2003a. "Interview with Ae Li," age 40, in Trapeang Chhouk village, Po Angkrang commune, Basaet district, Kampung Speu province, 20 March (TKI012—conducted by Vanthan Povdara, Isa Ohsman, and Phan Sochea).

DC-Cam 2003b. "Interview with Hau Li alias Soar" (I03922), age 44, in Anlung Krasang, Kampung Svay district, Kampung Thom province, 19 June (KTI0365—conducted by Vanthan Povdara and Phan Sochea).

DC-Cam 2004. "Interview with Hun Khor," 14 November (K07478—conducted by Sarin Vireak and Youk Chhang).

DC-Cam n.d. "PAT [Promoting Accountability Team] Reports." TKI09714 and TKI0079.

Hawk, David. 1986. "Limited Distribution: For Review Only. Not for Circulation or Quotation," 15 September. Typescript.

## Printed Materials and Other Unpublished Materials

Agence Khmère Presse. 1970a. "Déclaration de M. Boun Chan Mol, président de la délégation cambodgienne à la conférence mondiale des leaders bouddhistes à Seoul (République de Corée)." 2 November.

———. 1970b. "Discours du général Lon Nol, président du conseil des ministres, à l'occasion de la proclamation de la République Khmère." 9 October.

An Rasmey. 2004. "Culture and Memory of Vatt Mathar Village from Sangkum Reastr to the Present." Dissertation, Royal University of Phnom Penh.

Ang Chouléan. 1986. *Les êtres surnaturels dans la religion populaire khmère*. Paris: Cedoreck.

Armstrong, John P. 1964. *Sihanouk Speaks: Cambodia's Chief of State Explains His Controversial Policies*. New York: Walker.

Ba Swe, U. 1951. *The Burmese Revolution*. Rangoon: People's Literature House.

Bawden, C. R. 1989. *The Modern History of Mongolia.* London: Kegan Paul International.

Bayly, Susan. 2000. "French Anthropology and the Durkheimians in Colonial Indochina." *Modern Asian Studies* 34 (3): 581–622.

Becker, Elizabeth. 1979. "Communists Focus on Old Temple: Letter from Angkor Wat." *Guardian,* 4 January, 6.

———. 1986. *When the War Was Over: The Voices of Cambodia's Revolution and Its People.* New York: Simon and Schuster.

Benz, Ernst. 1965. *Buddhism or Communism: Which Holds the Future of Asia?* New York: Doubleday.

Bizot, François. 1976. *Le figuier à cinq branches: Recherche sur le bouddhisme khmer.* Paris: École Française d'Extrême-Orient.

———. 1980. "La grotte de la naissance." *Bulletin de l'École Française d'Extrême-Orient* 67:221–273.

———. 1988. *Les traditions de la pabbajjā en Asie du Sud-Est.* Göttingen: Vandenhoeck and Ruprecht.

———. 2000. *Le portail.* Paris: Table Ronde.

Blackburn, Anne M. 1999. "Looking for the *Vinaya:* Monastic Discipline in the Practical Canons of the Theravāda." *Journal of the International Association of Buddhist Studies* 22 (2): 281–309.

Boun Sokha. 1979. *Cambodge: La massue de l'Angkar.* Paris: Marcel Jullian.

Brown, John C. 1993. "Rockblasters Lay Siege to Temple That Defied KR." *Phnom Penh Post* 2 (10), 20.

*Buddha damnāy tām sāstra soḷasa nimitta* (Predictions of the Buddha according to the sastra of sixteen signs). Phnom Penh: Khemarak Pannakia, 1952.

"Buddhism Becomes the Cambodian State Religion." 1989. *Religion in Communist Lands* 17:337–339.

Buddhist Association of Cambodia. 1970. *Appeal Made by the Buddhist Association of Cambodia concerning the Aggression Committed by Vietcong–North Vietnamese Forces against Peaceful and Neutral Cambodia.* Phnom Pehn: Wat Unnalom, 18 September.

Bunchhan Mul (*P'uṇṇ Cand M"ul*). 1971. *Guk nayopāy* (Political prison). Phnom Penh: Banlī jāti.

Caldwell, Malcolm, and Lek Tan. 1973. *Cambodia in the Southeast Asian War.* New York and London: Monthly Review Press.

*Cambodge Nouveau.* 1970a. "Appel de l'Association des Écrivains Khmers." 5 (September), 16.

———. 1970b. "Messages bouddhistes." 2 (July), 20–21.

———. 1970c. "Message radiodiffusé de leurs éminences des chefs religieux des deux ordres à la nation." 6 (October), 23.

———. 1972. "Déclaration conjointe de leurs éminences samdech preah sanghareach, chefs des deux orders." 20 (October), 17.

———. 1973a. "Les communistes Indochinoise contre les moines bouddhistes." 26 (November), 13.

———. 1973b. "Un nouveau crime des aggresseurs." 24 (September), 48.

*Cambodia Daily.* 1997. "Mahaghosananda Meets Ieng Sary." 26 March, 2.

Carney, Timothy Michael. 1977. "Communist Party Power in Kampuchea (Cambodia): Documents and Discussion." Data Paper 106. Ithaca, NY: Cornell University Southeast Asia Program.

Centre for Advanced Studies and the Ministry of Cults and Religious Affairs. 1996. *Cambodia Report* 2 (2). Phnom Penh.

Chandler, David P. 1974. "Royally Sponsored Human Sacrifices in Nineteenth Century Cambodia: The Cult of *nak tā* Me Sa (Mahisāsuramardinī) at Ba Phnom." *Journal of the Siam Society* 62 (2): 207–222.

———. 1985. "Cambodia in 1984: Historical Patterns Re-asserted?" *Southeast Asian Affairs* 12:177–186.

———. 1986. "The Kingdom of Kampuchea, March–October 1945." *Journal of Southeast Asian Studies* 17 (1): 80–93.

———. 1990. "Aspects of Cambodian Politics—October 1989." In *Vietnam's Withdrawal from Cambodia: Regional Issues and Realignments,* Canberra Papers on Strategy and Defence 64, ed. Gary Klintworth, 55–65. Canberra: Australian National University.

———. 1991. *The Tragedy of Cambodian History: Politics, War, and Revolution since 1945.* New Haven, CT, and London: Yale University Press.

———. 1996. *A History of Cambodia.* 2nd ed., updated. Boulder, CO, and Oxford: Westview Press.

———. 1999. *Brother Number One: A Political Biography of Pol Pot.* Rev. ed. Boulder, CO: Westview Press.

———. 2000. *Voices from S-21: Terror and History in Pol Pot's Secret Prison.* Chiang Mai: Silkworm Books.

Chandler, David P., Ben Kiernan, and Chantou Boua, eds. 1988. *Pol Pot Plans the Future: Confidential Leadership Documents from Democratic Kampuchea, 1976–1977.* New Haven, CT: Yale University Southeast Asian Studies.

Chantou Boua. 1991. "Genocide of a Religious Group: Pol Pot and Cambodia's Buddhist Monks." In *State-Organized Terror: The Case of Violent Internal Repression,* ed. Timothy P. Bushnell, Vladimir Shlapentokh, Christopher K. Vanderpool, and Jeyaratnam Sundram, 227–240. Boulder, CO: Westview Press.

Chappell, David W. 1980. "Early Forebodings of the Death of Buddhism." *Numen* 27 (1): 122–154.

Ch'en, Kenneth. 1956. "The Economic Background of the Hui-ch'ang Suppression of Buddhism." *Harvard Journal of Asiatic Studies* 19 (1–2): 67–105.

———. 1965. "Chinese Communist Attitudes towards Buddhism in Chinese History." *China Quarterly* 22 (2): 14–30.

Chhang Song, ed. 1973. *Thousand Days of National Resistance.* Phnom Penh: Khmer Republic Magazine Co.

Christian, Pierre. 1952. "Le Viet Minh au Cambodge." *Indochine Sud-Est Asiatique.* February–March, 73–77.

Chuon Nath. 1938. *Vacanānukram Khmaer* (Cambodian dictionary). Phnom Penh: Buddhist Institute.

Chuon Nath, Jotañāno, and Samdech Preah Mahāsumedhādhipatī. 1976. "The Governing of the Buddhist Order in Cambodia." *Visakha Puja.* 3 May 2519 [1976], 40–47.

Ciorciari, John D., and Youk Chhang. 2005. "Documenting the Crimes of Democratic Kampuchea." In *Bringing the Khmer Rouge to Justice: Prosecuting Mass Violence before the Cambodian Courts,* ed. Jaya Ramji and Beth van Schaack, 221–306. Lewiston, NY: Edwin Mellen Press.

Collins, Steven. 1998. *Nirvana and Other Buddhist Felicities: Utopias of the Pali Imaginaire.* Cambridge: Cambridge University Press.

Collins, William. 1998. "Grassroots Civil Society in Cambodia." Unpublished report. Phnom Penh: Center for Advanced Study.

Communist Party of Kampuchea Central Committee. 1976. "Sharpen the Consciousness of the Proletarian Class to Be as Keen and Strong as Possible." Special issue, *Daṅ' Paṭivatt(n)* (Revolutionary flag), September–October, 33–97. Translation by Kem Sos and Timothy Carney in K. D. Jackson 1989, 269–291.

———. 1977a. "The Current Situation of the Kampuchean Revolution and the Building Up of Every Level of the Party's Cadres." *Daṅ' Paṭivatt(n)* (Revolutionary flag), October–November, 1–41. Translation by Steve Heder; held at DC-Cam.

———. 1977b. "Further Raise the Quality of Party Leadership in Order to Lead in Defence Duties and the Duties of Continuing the Socialist Revolution and Building Socialism." *Daṅ' Paṭivatt(n)* (Revolutionary flag), October–November, 42–74. Translation by Steve Heder; held at DC-Cam.

———. 1978. "Pay Attention to Pushing the Work of Building the Party and People's Cooperative Strength to Be Even Stronger." *Daṅ' Paṭivatt(n)* (Revolutionary flag) 3 (March), 37–53. Translation by Kem Sos and Timothy Carney in K. D. Jackson 1989, 293–298.

Corfield, Justin. 1991. "A History of the Cambodian Non-Communist Resistance, 1975–1983." Working Paper 72. Clayton, Victoria, Australia: Monash University Centre of Southeast Asian Studies.

———. 1994. *Khmers Stand Up! A History of the Cambodian Government, 1970–1975.* Clayton, Victoria, Australia: Monash University Centre for Southeast Asian Studies.

Danois, Jacques. 1980. "La force du pardon." *Sudestasie* 7, 72–75.

Davidson, Ronald M. 2002. *Indian Esoteric Buddhism: A Social History of the Tantric Movement.* New York: Columbia University Press.

Day, Tony, and Craig J. Reynolds. 2000. "Cosmologies, Truth Regimes, and the State in Southeast Asia." *Modern Asian Studies* 34 (1): 1–55.

de Beer, Patrice. 1978. "History and Policy of the Communist Party of Thailand." In *Thailand: Roots of Conflict,* ed. Andrew Turton, Jonathan Fast, and Malcolm Caldwell, 143–158. Nottingham: Spokesman.

de Bernon, Olivier. 1992. "Le retour de l'École au Cambodge: L'implantation du FEMC." *Bulletin de l'École Française d'Extrême-Orient* 79 (1): 243–246.

————. 1994. "Le Buddh Damnāy: Note sur un texte apocalyptique khmer." *Bulletin de l'École Française d'Extrême-Orient* 81:83–100.

————. 1997. "À propos du retour des bakous dans le palais royal de Phnom Penh." In *Renouveaux religieux en Asie,* Études Thématiques 6, ed. Catherine Clémentin-Ojha, 33–58. Paris: EFEO.

————. 1998a. "La prédiction du Buddha." *Aséanie* 1:43–66.

————. 1998b. "L'état des bibliothèques dans les monastères du Cambodge." In *Khmer Studies: Knowledge of the Past and Its Contributions to the Rehabilitation and Reconstruction of Cambodia—Proceedings of International Conference on Khmer Studies, Phnom Penh, 26–30 August 1996,* ed. Sorn Samnang, 2:872–882. Phnom Penh,

de Bernon, Olivier, Kun Sopheap, and Leng Kok-An, eds. 2004. *Inventaire provisoire des manuscrits du Cambodge. Première partie: Bibliothèques monastiques de Phnom Penh et de la province de Kandal.* Paris: École Française d'Extrême-Orient.

Debré, François. 1976. *Cambodge: La revolution de la forêt.* Paris: Flammarion.

de Nike, Howard J., John Quigley, and Kenneth J. Robinson, eds. 2000. *Genocide in Cambodia: Documents from the Trial of Pol Pot and Ieng Sary.* Philadelphia: University of Pennsylvania Press.

DeVoss, David. 1980. "Buddhism under the Red Flag." *Time,* 17 November, 62–63.

de Walque, Damien. 2005. "Selective Mortality during the Khmer Rouge Period in Cambodia." *Population and Development Review* 31 (2): 351–368.

"Dialogue between Pol Pot, Secretary of the Central Committee of the CPK and First Minister of the Democratic Kampuchea Government, and a Delegation of the Belgian-Kampuchean Association—Phnom Penh, August 1978." 2004. *Searching for the Truth,* special English edition, Second Quarter, 15–18. (Translated from DC-Cam document D00108.)

Dik Keam. 1972. "La persecution des religieux bouddhistes par les communistes Vietnamiens." *Cambodge Nouveau* 22 (December), 20–26.

Dobbs, Leo. 1992. "Aussies Repatriate Buddhist Scriptures." *Phnom Penh Post* 1 (7), 3.

*Dossier Kampuchéa.* Hanoi: Courrier du Vietnam, 1978.

Duiker, William J. 2000. *Ho Chi Minh: A Life.* New York: Theia Books.

Dunlop, Nic. 1999. "KR Torture Chief Admits to Mass Murder." *Phnom Penh Post* 8 (9), 1, 10.

————. 2005. *The Lost Executioner: A Story of the Khmer Rouge.* London: Bloomsbury.

Ea Meng-Try. 1987. "Recent Population Trends in Kampuchea." In *The Cambodian Agony,* ed. David A. Ablin and Marlow Hood, 3–15. Armonk, NY: M. E. Sharpe.

————. 2005. *The Chain of Terror: The Khmer Rouge Southwest Zone Security System.* Phnom Penh: Documentation Center of Cambodia.

Edwards, Penny. 1999. "Cambodge: The Cultivation of a Nation, 1860–1945." PhD thesis, Monash University, Clayton, Victoria.

————. 2004. "Making a Religion of the Nation and Its Language: The French Protectorate (1863–1954) and the Dhammakay." In *History, Buddhism, and New Religious Movements in Cambodia,* ed. John Marston and Elizabeth Guthrie, 63–85. Honolulu: University of Hawai'i Press.

————. 2007. *Cambodge: The Cultivation of a Nation.* Honolulu: University of Hawai'i Press.

Engel, D. M. 1978. *Code and Custom in a Thai Provincial Court.* Monographs of the Association of Asian Studies, no. 34. Tucson: University of Arizona Press.

Engelbert, Thomas, and Christopher E. Goscha. 1995. "Falling Out of Touch: A Study on Vietnamese Communist Policy towards an Emerging Cambodian Communist Movement, 1930–1975." Monash Papers on Southeast Asia, no. 35. Clayton, Victoria, Australia: Asia Institute.

Etcheson, Craig. 1984. *The Rise and Demise of Democratic Kampuchea.* Boulder, CO, and New York: Westview/Pinter.

————. 2005. *After the Killing Fields: Lessons from the Cambodian Genocide.* Westport, CT, and London: Praeger.

Evans, Grant. 1990. *Lao Peasants under Socialism.* New Haven, CT, and London: Yale University Press.

————. 1993. "Buddhism and Economic Action in Socialist Laos." In *Socialism: Ideals, Ideologies and Local Practice,* ed. C. M. Hann, 132–147. London and New York: Routledge.

————. 1998. *The Politics of Ritual and Remembrance: Laos since 1975.* Honolulu: University of Hawai'i Press.

Fawthrop, Tom, and Helen Jarvis. 2004. *Getting Away with Genocide? Elusive Justice and the Khmer Rouge Tribunal.* London and Ann Arbor, MI: Pluto Press.

Forest, Alain. 1980. *Le Cambodge et la colonisation française: Histoire d'une colonisation sans heurts (1897–1920).* Paris: L'Harmattan.

————. 1992. *Le culte des génies protecteurs au Cambodge: Analyse et traduction d'un corpus de textes sur les neak ta.* Paris: L'Harmattan.

Frings, K. Viviane. 1994. "Allied and Equal: The Kampuchean People's Revolutionary Party's Historiography and Its Relations with Vietnam (1979–1991)." Working Paper 90. Clayton, Victoria, Australia: Monash University Centre of Southeast Asian Studies.

————. 1997. "Rewriting Cambodian History to 'Adapt' It to a New Political Context: The Kampuchean People's Revolutionary Party's Historiography (1979–1991)." *Modern Asian Studies* 31 (4): 807–846.

Front d'Union pour l'Édification et la Défense de la Patrie Kampuchéenne. 1983a. *La communauté islamique au Kampuchea.* Phnom Penh.

————. 1983b. *La destruction de l'Islam dans l'ex-Kampuchea Démocratique.* Phnom Penh.

Gard, Richard A. 1962. "Buddhism and Political Authority." In *The Ethic of Power: Interplay of Religion, Philosophy and Politics,* ed. Harold D. Lasswell and Harland Cleveland, 39–70. New York: Harper and Brothers.

Giteau, Madeleine. 1969. *Le bornage rituel des temples bouddhiques au Cambodge.* Paris: EFEO.

Groupe de Juristes Cambodgiens. 1990. *Tribunal populaire révolutionnaire siégeant à Phnom Penh pour le jugement du crime de génocide commis par la clique Pol Pot—Ieng Sary: Août 1979—Documents.* Phnom Penh: Foreign Languages Publication House.

Guthrie, Elizabeth. 1992. "Khmer Buddhism in New Zealand." MA thesis, University of Otago, Dunedin.

———. 2002. "Buddhist Temples and Cambodian Politics." In *People and the 1998 National Elections in Cambodia,* ed. John L. Vijghen, 59–74. Phnom Penh: Experts for Community Research.

Gyallay-Pap, Peter. 1993. "From Conflict to Reconciliation in Cambodia? Toward an Indigenous Approach." Unpublished paper.

———. 2002. "Khmer Buddhism Resurfaces." In *People and the 1998 National Elections in Cambodia,* ed. John L. Vijghen, 109–116. Phnom Penh: Experts for Community Research.

Gyallay-Pap, Peter, and Michel Tranet. 1990. "Notes on the Rebirth of Khmer Buddhism." In *Radical Conservatism: Buddhism in the Contemporary World—Articles in Honour of Bhikkhu Buddhadasa's 84th Birthday Anniversary,* 360–369. Bangkok: Thai Inter-Religious Commission for Development/INEB.

Hang Chan Sophea. 2004. "Stec Gamlan and Yāy Deb: Worshipping Kings and Queens in Cambodia Today." In *History, Buddhism, and New Religious Movements in Cambodia,* ed. John Marston and Elizabeth Guthrie, 113–126. Honolulu: University of Hawai'i Press.

Hansen, Anne Ruth. 2007. *How to Behave: Buddhism and Modernity in Colonial Cambodia, 1860–1930.* Honolulu: University of Hawai'i Press.

Harris, Ian. 1999. "Buddhism *in Extremis:* The Case of Cambodia." In *Buddhism and Politics in Twentieth Century Asia,* ed. Ian Harris, 54–78. London and New York: Pinter.

———. 2000. "Magician as Environmentalist: Fertility Elements in South and Southeast Asian Buddhism." *Eastern Buddhist* 32 (2): 128–156.

———. 2001. "Buddhist Saṅgha Groupings in Cambodia." *Buddhist Studies Review* 18 (1): 73–106.

———. 2005a. *Cambodian Buddhism: History and Practice.* Honolulu: University of Hawai'i Press.

———. 2005b. "Onslaught on Beings: A Cambodian Buddhist Perspective on Crimes Committed in the Democratic Kampuchea Period." In *Bringing the Khmer Rouge to Justice: Prosecuting Mass Violence before the Cambodian Courts,* ed. Jaya Ramji and Beth van Schaack, 59–95. Lewiston, NY: Edwin Mellen Press.

———. 2006. "Entrepreneurialism and Charisma: Two Modes of Doing Business in Post–Pol Pot Cambodian Buddhism." In *Expressions of Cambodia: The Politics of Tradition, Identity and Change,* ed. Leakthina Chau Ollier and Tim Winter, 167–180. London: Routledge.

————. 2007. *Buddhism under Pol Pot.* Documentation Series, no. 13. Phnom Penh: Documentation Center of Cambodia.

————. 2008. "The Monk and the King: Khieu Chum and Regime Change in Cambodia." *Udaya: Journal of Khmer Studies* 9:81–112.

————. 2009. "Theravāda Buddhism among the Khmer Krom." In *The Khmer-Krom Journey to Self-determination,* ed. Daryn Reicherter and Joshua Cooper, 103–129. Pennsauken, NJ: Khmers Kampuchea Krom Federation.

————. 2010. "Rethinking Cambodian Political Discourse on Territory: Genealogy of the Buddhist Ritual Boundary (*sīmā*)." *Journal of Southeast Asian Studies* 41 (2): 215–239.

Hayashi Yukio. 2002. "Buddhism behind Official Organizations: Notes on Theravāda Buddhist Practice in Comparative Perspective." In *Inter-ethnic Relations in the Making of Mainland Southeast Asia and Southwestern China,* ed. Yukio Hayashi and Arunrat Wichiankhieo, 198–230. Bangkok: Amarin.

Heder, Stephen. 1979a. "The Kampuchean-Vietnamese Conflict." *Southeast Asian Affairs* 6:157–186.

————. 1979b. "Kampuchea's Armed Struggle: The Origins of an Independent Revolution." *Bulletin of Concerned Asian Scholars* 11 (1): 2–24.

————. 1980. *Kampuchean Occupation and Resistance.* Bangkok: Institute of Asian Studies, Chulalongkorn University.

————. 1983. "Interview with Chea Soth, Vice-Chairman, State Council, 16 June." Unpublished manuscript.

————. 1991. "Reflections on Cambodian Political History: Backgrounder to Recent Developments." Working Paper 239. Canberra: Australian National University, Strategic and Defence Studies Centre.

————. 1997. "Racism, Marxism, Labelling and Genocide in Ben Kiernan's *The Pol Pot Regime.*" *South East Asia Research* 5 (2): 101–153.

————. 1998. "The 1981 Elections: The Genesis of Polarization." *Phnom Penh Post* 7 (11), 9–10.

————. 1999. "A Fluid Policy Trail on How to Treat Ex-DK." *Phnom Penh Post* 8 (6), 10–11.

————. 2004. *Cambodian Communism and the Vietnamese Model.* Vol. 1, *Imitation and Independence, 1930–1975.* Bangkok: White Lotus.

————. 2005. "Reassessing the Role of Senior Leaders and Local Officials in Democratic Kampuchea Crimes: Cambodian Accountability in Comparative Perspective." In *Bringing the Khmer Rouge to Justice: Prosecuting Mass Violence before the Cambodian Courts,* ed. Jaya Ramji and Beth van Schaack, 377–423. Lewiston, NY: Edwin Mellen Press.

Heder, Stephen, and Brian D. Tittemore. 2004. *Seven Candidates for Prosecution: Accountability for the Crimes of the Khmer Rouge.* Washington, DC: War Crimes Research Office, Washington College of Law, American University and Coalition for International Justice; republished with a new preface, in cooperation with the Documentation Center of Cambodia, Phnom Penh.

Heuveline, Patrick. 1998. "'Between One and Three Million': Towards the Demographic Reconstruction of a Decade of Cambodian History (1970–79)." *Population Studies* 52:49–65.

Hinton, Alexander Laban. 1997. "Cambodia's Shadow: An Examination of the Cultural Origins of Genocide." PhD thesis, Emory University, Atlanta.

———. 1998. "Why Did You Kill? The Cambodian Genocide and the Dark Side of Face and Honor." *Journal of Asian Studies* 57 (1): 93–122.

———. 2002. "Purity and Contamination in the Cambodian Genocide." In *Cambodia Emerges from the Past: Eight Essays,* ed. Judy Ledgerwood, 60–90. De Kalb: Center for Southeast Asian Studies, Northern Illinois University.

———. 2005. *Why Did They Kill? Cambodia in the Shadow of Genocide.* Berkeley: University of California Press.

Hong Dy. 1989. "Jīvapravatti" (Biography [of Pen Sen]). Unpublished manuscript.

Huot Robiep. 2004. *Ekasār srāv jrāv pravatti vatta saṃroṅ knuṅ* (Research document on Wat Samraong Knong). Battambang: Wat Samraung Knong.

Huot Tat. 1929. "Tourné d'inspection dans les pagodes cambodgiennes de Sud-oeust de la Cochinchine." *Kambuja Surya* 2, 39–62.

Huxley, Andrew. 1991. "Sanction in the Theravāda Buddhist Kingdoms of S.E. Asia." *Recueil de la Société Jean Bodin* 58:335–370.

———. 1994. "The Reception of Buddhist Law in S.E. Asia, 200 BCE—1860 CE." In *La réception des systèmes juridiques: Implantation et destin,* ed. Michel Doucet and Jacques Vanderlinden, 139–237. Bruxelles: Bruylaut.

———. 1995. "Buddhism and Law—The View from Mandalay." *Journal of the International Association of Buddhist Studies* 18 (1): 47–95.

———. 2002. "Buddhist Law as a Religious System?" In *Religion, Law and Tradition: Comparative Studies in Religious Law,* ed. Andrew Huxley, 127–147. London: RoutledgeCurzon.

Huy Vannak. 2003. *The Khmer Rouge Division 703: From Victory to Self-Destruction.* Phnom Penh: Documentation Center of Cambodia.

Ieng Sary. N.d. *Cambodge 1972.* Gouvernement royal d'union nationale du Cambodge (GRUNC).

Imbert, Jean. 1961. *Histoire des institutions khmères.* Phnom Penh: Entreprise Khmère de Librairie.

Information Agency of the People's Republic of Kampuchea. 1982. *The Resurrection of Kampuchea, 1979–1982.* Phnom Penh.

Institut Bouddhique. 1963. *Centres d'etudes bouddhiques au Cambodge.* Phnom Penh.

International Commission of Jurists. 1960. *Tibet and the Chinese People's Republic: A Report to the International Commission of Jurists by Its Legal Inquiry Committee on Tibet.* Geneva.

Ishii, Yoneo. 1986a. *Sangha, State, and Society: Thai Buddhism in History.* Honolulu: University of Hawai'i Press.

———. 1986b. "The Thai Thammasat (with a Note on the Lao Thammasat)." In *The Laws of South-East Asia,* vol. 1, *The Pre-Modern Texts,* ed. M. B. Hooker, 143–203. Singapore: Butterworth.

Ith Sarin, 1973. *Sraṇoḥ braḷiñ khmaer* (Regrets for the Khmer soul). Phnom Penh: Ekareach.

Jackson, Karl D. 1989. *Cambodia, 1975–1978: Rendezvous with Death.* Princeton, NJ: Princeton University Press.

Jackson, Peter. 1989. *Buddhism, Legitimation and Conflict: The Political Functions of Urban Thai Buddhism.* Singapore: ISEAS.

Jarvis, Helen. N.d. "The National Library of Cambodia: Its 75 Year History since 1924." In *3rd National Socio-Cultural Research Congress on Cambodia, November 15–17, 2000,* 101–115. Phnom Penh: Royal University of Phnom Penh.

Jeldres, Julio, and Somkid Chaijiyvanit. 1999. *Royal Palace of Phnom Penh and Cambodian Royal Life.* Bangkok: Post Books.

Jerryson, Michael K., and Mark Juergensmeyer, eds. 2010. *Buddhist Warfare.* New York: Oxford University Press.

*Kambuja.* 1966. "Royal Funeral of Samdech Preah Sangharaj Phul-Tes." 2 (20), 42–49.

————. 1969. "Royal Funeral Rites of Samdech Preah Mongkol Tepeachar Keo Ouch, 14th–18th March 1969." 5 (49), 72–75.

*Kampuchea.* 1981a. "All People Support the Fourth Bright Congress of the Party" [in Khmer]. 11 July.

————. 1981b. "Feelings of People in All Classes about the First Congress of the National Assembly" [in Khmer]. 2 July.

————. 1982. "The Successful National Monk Congress" [in Khmer]. 10 June.

Kane, Solomon. 2007. *Dictionnaire des Khmers rouges.* Bangkok: Irasec.

Karmay, Samten G. 2003. "King Lang Darma and His Rule." In *Tibet and Her Neighbours: A History,* ed. Alex McKay, 57–66. London: Hansjörg Mayer.

Ken Khun. 1994. *De la dictature des Khmers rouges à l'occupation Viêtnamienne, Cambodge, 1975–1979.* Paris: L'Harmattan.

Keng Vannsak. 1966. *Mūlabhāb nai kār paṅkoet bāky thmī* (Principles for the creation of new words). Phnom Penh: Faculté des Lettres et des Sciences Humaines.

"Ke Pauk Defended Himself to His Death." 2002. *Searching for the Truth* 27 (March), 2–7.

Ketelaar, James Edward. 1993. *Of Heretics and Martyrs in Meiji Japan: Buddhism and Its Persecution.* Princeton, NJ: Princeton University Press.

Keyes, Charles F. 1990. "Buddhism and Revolution in Cambodia." *Cultural Survival Quarterly* 14 (3): 60–63.

————. 1994. "Communist Revolution and the Buddhist Past in Cambodia." In *Asian Visions of Authority: Religion and the Modern States of East and Southeast Asia,* ed. Charles F. Keyes, Laurel Kendall, and Helen Hardacre, 43–73. Honolulu: University of Hawai'i Press.

————. 2006. "Communism, Peasants and Buddhism: The Failure of 'Peasant Revolutions' in Thailand in Comparison to Cambodia." Unpublished manuscript.

Khieu Chum (Khīev Juṃ). 1971. *Buddhasāsanā prajādhipateyy sādhāraṇaraṭṭh* (Buddhism, democracy, and republic). Phnom Penh: Banḷi jāti.

————. 1972a. *Prajādhipateyy cās' duṃ* (Ancient democracy). Phnom Penh: Banḷi jāti.

————. 1972b. *Sakal cintā gaṃnit srāv jrāv* (Universal mind: Thoughts for research). Phnom Penh: Trai rat(n).

Khieu Samphan. 1959. *L'économie du Cambodge et ses problèmes d'industrialisation.* Thèse d'etat. Université de Paris.

———. 1975. *Declaration of the Second National Congress of Cambodia, February 24–25, 1975.* Paris: GRUNK Mission Information Bulletin. (Translated by the Indochina Resource Centre, Berkeley, CA.)

Khin Sok. 1999. *La grammaire du Khmer moderne.* Paris: You-Feng.

———. 2002. *L'annexation du Cambodge par les Vietnamiens au XIX° siècle: D'après les deux poèmes du Vénérable Bâtum Baramey Pich.* Paris: You-Feng.

Khing Hoc Dy. 1990. *Contribution à l'histoire de la littérature khmère.* 2 vols. Paris: L'Harmattan.

———. 2006–2007. "Suzanne Karpelès and the Buddhist Institute." *Siksacakr* 8–9:55–59.

Khmer Peace Committee. 1952. *Khmer Armed Resistance.* Rangoon: Viet Nam News Service.

*Khmer Republic.* 1971a. "The Murdered Monk." 1 (2; October–November), 23–26.

———. 1971b. "The Silent Protest." 1 (2; October–November), 37–42.

———. 1972. "Chronology." 1 (5; December), 27.

Kiernan, Ben. 1975. *The Samlaut Rebellion and Its Aftermath, 1967–70: The Origins of Cambodia's Liberation Movement.* Clayton, Victoria, Australia: Monash University Centre of Southeast Asian Studies.

———. 1981. "Origins of Khmer Communism." *Southeast Asian Affairs* 8:161–180.

———. 1982. "Kampuchea 1971–81: National Rehabilitation in the Eye of an International Storm." *Southeast Asian Affairs* 9:167–195.

———. 1985. *How Pol Pot Came to Power: A History of Communism in Kampuchea, 1930–1975.* London: Verso.

———. 1988. "Orphans of Genocide: The Cham Muslims of Kampuchea under Pol Pot." *Bulletin of Concerned Asian Scholars* 20 (4): 2–33.

———. 1989. "The American Bombardment of Kampuchea, 1969–1973." *Vietnam Generation* 1:4–41.

———. 1990. "The Genocide in Cambodia, 1975–79." *Bulletin of Concerned Asian Scholars* 22 (2): 35–40.

———. 1991. "Genocidal Targetting: Two Groups of Victims in Pol Pot's Cambodia." In *State-Organized Terror: The Case of Violent Internal Repression,* ed. Timothy P. Bushnell, Vladimir Shlapentokh, Christopher K. Vanderpool, and Jeyaratnam Sundram, 207–226. Boulder, CO: Westview Press.

———. 1996. *The Pol Pot Regime: Race, Power, and Genocide in Cambodia under the Khmer Rouge, 1975–79.* New Haven, CT, and London: Yale University Press.

———. 2003. "The Demography of Genocide in Southeast Asia: The Death Tolls in Cambodia, 1975–79, and East Timor, 1975–80." *Critical Asian Studies* 35 (4): 585–597.

———. 2006. "External and Indigenous Sources of Khmer Rouge Ideology." In *The Third Indochina War: Conflict between China, Vietnam and Cambodia, 1972–79,* ed. Odd Arne Westad and Sophie Quinn-Judge, 187–206. Abingdon, Oxford: Routledge.

———. 2007. *Genocide and Resistance in Southeast Asia: Documentation, Denial and Justice in Cambodia and East Timor.* New Brunswick, NJ, and London: Transaction Publishers.

Kiernan, Ben, and Chantou Boua, eds. 1982. *Peasants and Politics in Kampuchea, 1942–1981.* London: Zed Books.

Kissinger, Henry. 2003. *Ending the Vietnam War: A History of America's Involvement in and Extrication from the Vietnam War.* New York: Simon and Schuster.

Kobayashi, Satoru. 2005. "An Ethnographic Study on the Reconstruction of Buddhist Practice in Two Cambodian Temples: With Special Reference to Buddhist *Samay* and *Boran.*" *Southeast Asian Studies* 42 (4): 489–518.

*Koḥ Santibhāb.* 1972a. "Enemy Exerts Pressure on National Road No. 2" [in Khmer]. No. 1580 (28 September).

———. 1972b. "Operation to Get Rid of Enemy on National Road No. 5" [in Khmer]. No. 1555 (30 August).

———. 1972c. "War Still Causing Harm on National Road No. 2" [in Khmer]. No. 1557 (1 September).

Kong Sophear, ed. 1972. *Braḥ Pāḷāt' Ghosanāg Haem Cīev, vīrapurus jāti* (Preah Achar Haem Chieu, national hero). Phnom Penh: Niseth N. V.

Lafont, P.-B. 1982. "Buddhism in Contemporary Laos." In *Contemporary Laos: Studies in the Politics and Society of the Lao People's Democratic Republic,* ed. Martin Stuart-Fox, 148–162. St. Lucia: University of Queensland Press.

Lamant, P.-L. 1987. "Les partis politiques et les mouvements de résistance khmers vus par les services de renseignement français (1945–1952)." *Guerres Mondiales* 148, 79–96.

———. 1989. *L'affaire Yukanthor: Autopsie d'un scandale colonial.* Paris: Société d'Histoire d'Outre-Mer.

Lao Mong Hay. 2000. "Cambodia's Past: Another Solution." In *Discussion Guide: Truth, Justice, Reconciliation and Peace in Cambodia,* ed. Laura McGrew and Heang Path, 20. Phnom Penh: Embassy of Canada.

Lê Hương. 1969. *Người Việt gốc Miên* (Khmer Vietnamese).Saigon.

Lê Hũu Dan. 1995. *Tài liệu soi sáng sự thật* (Document that sheds light on the truth). Fremont, CA: Lê Hũu Dan.

Lê Minh Quí. 1981. *Hòa thượng Hồ-Tông* ([Biography of] Maha Thera Ho-Tong). Ho Chi Minh City.

*Le Republicain.* 1974a. "Lettre du Maréchal Lon Nol au chef de l'association bouddhiste theravāda." 25 February.

———. 1974b. "Lettre ouverte de samdech preah sanghareach, chefs suprêmes des deux orders religieux." 21 February.

———. 1974c. "17 moines ont choisi le chemin de la liberté." 22 February.

Leclère, Adhémard. 1894. *Recherches sur la legislation criminelle et la procédure des Cambodgiens.* Paris: Augustin Challamel.

———. 1898. *Les codes cambodgiens.* 2 vols. Paris: Ernest Leroux.

Lee, Oey Hong. 1976. *Power Struggle in South-East Asia.* Bibliotheca Asiatica 13. Zug, Switzerland: Inter Documentation Co.

Lester, Robert C. 1973. *Theravāda Buddhism in Southeast Asia.* Ann Arbor: University of Michigan Press.

Lewitz, Saveros. 1969. "Note sur la translittération du cambodgien." *Bulletin de l'École Française d'Extrême-Orient* 55 (1): 163–169.

Leys, Simon. 1986. *The Burning Forest: Essays on Chinese Culture and Politics.* New York: Holt, Rinehart and Winston.

Locard, Henri. 1996. *Le "Petit Livre Rouge" de Pol Pot ou les paroles de l'Angkar.* Paris: L'Harmattan.

———. 1998. "Les chants révolutionnaires Khmers rouges et la tradition musicale cambodgienne." In *Khmer Studies: Knowledge of the Past and Its Contributions to the Rehabilitation and Reconstruction of Cambodia—Proceedings of International Conference on Khmer Studies, Phnom Penh, 26–30 August 1996,* ed. Sorn Samnang, 308–336. Phnom Penh.

———. 2004. "The Khmer Rouge Prison System in the Provinces of Kampong Thom and Siemreap (1970–1979)." Unpublished manuscript.

———. 2005. "Haem Chieu (1898–1943), the 'Umbrella Demonstration' of 20th July 1942 and the Buddhist Institute under the Vichy Regime." Paper delivered at the "Researching Buddhism and Culture in Cambodia, 1930–2005" Colloquium, Buddhist Institute, Phnom Penh, 17 June.

———. 2006–2007. "*Achar* Hem Chieu (1898–1943), the 'Umbrella Demonstration' of 20th July 1942 and the Vichy regime." *Siksacakr* 8–9:70–81.

Locard, Henri, and Mœung Sonn. 1993. *Prisonnier de l'Angkar.* Paris: Fayard.

Lon Nol. 1970. *Campāṃṅ sāsanā* (The religious war). Phnom Penh.

Löschmann, Heike. 1989. "Die Rolle des Buddhismus in der gesellschaftlichen Entwicklung der Volksrepublik Kampuchea nach der Befreiung vom Pol-Pot-Regime 1979 bis Mitte der achtziger Jahre." PhD thesis, Humboldt-Universität, Berlin.

———. 1991. "Buddhismus und gesellschaftliche Entwicklung in Kambodscha seit der Niederschlagung des Pol-Pot-Regimes im Jahre 1979." *Asien* 41:13–27.

———. 2000. "The Revival of the Don Chee Movement in Cambodia." In *Innovative Buddhist Women: Swimming against the Stream,* ed. K. L. Tsomo, 91–95. Richmond, Surrey, UK: Curzon Press.

———. 2005. "The Role of Buddhism in the Social Development of Cambodia Following the Overthrow of Pol Pot." In *The Buddhist Institute Colloquium: Researching Buddhism and Culture in Cambodia, 1930–2005,* 6–7, 43–61. Phnom Penh: Buddhist Institute.

Luciolli, Esmeralda. 1988. *Le mur de bambou: Le Cambodge après Pol Pot.* Paris: Médecins sans Frontières.

Luco, Fabienne. 2002. *Between a Tiger and a Crocodile: Management of Local Conflict in Cambodia.* Phnom Penh: UNESCO.

Ly Heng and F. Demeure. 1992. *Cambodge: Le sourire bâillonné.* Xonrupt-Longemer, France: Anako.

Ly Sophal. 2002. "Social Classes in Democratic Kampuchea." *Searching for the Truth* 34 (October), 14–17.

Ly Sovir. 1999. *Pravatti braḥ saṅgh khmaer* (History of the Cambodian Buddhist order). Phnom Penh: École Française d'Extrême-Orient.

MacInnes, Donald E., ed. 1972. *Religious Policy and Practice in Communist China: A Documentary History.* London: Hodder and Stoughton.

Maha Ghosananda. 1992. *Step by Step: Meditations on Wisdom and Compassion.* Ed. Jane Sharada Mahoney and Philip Edmonds. Berkeley, CA: Parallax Press.

Mak, Kanika. 2004. "Genocide and Irredentism under Democratic Kampuchea (1975–79)." Yale Center for International and Area Studies, Genocide Studies Program, Working Paper 23. http://www.yale.edu/cgp/.

Mak Phœun. 1989. "La frontière entre le Cambodge et le Viêtnam du XVII$^e$ siècle à l'instauration du protectorat français presentée à travers les chroniques royales khmères." In *Les frontières du Vietnam: Histoire des frontières de la péninsule indochinoise,* ed. P. B. Lafont, 136–155. Paris: L'Harmattan.

———. 2003. "Cambodge: Le bouddhisme et les croyances traditionelles face à l'angkar (1975–1979)." In *Religions et états en Indochine contemporaine,* ed. G. Delouche, 47–75. Paris: Centre d'Histoire et Civilisations de la Péninsule Indochinoise.

Manu. 1874. *The Damathat, or the Laws of Menoo.* Trans. from the Burmese by D. Richardson. Rangoon.

Mao Tse-tung. 1967. "On New Democracy." In *Selected Works of Mao Tse-tung,* 2:339–384. Peking: Foreign Languages Press.

Marston, John. 1994. "Metaphors of the Khmer Rouge." In *Cambodian Culture since 1975: Homeland and Exile,* ed. May M. Ebihara, Carol A. Mortland, and Judy Ledgerwood, 105–118. Ithaca, NY: Cornell University Press.

———. 1997. "Cambodia 1991–94: Hierarchy, Neutrality and Etiquettes of Discourse." PhD thesis, University of Washington, Seattle.

———. 2008. "Re-establishing the Cambodian Monkhood." Unpublished paper.

———. 2009. "Cambodian Religion since 1989." In *Beyond Democracy in Cambodia: Political Reconstruction in a Post-Conflict Society,* ed. Joakim Öjendal and Mona Lilja, 224–249. Copenhagen: NIAS Press.

Martin, Marie Alexandrine. 1981. "La riziculture et la maîtrise de l'eau dans le Kampuchea démocratique." *Études Rurales* 83 (July–September), 7–44.

———. 1994. *Cambodia: A Shattered Society.* Berkeley: University of California Press.

———. 1997. "L'implantation du bouddhisme dans le massif des Cardamones (Cambodge)." In *Living Life according to the Dhamma: Papers in Honour of Professor Jean Boisselier on His Eightieth Birthday,* ed. R. L. Brown and N. Eilenburg, 357–376. Bangkok: Silpakorn University.

Mazlish, Bruce. 1976. *The Revolutionary Ascetic: Evolution of a Political Type.* New York: Basic Books.

McCargo, Duncan. 2004. "Buddhism, Democracy and Identity in Thailand." *Democratization* 11 (4): 155–170.

Meyer, Charles. 1971. *Derrière le sourire khmer.* Paris: Plon.

Migozzi, J. 1973. *Cambodge: Faits et problèmes de population.* Paris: Éditions du CRNS.

Ministère de l'Information. 1971. *L'agression Vietcong et Nord-Vietnamienne contre la Republique Khmere (Nouveaux Documents).* Phnom Penh.

Ministère de l'Information de la Presse et des Affaires Culturelles du Conseil Populaire Révolutionnaire du Kampuchea. 1979. *La naissance du nouveau Kampuchea.* Phnom Penh.

Min Khin. 1983. *Ukriṭṭhakamm rapas' pan vāt dī anukarbhāb niyam cin pekāṃṅ nin parivār pul bat īeṅ sārī khīev saṃphan knuṅ aṃḷaṅ chnāṃ 1975–1978* (Record on the total crimes of China, Beijing, and their servants: Pol Pot, Ieng Sary, [and] Khieu Samphan on the Cambodian people during 1975–1978). Phnom Penh: Research Committee on Pol Pot's Genocidal Regime.

Miwa Takahashi. 2000. "Some Aspects of Reconstruction of Buddhist Monasteries in Cambodia: A Case Study of Kien Svay District, Kandal Province." In *Proceedings of the Second International Conference on Khmer Studies: 26–28 January 2002,* ed. Neth Barom, Khus Chiev, and Henri Locard, 465–471. Phnom Penh.

Morell, David, and Susan Morell. 1972. "Impermanence of Society: Marxism, Buddhism and the Political Philosophy of Thailand's Pridi Banomyong." *Southeast Asia* 2 (4): 397–426.

Morris, Stephen J. 1999. *Why Vietnam Invaded Cambodia: Political Culture and the Causes of War.* Stanford, CA: Stanford University Press.

Moses, Larry William. 1977. *Political Role of Mongolian Buddhism.* Bloomington: Indiana University Press.

Moung Ra and Chheung Bun Chhea. 2001. *Braḥ rāja jīvapravatti samtec braḥ mahāsumedhādhipatī Tep Vong* (Biography of Tep Vong). Phnom Penh.

Murashima, Eiji. 2009. "The Young Nuon Chea in Bangkok (1942–1950) and the Communist Party of Thailand: The Life in Bangkok of the Man Who Became 'Brother No. 2' in the Khmer Rouge." *Journal of Asia-Pacific Studies* 12:1–42.

Mus, Paul. 1952. *Viêt-Nam: Sociologie d'une guerre.* Paris: Éditions du Seuil.

———. 1971. *Ho Chi Minh: Le Vietnam, L'Asie.* Paris: Éditions du Seuil.

———. 1977. *L'angle de l'Asie.* Paris: Hermann.

My Samedy. 2000. *We Live in Order to Participate in Life.* Phnom Penh.

National Council of the United Front for the Construction and Defense of the Motherland Kampuchea. 1989. *Circular concerning Becoming a Buddhist Novice* [in Khmer]. No. 03, 89KJRS, signed by Chea Sim, 24 April.

National United Front of Cambodia. 1971a. *The Armed Struggle and the Life of the Khmer People in the Liberated Areas in Pictures.* NUFC Press.

———. 1971b. *The P.N.L.A.F. (The People's National Liberation Armed Forces) in Pictures.* NUFC Press.

Newman, Robert S. 1978. *Brahmin and Mandarin: A Comparison of the Cambodian and Vietnamese Revolutions.* Clayton, Victoria, Australia: Monash University.

Nguyên Thê Anh. 1993. "Buddhism and Vietnamese Society throughout History." *South East Asia Research* 1 (1): 98–114.

Nguyễn Văn Hiếu. 1971. *Công tác Xây dựng Phật giáo Nguyên thủy tại Việt Nam* (On the work of establishing Theravāda Buddhism in Vietnam). Saigon.

*Nokor Thom.* 1972. "Phcum Ben in zone of insecurity" [in Khmer]. No. 842 (27 September).

Norodom Sihanouk. 1958. "Le communisme au Cambodge." *France-Asie* 15 (144): 192–206, 290–306.

———. 1962. "Inaugural Address: 6th Conference of the World Fellowship of Buddhists; Phnom Penh, November 14–22, 1961." *France-Asie* 171:25–28.

———. 1964. "Remise des armes aux forces paramilitaries à Prasaut, Srok Svay Teap, Svay Rieng (12 Août 1964)." In *Les paroles de Samdech Preah N. Sihanouk.* Phnom Penh: Ministère de l'Information.

———. 1970. "Message spécial du Prince Sihanouk aux moines bouddhistes khmers." *La Documentation Française* 50 (11 December), 16–18.

———. 1980. *War and Hope: The Case for Cambodia.* Trans. from the French by Mary Feeney. London: Sidgwick and Jackson.

Nuon Chea. 1987. "Statement of the Communist Party of Kampuchea (CPK) to the Communist Workers' Party of Denmark, July 1978." Trans. Peter Bischoff; ed., abr., and annotated by Laura Summer. *Journal of Communist Studies* 3 (1): 19–36.

Öjendal, Joakim, and Mona Lilja, eds. 2009. *Beyond Democracy in Cambodia: Political Reconstruction in a Post-Conflict Society.* Copenhagen: NIAS Press.

Ong Thong Hoeung. 2003. *J'ai cru aux Khmers rouges.* Paris: Buchet-Chastel.

Operations Coordinating Board. 1957. *Outline Plan regarding Buddhist Organizations in Ceylon, Burma, Thailand, Laos, Cambodia.* Washington, DC. (Secret document dated 16 January 1957, declassified with deletions 26 October 1998.)

Ouch Sophany. 2004. "Culture and Memories of Sre Ampil Villagers from Sangkum Reastr Niyum to Present." Dissertation, Royal University of Phnom Penh.

Owen, Taylor, and Ben Kiernan. 2006. "Bombs over Cambodia." *Walrus,* October, 62–69.

*Peace through Harmony: Proceedings of the ABCP Sixth General Conference, Ulan-Bator, August 16–18, 1982.* 1982. Ulan Bator: Asian Buddhists' Conference for Peace Headquarters.

Phat, Kosal. 2000. "Meeting with a Student and a Close Friend of Kaing Kek Iev, Alias 'Comrade Deuch,' in Kampong Thom." *Searching for the Truth* 6 (June), 4–6; and 7, July, 14–18.

*Phnom Penh News.* 1982. "The Interest of Monks in the City." 16 July, 69.

*Phnom Penh Post.* 1994. "Buddha Books Back." 3 (25), 14.

Picq, Laurence. 1989. *Beyond the Horizon: Five Years with the Khmer Rouge.* Trans. from the French (*Au-delà du ciel: Cinq ans chez les Khmers rouges*) by Patricia Norland. New York: St. Martin's.

Pin Yathay. 1980. *L'utopie meurtrière.* Paris: Laffont.

Pok Sokundara and Beth Moorthy. 1998. "Monks Walk Tightrope between Peace and Politics." *Phnom Penh Post* 7 (22), 4.

Ponchaud, Francois. 1978. *Cambodia Year Zero.* London: Allen Lane.

———. 1989. "Social Change in the Vortex of Revolution." In *Cambodia, 1975–1978: Rendezvous with Death,* ed. Karl D. Jackson, 151–177. Princeton, NJ: Princeton University Press.

———. 1990. *La cathédrale de la riziere: 450 ans d'histoire de l'église au Cambodge.* Paris: Fayard.

Porée-Maspero, Éveline. 1962–1969. *Étude sur les rites agraires des Cambodgiens.* 3 vols. Paris: Mouton.

Pridi, Banomyong. 1957. *Khwampen'anitchang khong sangkhom* (Impermanence of society). Bangkok.

Quinn, Kenneth M. 1976. "Political Change in Wartime: The Khmer Krahom Revolution in Southern Cambodia, 1970–1974." *Naval War College Review* 28:3–31.

———. 1982. "The Origins and Development of Radical Cambodian Communism." PhD thesis, University of Maryland, College Park.

Quinn-Judge, Sophie. 2006. "Victory on the Battlefield: Isolation in Asia; Vietnam's Cambodia Decade, 1979–1989." In *The Third Indochina War: Conflict between China, Vietnam and Cambodia, 1972–79,* ed. Odd Arne Westad and Sophie Quinn-Judge, 207–230. Abingdon, Oxford: Routledge.

*Rāstracakr.* 1972a. "Salary Should Be Increased" [in Khmer]. No. 927 (7 November).

———. 1972b. "Salary Should Be Increased Too" [in Khmer]. No. 932 (14 November).

"Recherche sur le Parti Cambodgien." N.d. Document 3KN.T.8572. Hanoi: Vietnamese Archives.

Reinders, Eric. 2004. "Monkey Kings Make Havoc: Iconoclasm and Murder in the Chinese Cultural Revolution." *Religion* 34:191–209.

"Religion in Kampuchea." 1988. *Religion in Communist Lands* 16 (2): 169–170.

Ros Chantrabot. 2000. *Cambodge: La répétition de l'histoire (de 1991 aux élections de juillet 1998).* Paris: You-Feng.

Roveda, Vittorio, and Sothon Yem. 2009. *Buddhist Painting in Cambodia.* Bangkok: River Books.

Roy, Daniel. 1970. "70 000 bonzes et la guerre civile." *La Documentation Française* 50 (11), 14–15.

Sak Sutsakhan, Lt. Gen. 1980. *The Khmer Republic at War and the Final Collapse.* Washington, DC: US Army Center of Military History.

Saloth Sar. 1952. "Monarchy or Democracy." *Khmer Nissit.* (Trans. into French in Thion and Kiernan, 1981.)

*Samdech Sihanouk's Inspection Tour of the Cambodian Liberated Zone.* 1973. Supplement to *China Pictorial,* no. 6 (March). Peking.

Sann, Kalyan. 2000. "I Only Want Justice." *Searching for the Truth* 8, 6–8.

Sarkisyanz, Emanuel. 1958. "Communism and Lamaist Utopianism in Central Asia." *Review of Politics* 20 (4): 623–633.

———. 1965. *Buddhist Backgrounds of the Burmese Revolution.* The Hague: Martinus Nijhoff.

Scott, James C. 1985. *Weapons of the Weak: Everyday Forms of Peasant Resistance.* New Haven, CT: Yale University Press.

Shapiro-Phim, Toni. 2002. "Dance, Music, and the Nature of Terror in Democratic Kampuchea." In *Annihilating Difference: The Anthropology of Genocide,* ed. Alex Hinton, 179–193. Berkeley: University of California Press.

Sher, Sacha. 2003. "Le parallèle éminemment douteux entre l'*angkar* révolutionnaire et Angkor." *Aséanie* 11:21–38.

———. 2004. *Le Kampuchéa des "Khmers rouges": Essai de compréhension d'une tentative de révolution.* Paris: L'Harmattan.

Short, Philip. 2004. *Pol Pot: The History of a Nightmare.* London: John Murray.

Simon-Barouh, Ida, and Yi Tan Kim Pho. 1990. *Le Cambodge des Khmers rouges.* Paris: L'Harmattan.

Sliwinski, M. 1995. *Le génocide Khmer rouge: Une analyse démocratique.* Paris: L'Harmattan.

Slocomb, Margaret. 2001. "The K5 Gamble: National Defence and Nation Building under the People's Republic of Kampuchea." *Journal of Southeast Asian Studies* 32 (2): 195–210.

———. 2003. *The People's Republic of Kampuchea, 1979–1989.* Chiang Mai: Silkworm Books.

———. 2004. "Commune Elections in Cambodia: 1981 Foundations and 2002 Reformulations." *Modern Asian Studies* 38 (2): 447–467.

———. 2006. "The Nature and Role of Ideology in the Modern Cambodian State." *Journal of Southeast Asian Studies* 37 (3): 375–395.

Smith, Donald Eugene. 1965. *Religion and Politics in Burma.* Princeton, NJ: Princeton University Press

Smith, Frank. 1989. *Interpretive Accounts of the Khmer Rouge Years: Personal Experience in Cambodian Peasant World View.* Occasional Paper 18. Madison: University of Wisconsin Center for Southeast Asian Studies.

Sorn Samnang, ed. 1998. *Khmer Studies: Knowledge of the Past and Its Contributions to the Rehabilitation and Reconstruction of Cambodia—Proceedings of International Conference on Khmer Studies, Phnom Penh, 26–30 August 1996.* 2 vols. Phnom Penh.

Stanic, S. 1978. "Cambodia: A Path without a Model. Buddha Is Dead! Long Live the Revolution." Belgrade Domestic Service. *FBIS (Foreign Broadcast Information Service)* 4, 24 April.

Steinberg, David J., et al. 1959. *Cambodia: Its People, Its Society, Its Culture.* New Haven, CT: HRAF Press.

Strong, John S. 1983. *The Legend of King Aśoka: A Study and Translation of the Aśokāvadāna.* Princeton, NJ: Princeton Library of Asian Translations.

Stuart-Fox, Martin. 1983. "Marxism and Theravāda Buddhism: The Legitimation of Political Authority in Laos." *Pacific Affairs* 56 (3): 428–454.

———. 1996. *Buddhist Kingdom, Marxist State.* Bangkok: White Lotus.

Stuart-Fox, Martin, and Bunhaeng Ung. 1998. *The Murderous Revolution.* Bangkok: Orchid Press.

Summary of World Broadcasts. 1979. "Vietnamese Buddhists in Cambodia," FE/6255/A3/7, September 21; "Reordination of Buddhist Monks" and "Vietnamese Buddhist Delegation in Cambodia," FE/6231/A3/6–7, 28 September.

Suwanna Satha-Anand. 2006. "Buddhism for Social Justice in Thai Society: An Analysis of Buddhadasa's Teachings." In *Buddhist Exploration of Peace and Justice,* ed. Chanju Mun and Ronald S. Green, 173–182. Honolulu: Blue Pine.

Svay Muoy. 1972. "Histoire de Keo Preah Phleung." *Bulletin de la Société des Études Indochinoises,* n.s. 47 (3): 375–392.

Tambiah, S. J. 1992. *Buddhism Betrayed? Religion, Politics, and Violence in Sri Lanka.* Chicago: University of Chicago Press.

Taylor, Jim. 1999. "(Post-)Modernity, Remaking Tradition and the Hybridization of Thai Buddhism." *Anthropological Forum* 9 (2): 163–187.

Témoignages: Les moines bouddhistes Khmers krom parlent. 1963. *Les persécutions religieuses au sud Vietnam.* Phnom Penh.

Thach Reaksa. 1970. *Au Sud-Vietnam 2600000 Khmers-Krom revendiquent.* Monaco: Éditions du Rocher.

Thach Saret. 1971. *Braḥ saṅgh jā jhloeṅ maen ṛ?* (Are monks leeches?). Phnom Penh: Group of Nationalist Buddhists.

Thayer, Nate. 1997a. "Am I a Savage Person?" *Phnom Penh Post* 6 (21), 1.

———. 1997b. "Forbidden City." *Far Eastern Economic Review,* October, 22.

Thion, Serge. 1983. "Chronology of Khmer Communism." In *Revolution and Its Aftermath in Kampuchea: Eight Essays,* ed. David P. Chandler and Ben Kiernan, 291–319. New Haven, CT: Yale University Southeast Asia Studies.

———. 1987. "The Pattern of Cambodian Politics." In *The Cambodian Agony,* ed. David A. Ablin and Marlow Hood, 149–164. Armonk, NY: M. E. Sharpe.

———. 1993. *Watching Cambodia: Ten Paths to Enter the Cambodian Tangle.* Bangkok: White Lotus.

Thion, Serge, and Ben Kiernan. 1981. *Khmers rouges: Matériaux pour l'histoire du communisme au Cambodge.* Paris: J. E. Hallier–Ablin Michel.

Trannin, Sabine. 2005. *Les ONG occidentals au Cambodge: La réalité derrière le mythe.* Paris: L'Harmattan.

Try, Jean-Samuel S. 1991. "Le bouddhisme dans la société khmère moderne." Doctoral thesis, École Pratique des Hautes Études, Section Sciences Religieuses, Paris.

United Nations. 1979. "Elimination of All Forms of Religious Intolerance: The Situation in Kampuchea." Letter dated 12 October 1979 from the Permanent Representative of Vietnam [Ha Van Lau] to the United Nations addressed to the Secretary-General. UN document A/34/569. http://daccess-dds-ny.un.org/doc/UNDOC/GEN/N79/259/72/PDF/N7925972.pdf?OpenElement/.

Vairon, Lionel. 2004. "Les intellectuals cambodgiens face au régime Khmer rouge, 1975–1979." *Aséanie* 13:47–61.

Vajirananavarorasa, Somdet P. 1984. *The Entrance to the Vinaya: Vinayamukha.* Vol. 3. Bangkok: Mahamakut Rajavidyalaya Press.

Vickery, Michael. 1984. *Cambodia 1975–1982.* Sydney and Boston: Allen and Unwin.

———. 1986. *Kampuchea: Politics, Economics and Society.* Marxist Regimes Series. London and Boulder, CO: Pinter and Rienner.

———. 1988. "Letter to the Editor." *Bulletin of Concerned Asian Scholars* 20:70–73.

———. 1992. "Comments on Cham Population Figures." *Bulletin of Concerned Asian Scholars* 22 (1): 31–33.

———. 1994. "The Cambodian People's Party: Where Has It Come From, Where Is It Going?" *Southeast Asian Affairs* 21:102–117.

Vickery, Michael, and Naomi Roht-Arriaza. 1995. "Human Rights in Cambodia." In *Impunity and Human Rights in International Law and Practice,* ed. Naomi Roht-Arriaza, 243–251. New York and Oxford: Oxford University Press.

Vietnam Buddhist Saṅgha. 1990. *Vietnam Buddhism and Its Activities for Peace.* Ho Chi Minh City: Vietnam Buddhist Research Institute.

Vittachi, Imran. 1997. "Ieng Sary's Redemption." *Phnom Penh Post* 6 (6), 17.

Vong Sokheng and Christine Chaumeau. 2001. "Brother's Buddhist Embrace in Doubt." *Phnom Penh Post* 10 (15), 12.

Vu Can. 1982. "Buddhism and Socialism in Kampuchea." *Vietnam Courier* 18 (9), 28–30.

Wagner, Carol. 2002. *Soul Survivors: Stories of Women and Children in Cambodia.* Berkeley, CA: Creative Arts Book Co.

Welch, Holmes. 1969. "Buddhism since the Cultural Revolution." *China Quarterly* 40:127–136.

———. 1972. *Buddhism under Mao.* Cambridge, MA: Harvard University Press.

Willmott, W. E. 1981. "Analytical Errors of the Kampuchean Communist Party." *Pacific Affairs* 54:209–227.

Wipulasara, M. Thero. 1994. "Thanks for the Memories." *Phnom Penh Post* 3 (18), 8–9.

Yamaguchi, Zuihō. 1996. "The Fiction of King Dar-ma's Persecution of Buddhism." In *Du Dunhuang au Japon: Études chinoises et bouddhiques offertes à Michel Soymié,* ed. Jean-Pierre Drège, 231–258. Geneva: Droz.

Yang Sam. 1987. *Khmer Buddhism and Politics from 1954 to 1984.* Newington, CT: Khmer Studies Institute.

———. 1990. "Buddhism in Cambodia, 1795–1954." MA thesis, Cornell University, Ithaca, NY.

Ysa, Osman. 2002. *Oukoubah.* Monograph 2. Phnom Penh: Documentation Center of Cambodia.

———. 2006. *The Cham Rebellion: Survivors' Stories from the Villages.* Monograph No. 9. Phnom Penh: Documentation Center of Cambodia.

Yu, David. 1987. "Religion and Politics in Asian Communist Nations." In *Movements and Issues in World Religions: A Sourcebook and Analysis of Developments since 1945,* ed. Wei-hsun C. Fu and G. E. Spiegler, 371–392. New York and Westport, CT: Greenwood Press.

Yuangrat (Pattanapongse) Wedel. 1981. *Modern Thai Radical Thought: The Siamization of Marxism and Its Theoretical Problems.* PhD thesis, University of Michigan, Ann Arbor.

# INDEX

Page numbers in boldface type refer to illustrations.

Production Notes for Harris | *Buddhism in
    a Dark Age*
Cover design by Julie Matsuo-Chun
Text design and composition by Jansom
    with display type in Heroic Condensed
    and text type in Times New Roman
Printing and binding by Integrated Book Technology, Inc.
Printed on 60 lb. offset, 435 ppi.

# THIS SAME EARTH
## ELEMENTAL MYSTERIES BOOK TWO

## ELIZABETH HUNTER

Cover Design: Karen Dimmick/ArcaneCovers.com
Edited by: Amy Eye
Formatted by: Elizabeth Hunter

Recurve Press LLC
PO Box 4034
Visalia, California 93278
USA

For more information about Elizabeth Hunter, please visit: ElizabethHunter-Writes.com